THE ROLE OF INTELLIGENCE

IN THE

BATTLE OF BRITAIN

All the business of war, and indeed all the business of life, is to endeavour to find out what you don't know by what you do; that's what I called 'guess what was at the other side of the hill'.

Duke of Wellington

THE ROLE OF INTELLIGENCE
IN THE
BATTLE OF BRITAIN

NORMAN RIDLEY

AIR WORLD

AIR WORLD

THE ROLE OF INTELLIGENCE IN THE BATTLE OF BRITAIN

First published in Great Britain in 2021 by
Air World
An imprint of
Pen & Sword Books Ltd
Yorkshire – Philadelphia

Copyright © Norman Ridley, 2021

ISBN 978 1 39901 038 2

Typeset by SJmagic DESIGN SERVICES, India.

Printed and bound in the UK by CPI Group (UK) Ltd, Croydron, CR0 4YY.

Pen & Sword Books Limited incorporates the imprints of Atlas, Archaeology,
Aviation, Discovery, Family History, Fiction, History, Maritime, Military, Military
Classics, Politics, Select, Transport, True Crime, Air World, Frontline Publishing, Leo
Cooper, Remember When, Seaforth Publishing, The Praetorian Press, Wharncliffe
Local History, Wharncliffe Transport, Wharncliffe True Crime and White Owl.

For a complete list of Pen & Sword titles please contact

PEN & SWORD BOOKS LIMITED
47 Church Street, Barnsley, South Yorkshire, S70 2AS, England
E-mail: enquiries@pen-and-sword.co.uk
Website: www.pen-and-sword.co.uk

Or
PEN AND SWORD BOOKS
1950 Lawrence Rd, Havertown, PA 19083, USA
E-mail: Uspen-and-sword@casematepublishers.com
Website: www.penandswordbooks.com

MIX
Paper from
responsible sources
FSC® C013604

Contents

Preamble   vii

Introduction   ix

Chapter 1   Luftwaffe Intelligence   1

Chapter 2   Reichsmarschall Hermann Wilhelm Göring   53

Chapter 3   German Radar   75

Chapter 4   RAF Intelligence   82

Chapter 5   Air Chief Marshal Sir Hugh Caswall
              Tremenheere Dowding   113

Chapter 6   British Radar   123

Chapter 7   The Dowding System   142

Chapter 8   Testing the Dowding System to Destruction   165

Chapter 9   The Tizard Committee   175

Chapter 10   Enigma   192

Chapter 11   Polish Codebreakers   207

Appendix A   The Oslo Report   221

Appendix B   British Intelligence on Luftwaffe Aircraft   223

Appendix C   How the Enigma Machine Works   226

Appendix D   Giulio Douhet   237

Sources   241

Notes   244

Index   256

Preamble

Professor F.H. Hinsley, in his book *British Intelligence in the Second World War*, described intelligence as 'an activity which consists, essentially, of three functions. Information has to be acquired; it has to be analysed and interpreted; and it has to be put into the hands of those who can use it.' These criteria are applied here to examine the way in which both British and German Intelligence played a part in the Battle of Britain.

Both the RAF and the Luftwaffe were hamstrung in their endeavours during the Battle of Britain by poor intelligence. The most egregious Luftwaffe blunder was its failure to appreciate the true nature of Fighter Command operational systems and consequently it made fundamental strategic errors when trying to degrade them. This was compounded by Luftwaffe intelligence chief, Oberst Josef 'Beppo' Schmid, consistently underestimating Fighter Command's capabilities which resonated with Luftwaffe chief Reichsmarschall Göring's own prejudices and influenced German decision-making at all stages of the conflict.

Each side had trouble building a picture of the other's strengths, having previously failed to acquire detailed intelligence about each other's war production capacity. In the case of the Luftwaffe, they had not seriously considered the prospect of an air war over Britain, and in the case of the RAF, they had only belatedly – and reluctantly – faced up to the reality of war, having for so long tried to avoid it. While the Luftwaffe did have the benefit of rudimentary pre-war aerial surveillance data, it had been unable to update it significantly after the declaration of war in September 1939. British knowledge of German strategic industrial and military assets was even worse, having made no comprehensive pre-war aerial survey of potential targets to inform their bombing operations.

RAF Fighter Command did have an 'ace in the hole' with its radar surveillance systems giving early warnings of Luftwaffe raids, but this was, in the early stages of the conflict at least, less than totally reliable and it was often difficult to interpret the data coming through due to the inexperience of many of its operators. British radio-monitoring stations laboriously probed Luftwaffe communications looking for the tiniest snippets of intelligence, with which it painstakingly built up a picture of its foe's capabilities and intentions. Vital information about the German 'Enigma' coding machines supplied by Polish Intelligence allowed Bletchley Park analysts to start breaking the German codes, but it was a slow and hugely complicated process which did not really pay significant dividends until much later in the war.

Good intelligence, used correctly, helps a combatant to magnify such advantages as they may have and minimise the debilitating effects of their weaknesses. In this way intelligence acts as a 'force multiplier', but faulty intelligence, or good intelligence misapplied, has the opposite effect of misdirecting operations. In the case of the Luftwaffe, the degree to which it mishandled intelligence threatened to act as a 'force diluter', by throwing its campaign into a negative spiral where material and strategic advantages were squandered even at the very moment when victory was within reach. Fighter Command, however, struggling to mount a credible defence found, through exploitation of its own intelligence, a feedback mechanism that allowed them to improve the working of the 'Dowding System' of air defence on a daily basis, and respond quickly to every new strategic initiative rolled out by the Luftwaffe – right up to the moment that the British people stood on the precipice beyond which catastrophe loomed.

Introduction

The Battle of Britain was notable for several reasons, not least of which was the role played by intelligence on both sides. During the years immediately preceding the Second World War, both German and British Intelligence was fragmented, disjointed, and lacked focus. Little time or effort had been spent on identifying intelligence priorities since neither side had more than a vague notion of what circumstances might prevail in the event of war, and consequently what aspects of such a conflict might be worthy of detailed investigation. The fighting services on both sides had their own intelligence resources, but these were directed to work within the limited field of their own interests and were given little incentive to share either their sources or information. Intelligence agencies outside their direct control were seen as insecure and dilettante, their work unworthy of serious consideration.

The modern ideas of military Intelligence as 'a significant instrument of war' emerged from First World War experiences in which the military had discovered that assigning a few thousand men to ascertain enemy troop deployments proved more productive than putting them in trenches with rifles.[1] The role of reconnaissance aircraft and the growth of radio communications were fundamental to this development. In all cases, sound intelligence promoted efficient decision-making by recognising an enemy's strengths and exposing its weaknesses. This important realisation prompted German military leaders, in the wake of their defeat, to retain an intelligence evaluation capability, albeit in the face of opposition from within. This capability laid the foundation for the whole intelligence regime that grew during the inter-war years.

In Britain, there was a tacit understanding that the Foreign Office was responsible for political intelligence and would advise the government on foreign policy and foreign relations, while the War Office conducted Military Intelligence activities free from civilian interference.[2] The Army and Navy had well-established intelligence directorates, but it was not until 1935 that the Air Ministry saw fit to create an intelligence staff of equal status. The gathering and dissemination of Air Intelligence was formalised in 1938, but bureaucratic overload impeded efficient use of raw intelligence coming through the radio intercept station at Cheadle, which was the main investigative source of Luftwaffe Intelligence, by insisting that it go through Air Intelligence Branch for analysis before going out to operational units. By the time war broke out in 1939 such impediments were being removed, but it gave precious little time for an effective, integrated intelligence operation to establish itself.

In Germany, the intelligence services were subject to immense political pressures: 'All German politicians of consequence sought to set up their own information bureaus … as additional supports for their personal authority.'[3] The most glaring example of which was the Forschungsamt (Research Office of the Reich Air Ministry) set up on 10 April 1933 and run by Hermann Wilhelm Göring as an individual, not as a minister of the Reich. When the Luftwaffe did establish a number of Air Intelligence agencies they failed to work together effectively, primarily because the most influential agency was run by Josef Schmid, a low-ranking but politically well-connected officer characterised by a jealous scorn for his contemporaries and a grovelling willingness to please (and not disconcert) his superiors. Schmid started out with the best of intentions and produced a comprehensive report, Studie Blau (Study Blue), in 1939, with a realistic appreciation of British air power, upon which he expected the Luftwaffe to formulate an air policy towards Britain; the indifference with which the report was received, and the distortion of German military policy after its startling victories over France and the Low Countries, alerted him to the reality that his personal standing within the Luftwaffe was founded more upon his ability to exaggerate German superiority than to draw attention to any areas in which it might be inferior to its enemy. Much has been written about Schmid's culpability for the Luftwaffe's failure in the summer of 1940, and indeed his performance as intelligence chief is widely seen as lamentable, but it is questionable whether his actions had any great influence on the outcome of the Battle of Britain. It is not so much the case that Göring was swayed by Schmid's various erroneous assessments of British strength and capabilities, more that Göring, with his driving ambition for personal glory, simply accepted Schmid's reports as a convenient confirmation of his own overblown belief in Luftwaffe superiority and the inevitability of victory. Had Schmid pursued a different strategy, by taking a more guarded and nuanced view based on close scrutiny of intelligence rather than fatuous wishful-thinking, and told Göring a few home truths, there is little doubt that he would not have survived for five minutes in his role and would have been replaced by someone whose sycophancy was more soothing of Göring's vanity.

In Britain, as the political humiliations of Munich and Czechoslovakia dragged the government unwillingly to the brink of war, it found itself scrambling for intelligence about German capabilities and intentions. Its moat-like defences of the North Sea and English Channel, combined with the biggest Navy in the world, gave it considerable protection against invasion which left aerial attack as the most likely threat if it came to open conflict, and this was a threat that Britain had started to take very, very seriously. That is not to say, however, that it had any plans to deal with such an eventuality. Indeed, its lack of intelligence had given it no clear idea of what the true nature of the threat really was. As early as 1934, Britain had set up the Sub-Committee on the Reorientation of Air defence Systems of Great Britain, which soon discovered that far from finding answers, it hardly knew what questions to ask. Its great achievement, however, was its willingness to look beyond the military and reach out to the scientific community to find a way forward.

Alongside, and closely allied to, scientific research was another equally important development that found its champion in the person of Air Marshal Sir Hugh Dowding, namely the system of control and command of aircraft based upon radar intelligence. The development of radar is of crucial importance to any intelligence assessment of the Battle of Britain. German radar was, in fact, quite as well-developed as Britain's, but it was the different ways in which it was applied that gave Britain the advantage. Germany, while justifying its military build-up as a necessary defensive measure, in reality prepared its forces for offensive action which left little time, enthusiasm or resources for the development of a defensive strategy, a significant part of which was its radar systems. This association of radar with anti-aircraft defences meant that, while its development continued, radar came very much under the purview of the Army, and the Luftwaffe tended to concentrate its resources more on developing navigation aids to its bomber fleet. As a purely attack-minded option this could not be faulted, but alongside it, taking a greater interest in radar as such might well have alerted the Luftwaffe to the ways in which radar could, if properly resourced, be integrated into a formidable air defence system such as that developed by Fighter Command, and that could have influenced its decision-making in a fundamental way. Britain, on the other hand, saw its only attacking resources as its bomber fleet which it believed, rightly, to be inferior to that of Germany, putting it in a distinctly weak position in the event of a head-to-head war of attrition. Prudence advised a reorientation of focus onto defence, where radar now assumed an importance which attracted huge resources and effort to speed development.

Neither Fighter Command, with its limited resources, nor the Luftwaffe, with its flawed strategy, were able to bring decisive material force to bear at any stage of the conflict and both would have benefited enormously from other means of acquiring dominance, the most important of which was good intelligence. It will be shown that, in this respect, it was Fighter Command which made best use of its intelligence resources, through surveillance of Luftwaffe aircraft movements and its exploitation of knowledge acquired through radar to manage deployment of its aircraft in the face of attack. The Luftwaffe, by comparison, failed to know its enemy and seemingly lacked the will to learn about it through analysis of day-to-day contact.

Chapter 1

Luftwaffe Intelligence

To set up an intelligence organisation for the largest air force in the world, appoint its commanding officer in the rank of Major (Oberst) and then deny it the facilities to do the job was sheer folly. The outcome was inevitable.[1]

One of the first things to be said about Luftwaffe Intelligence is that OKL (Oberkommando der Luftwaffe), the German Air Force High Command, had so little time for it that its headquarters' General Staff in Berlin did not include one single intelligence agency of their own when it was created.[2] Germany had been denied an air force under the 1919 Treaty of Versailles, so when the OKL was formed in 1936 it had no traditions or precedents upon which to build. It created itself according to the ambition and requirements of the age, which envisioned a mobile and flexible component of national defence in which intelligence would be collected, analysed and its lessons applied within flexible, localised areas of operations and not through rigid centralised channels. This placed the Luftwaffe uneasily within a German Intelligence system 'consisting of numerous uncoordinated and often competing mechanisms', overseen by 'jealous ministers, arrogant party officials and proud warlords' scrambling to 'bring their titbits' to their masters.[3]

During peacetime, the Luftwaffe relied heavily on the OKW (Armed Forces High Command) Counterintelligence Office (Abwehr) headed up by Konteradmiral Wilhelm Franz Canaris, but began to exercise more independence once war threatened.[4] It is worth noting also that the Luftwaffe was the most highly politicised of the three armed services and some in the Abwehr, most conspicuously Canaris himself and the chief of the Central Branch, Colonel Hans Oster, were becoming seriously disaffected with Nazi ideology.[5] Canaris had been brought out of semi-retirement to fill the post and 'lacked both the moral courage to challenge the Nazis … and the skills to run an effective secret service.'[6] Cooperation between the intelligence services was unlikely to survive the separation.

The first intelligence organisation that had any connection to the Luftwaffe was the Forschungsamt (Research Bureau), one of ten independent and frequently feuding intelligence agencies within the German armed forces. The Forschungsamt had been set up by Göring in 1933, ostensibly as part of the, then secret, German Air Force, but which was, in reality, a bureau used almost exclusively to serve him personally and his political associates.[7] The Forschungsamt had initially operated from Göring's personal residence with its twenty operatives tapping telephone wires, but later moved into the Schiller Colonades at Schillerstrasse. It grew to establish offices in most major German cities.[8] Other intelligence agencies struggled to protect themselves from Nazi domination with the assistance of the anti-Nazi Foreign Minister, Konstantin von Neurath, but he could do little more than fight a rearguard action until his death in 1938 opened up the floodgates to a political tsunami.[9] Many of the more ambitious and more strident operatives, although by no means the most effective, were attracted to those agencies that promised greater advancement, the Luftwaffe being the first option. The nature of German Intelligence agencies within an increasingly authoritarian regime during the immediate pre-war years inevitably ensured that they spent as much time spying on each other as they did on the enemy.

When the role of centralised intelligence gained a modicum of recognition as the political situation in Europe became more unstable, OKL bowed to the inevitable and established a range of intelligence sections, but its response was grudging and half-hearted. On 1 January 1938, weeks after the Reich Air Ministry had been reorganised, an intelligence organisation, the 5th Abteilung (5th Branch Foreign Powers Section D5, Operations Staff/Ic) of the Luftwaffe General Staff, was formed, under the command of Oberst Josef 'Beppo' Schmid, to acquire information about foreign air forces and identify strategic targets in the event of war. Schmid had been plucked out of the Operations Division on the recommendation of the Chief of the Luftwaffe General Staff, Hans Jeschonnek, and this promotion also saw him attached to Göring's personal General Staff, giving him prestige and influence far above his rank. The intensely ambitious Schmid, considered 'more cunning than intelligent', was born in Bavaria in 1901 and had been a member of the National Socialist Party in Germany since November 1923, when he had taken part in Hitler's abortive Beer Hall Putsch in Munich.[10] Thus, Schmid had established a crucial relationship with Hitler who commemorated the event annually and had presented a special award to all those who had participated in it. While Hitler served a prison term for his actions, Schmid went on to become an infantry private in the German Army. General Hermann Plocher called him 'a colourful and sometimes controversial character'.[11] He consolidated his personal position by shrewd manipulation of his political connections to Göring, but notwithstanding his many years of service to the Nazi Party, he still essentially lacked the seniority that would allow him to give his department any real status or authority.

His early involvement with the Nazi Party meant that Schmid was well known to Hitler and had also enjoyed a close association with Göring over the years. It is a clear example of the way the Luftwaffe operated at staff level that Schmid, with no experience of, or expertise in, intelligence, had been assigned his position without proper scrutiny of his suitability. His General Staff officers were similarly unqualified, for the most part, for the roles they were asked to play. Few were trained in analysis and evaluation techniques which meant that reports lacked rigour and coordination, sometimes resulting in contradictory assessments of the same intelligence. This inevitably tended to reinforce the jaundiced view of the High Command when considering intelligence from any source other than those over which they had direct control. Schmid found himself, more often than not, in little more than a propaganda role feeding upbeat stories to the German media. The higher echelons of Luftwaffe command, aware both of his political connections and penchant for intrigue, were wary of him but were, nevertheless, unimpressed by his abilities. On the other hand, for Schmid, it was considered neither proper nor advisable for a mere Oberst to offer up any opinion that disturbed the confidence of a totalitarian policy-making hierarchy. He very quickly understood the lie of the land and was careful not to make himself unpopular on any level.

Schmid's main attributes were a penchant for bribery, a persuasive tongue and his proverbial conviviality – he was a heavy drinker; he created about himself a circle of officers who lacked intelligence skills but were completely under his control. Given the attitude of OKW to intelligence per se, there was little incentive for him to excel professionally in a role that encouraged him to focus more on political correctness than operational efficiency. Indeed, Göring valued him for his 'good company' which, in the pre-war years at least, was more than enough to keep him in place. While it is not wise to rely too much on the opinions of protagonists after the event, especially ones on the losing side, it is worth noting that the decorated Luftwaffe fighter pilot, Adolph Galland, later called Schmid 'a complete wash-out', and Milch said he had 'trimmed his sails to the wind.'[12] When considering Schmid's qualities it is important to note that, whatever assessment is made of his performance in intelligence, he served throughout the war with increasing rank, thanks to Göring, ending up as a generalleutnant in control of the 1st Jagdkorps, then Luftflotte 3 and finally in command of all units charged with Defence of the Reich in 1945. Having said that, there is no record of any historian claiming that he served with distinction in any of these roles.

The Luftwaffe had suffered from an accelerated development which outstripped its organisational capabilities and, through Göring's leadership, was too much wedded to political dogma to have ever had the chance of becoming a balanced and properly organised service. For instance, there were no adequate facilities for scientific aeronautic research. Neither was there sufficient attention given to providing logistical support units which would later prove to be a crucial failing in the Battle of Britain, when the shortage of replacement fighters weakened the *Jagdgeschwader* in September and October. Intelligence was also neglected alongside these auxiliary elements, all of which somehow were considered to be un-military and rather a bit too highbrow for Nazi ideology.

Many of the 5th Abteilung personnel had been drawn from the Foreign Air Forces Branch of the General Staff and consisted of civilians and reserve officers who, in their previous roles, had been used to following a strategy which did little more than exaggerate the strength of foreign air forces in order to justify German armament production. The section was tasked with 'evaluation of intelligence on foreign states, their military-political appreciation, especially on all questions in connection with the area of air war command' and 'target study'.[13] Schmid, for all his personality shortcomings, however, was a clever man and realised that the impending war required something more in the way of intelligence appraisals than had hitherto been the case. He adjusted his departmental priorities to focus more on acquiring intelligence about potential enemy targets. Technical Staff Officers were given extended leave in order to travel to foreign countries to become acquainted with the political and economic environment there.[14] This practice had been an intrinsic part of German intelligence-gathering since the 1920s, when Reichswehr officers had travelled extensively in the United States. There was a general shake-up of staff which saw younger and more suitably qualified officers brought in, but qualified men were few and far between and until a sufficient number could be recruited the department still relied on the knowledge and experience of its older reservist personnel who, for the most part, were unsuitable from both a physical and intellectual perspective. It was often the case, also, that the efficiency of intelligence gathering was undermined by Göring and Milch insisting on having their friends or personal favourites appointed to desirable positions such as attachés serving with diplomatic missions.[15] The attaché service was particularly inept at intelligence gathering as a result, especially given that reports from embassies were thoroughly vetted and amended as required in order to conform to political imperatives.[16] The whole attachés service was undermined by its never having 'trained men specifically for the job', and selected personnel on the basis of 'good character, military knowledge, social skills and handsome appearance'.[17]

The Press Group, part of the 5th Abteilung, was responsible for monitoring both local and foreign news media. Foreign newspapers could have been used much more effectively as a source of potential target intelligence, but again a shortage of foreign language personnel restricted its performance. One major source of intelligence was a column written by a French Major Longeront for the right-wing *L'Intransigeant* newspaper, in which he reported on personnel transfers, promotions and movement of air squadrons.[18] German media was scoured for indiscretions and censorship became widespread to restrict reporting and exposure of its own sensitive material.[19]

The main departments of Schmid's new organisation were set up as a second echelon at their Wildpark-Werder headquarters near Potsdam, and other departments at Kurfürst, in Berlin. Schmid, and his immediate staff, however, lived and worked in the Sonderzug 'Robinson' command train mobile headquarters of the Luftwaffe General Staff. Daily conferences were held at Kurfürst and chaired by Jeschonnek or his deputy, where the minutes of the previous day's Führer conference were discussed and all necessary orders issued to field commanders.[20]

There was clearly a general systemic mindset throughout the German armed forces which viewed intelligence departments as low priority. They were usually underfunded, lacked authority and were 'not a strong suit in the German military tradition'.[21] With each intelligence department vainly seeking recognition only to be rebuffed, each tended to become suspicious and jealous of the others generating debilitating inter-departmental rivalries. Schmid had an advantage over other, more competent, rivals because of his Nazi credentials and closeness to Göring, which gave him unparalleled access to the highest levels of command. In an atmosphere where personal advancement in this field often tended to depend upon operatives varnishing the truth according to what might be acceptable, Schmid excelled. He was a fine example of an ex-Army Nazi-party hack who had great personal ambition, but lacked any experience of intelligence gathering or its analysis. His department was actually quite small and incapable of wide-ranging research and monitoring, but Göring, who seemed not to rely too much on Schmid's opinions anyway, was often willing to take him at his word, which usually avoided uncomfortable details. The 5th Abteilung, under-resourced and lacking rigorous practices, acquired the habit of relying on whatever information it could surreptitiously glean from rival departments, from perusal of foreign press coverage and generally outdated pre-war publications. As a result, despite Schmid's personal relationship with Göring, his staff were seen as low-grade personnel who did not fit into the normal military structure and whose advice was generally treated with disdain by their operational superiors. Nevertheless, Schmid had moderate success in acquiring intelligence sufficient to inform his early reports which were considered wide-ranging but lacked depth owing to staff shortages. Göring at that time called Schmid's work 'exemplary' in reference to its photoreconnaissance component.[22] Possibly Schmid's most important contribution to the Luftwaffe war effort against Britain was his dossier consisting of detailed lists of potential targets, many with aerial photographs supplied by the Strategic Reconnaissance Group, headed by Oberst Theodor Rowehl. These files were copied and distributed to all bomber *geschwader* of Luftflotten 2 and 3.[23]

Intelligence within the Luftwaffe was judged more on how it supported the ambitions of the Luftwaffe leadership, especially Göring, rather than on its intrinsic value. Throughout the whole Battle of Britain, Schmid never failed to provide his commander with precisely the information he required to justify and explain away one setback after another and confidently predict an imminent turnaround of fortunes. His attitude may well have been permanently coloured by the way in which a report had been received during 1939, pointing out that unless Germany increased her air strength, the combined air resources of France and Great Britain would outstrip those of Germany by the beginning of 1940. This report had the powerful backing of the then Luftflotte 5 Commander, General Erhard Milch, but when Göring read it he summoned his Chief of the General Staff, General Hans Jeschonnek, and Schmid to a severe dressing-down for their defeatist analysis and ordered the report to be destroyed.

During 1939, the German High Command had expanded its intelligence-gathering facilities by creating a new decryption agency,

OKW Chi (Oberkommando der Wehrmacht, Chiffrierabteilung), headed up by Oberstleutnant Friedrich (Fritz) Boetzel, 'a man of some charm and broad cultural interests'.[24] This service was increasingly staffed by experts in the fields of linguistics, mathematics, electronics and such like, who were beginning to transform intelligence gathering and its analysis. They specialised in the interception and decryption of secret diplomatic and military communications. There still remained, however, the thorny problem of getting the authorities to take intelligence seriously and act on it swiftly and decisively.

In October of that year, a sister agency, OKL Chi-Stelle (the Luftwaffe equivalent of OKW-Chi) had a stroke of luck when an RAF Wellington bomber was shot down by flak at Erfurt, and yielded up a series of cards with seemingly random characters printed on them. Someone was curious enough to pass them on to the local Luftwaffe Intelligence operative and they ended up at Chi-Stelle headquarters with cryptanalyst Ferdinand Voegele. Voegele, an accomplished linguist with hands-on experience of radio-traffic interception, was absorbed in his work and had remained aloof from politics. He had worked for some time on trying to break the RAF codes which many believed to be undecipherable. He recognised the symbols on the captured cards as belonging to the RAF Syko encryption system. This was used in conjunction with radio traffic to the aircraft as a means of secure communications, but the codes, which were changed daily, could only be cracked if the cards were examined on the day they were issued and at the time of a live radio transmission. Fortunately, the service was also routinely listening to RAF radio traffic. The two, in combination, opened a window on RAF codes, but manpower limitations threatened to thwart all efforts to exploit the opportunities opening up until Generalleutnant Wolfgang Martini of the 3rd Abteilung Signals Corps sent him fifty men to work on breaking the code.[25]

Because of the way that the British communicated with their French allies, parts of the same message were often sent in both languages, which was a gift for the German cryptanalysts. They also discovered that the RAF routinely published monthly Air Force Lists, freely available at bookshops, that listed registration numbers and type of all their aircraft. Together with radio intercepts of RAF training flights, this allowed the Luftwaffe to build up a picture of RAF aircraft types in use, where they were located and in what numbers. All this information gave German Intelligence a vital 'crib' to break what had been previously thought to be impenetrable ciphers. It was painstaking work to identify 'crib' words (the most frequently used words) and work out how they had been encrypted, but the process was accumulative and once a 'crib' was uncovered it made it slightly easier to identify others. A second line of investigation was weather reports, which were sent twice a day in five-figure code. The limited lexicon of these messages reduced enormously the task of decrypting, so that by early 1940 the Syko codes had been broken and up to 600 radio intercepts per day were yielding usable intelligence in real time.[26]

Generalleutnant Wolfgang Martini, 'an officer with great initiative, creativeness, and an intuitive sense [who] spared no effort in developing his group into a model unit', was head of the 3rd Abteilung (Funkhorchdienst), which had been set up in 1936 specialising in monitoring the radio traffic of potential enemies.[27] The officer with specific responsibility for radio intelligence was Kurt Gottschling. The Luftwaffe was still shrouded in secrecy and so, in order to conceal their true purpose, the monitoring stations had been set up ostensibly as research centres to record weather data. These 'weather stations' were stone buildings which incorporated radio-receiving rooms, direction-finding control, data evaluation and communications. They were surrounded by tall wooden towers supporting the aerials. A station at Telgte (weather station 12), just outside Munster with forward stations at Emden and Husum (weather station 22) were assigned to cover the area Holland-Belgium-England. The two main functions of these radio stations were first, using radar, to detect and track enemy aircraft entering German air space, and second, to monitor enemy radio traffic to determine their air control systems. Having no specialist of its own, the Luftwaffe had to beg staff from the Army, who offered fourteen, and the Kriegsmarine who ignored the request.[28]

Despite this inauspicious start, under Martini's sound leadership, the service soon grew into a very strong organisation. It was tasked with a) establishing lines of communication between Luftwaffe command posts and all subordinate agencies in the field, static and mobile; b) establishing lines of communication between weather observation stations and airfields and setting up a network of direction-finding beacons; c) maintaining air surveillance over important areas to detect intruders; and d) continuing the expansion of a radio intercept network to monitor radio communications of neighbouring countries. By the end of 1939, Martini had four radio monitoring command posts with nine intercept stations.[29]

This 3rd Abteilung was another department run almost as a private enterprise with little inter-departmental contact, but it did have direct lines to the Cryptographic Centre of the Luftwaffe at the New Palace in Potsdam, which had the necessary staff for decoding many of the signals.[30] The whole Luftwaffe radio intelligence organisation employed about 5,000 men and was under the command of Major Ulrich Freudenfeld. Its prime function was to ascertain the enemy air organisations and operations by eavesdropping on radio communications. Martini's section was well organised and adequately equipped, but was subordinate to Schmid's 5th Abteilung in the selection of mission targets and was obliged to feed its reports back through the same channels, denying it the means of evaluating its own intelligence in close collaboration with other field agencies and then planning further missions based upon their findings.[31] Martini's work was kept so secret and isolated that when Generalleutnant Nielsen became Chief of Staff of the Luftwaffe in 1940, he had never heard of the 3rd Abteilung. Martini was not unaffected by intrigue all around him and maintained a strict security blanket over his operations, even to the point of refusing access to very senior commanders to his field stations. Nielsen claims that it 'could have been an extremely valuable source for obtaining or supplementing elements of information if the evaluation had been properly organised but this was never the case, neither before nor during the war.'[32]

After the fall of France the new radio intercept stations set up along the Channel coast found communications with Potsdam to be problematic owing to the distance between them, so a new cryptographic centre was established at Noisy, just north of Paris; but not before October 1940. Through his work Martini built up an excellent picture of Fighter Command control systems and especially of its radar experiments. He had personally flown in a dirigible, the 'Graf Zeppelin', along the British east coast on two occasions in May and August of 1939 to try and monitor signals emanating from the new towers being constructed there, suspecting that they were part of an electronic early warning system. He packed the airships with large quantities of electronic receivers to try and determine exactly what was the function of the transmitters. On each occasion the airship was detected by a number of British radar stations, but they chose not to investigate with aircraft fearing that such a response might alert the interloper that they had been spotted. It turned out that Martini was monitoring on the wrong wavelengths and so failed to pick up any of the signals which, rather than diminish his suspicions, led him to conclude that the stations were not operating at the time of his missions. He remained convinced that the stations were part of a radar chain, but the failure of his missions did not help his cause and it remained an uphill struggle to get Göring interested in British radar. Göring seemed to think that Martini was exaggerating the importance of his work for personal advancement. The almost total lack of cooperation with other intelligence departments also robbed Martini of the chance to correlate his own information with that of other sections, such as that which interrogated captured British airmen. Martini reported directly to Schmid, who was very judicious in his use of Martini's reports and generally gave them scant attention. It was Schmid's general policy to ignore or downplay information for which he could not take personal credit.

Even had Martini discovered the true nature of the spindly towers, he would have had no way of understanding how radar detection fitted into the Dowding System of fighter control. German research into radar was conducted, for the most part, by departments outside the Luftwaffe which had never considered it to be a basic requirement of air policy. Radar was, if anything, a component of defence rather than attack and had been side-lined within the Luftwaffe, considered to be of interest mainly to the Army; it was generally outside Luftwaffe operational needs. Crucially, however, neither had given any thought to how radar might be developed as a component of an enemy defensive system which the Luftwaffe might come up against. Neither Poland nor France had employed radar to any significant extent and so the Luftwaffe had no experience of how it might be used by an enemy, nor how it could be countered. Little thought had been given as to how a more scientifically orientated air force, such as the RAF, might use it. The sheer power of the Luftwaffe, the report seemed to say, obviated the need to look closely at British defensive capability, which would crumble under the crushing blows of the first mass attack. Had Schmid consulted with other intelligence units, such as Martini's 3rd Abteilung, he might have been able to build up a more comprehensive understanding of the sophistication of the Dowding System but, of course, that was never likely to happen.

The daily monitoring of British radio traffic by Martini's twenty-four mobile and fixed listening stations, many of which were on the Channel coast, allowed Chi-Stelle to work out the RAF fighter and bomber deployment. Once his listeners were in place, Martini's stations also started picking up signals radiating out from the tall coastal towers which he suspected, but crucially could not prove, to be radar transmissions. Most of his efforts were focused on early detection of night-time RAF bombing raids over Germany. A message intercepted early in the day could be decoded by the afternoon and information passed on to the relevant target areas in good time to alert the defences. Intercepting traffic about British bomber raids was one thing, but accumulating usable information about RAF defences, especially their fighter squadron deployment against Luftwaffe raids going in the other direction, was quite a different matter. The emphasis remained on defence and in this regard Luftwaffe operations closely resembled the British Intelligence priorities, but it was the British who would benefit most when the Luftwaffe found itself, for the most part, in an offensive role. While the several hours required to decrypt British signals was sufficient to prepare against a night-time bombing raid, the signals calling for RAF fighter deployment against Luftwaffe bombers would still be un-decoded long after the action had concluded.

While interception and deciphering of radio traffic should have been seen as a clear priority, the way that intelligence was managed in the German forces, and the Luftwaffe in particular, gave little confidence to Martini that he might have a positive role to play in the Luftwaffe's battle. The component parts tended to work independently rather than cooperatively. Göring's Forschungsamt was barely even a part of the Luftwaffe, more his private service, and had creamed off many of the more talented codebreakers in a bid to win more control of the Intelligence services, but had made little practical use of them other than to spy on his enemies within Germany. The German head of cryptanalysis, William Fenner, described the Forchungsamt as 'the inner foe'.[33] This ensured that the Luftwaffe operational leadership had a low opinion of its own intelligence-gathering capabilities, and also did not view it as a prerequisite for military victory and paid it little heed.

As we have seen, the Luftwaffe had not considered it necessary to create a centralised intelligence-gathering agency when it was formed, choosing instead, in keeping with its modern, dynamic image, to place greater emphasis on mobility of its flying units and ground support organisation. It was thought that, in time of war, its *geschwader* stations would be constantly shifting so that an intelligence headquarters based in Berlin would be unable to maintain fixed lines of communication to whatever theatre of operations was most active at the time. This was especially true of the radio intercept services which had to rely on bare wire link, which attracted much interference and often made communications unintelligible. Although each Luftwaffe unit had its own intelligence officer, he would be expected to get all his information from a central source and would have no active intelligence-gathering role.

There were no less than ten separate signals intelligence agencies, each deeply suspicious of the others and jealously guarding its own operations. Fenner tried hard to integrate them under OKW-Chi but it was an impossible task.[34] Neither was there any mechanism for collecting intelligence from subordinate agencies despite, or possibly because of, Schmid's strenuous efforts to create an inter-service section in OKW, headed by Schmid himself, which was bitterly resisted by his rivals.

The Luftwaffe was the newest of the German military arms and as such was not restrained by precedent, tradition or institutional conservatism. Göring, upon taking command, had imbued the service with National Socialist (Nazi) doctrine which had impressed and delighted Hitler who, despite the professionalism and recent successes of his Army, saw the Luftwaffe as the embodiment of his political ambition. As a result, the Luftwaffe was staffed, at least administratively, by people who were chosen more for their political correctness than military expertise, and that was to prove decisive when the Luftwaffe was tasked with delivering military success without the support of either the Army or the Navy.

On an operational level, when the intelligence departments were established, information was collected through a variety of channels of field intelligence then funnelled up to headquarters where it was collated, and digests then sent back down to the operational units. By far the most productive arm of field intelligence was the Strategic Reconnaissance Group, headed by Rowehl, which operated the Aufklärer aerial reconnaissance units producing daily up-to-date reports. Rowehl, a former First World War naval observer, said, 'One of the most important and valuable organisations for collecting information on conducting the air war both before and during hostilities was the Strategic Reconnaissance Group of the Luftwaffe High Command.'[35]

German political aspirations included the amalgamation of all German-speaking peoples in eastern Europe into a greater Reich and the return of the Danzig corridor to German control. It was the Danzig situation which led to the creation of what became the major tool of Luftwaffe Intelligence, aerial reconnaissance. The German military were anxious to survey the border areas, but scheduled civilian flights were banned from overflying the Polish controlled area. A former Navy flyer, the 'lanky, easygoing' Rowehl, although no longer a serving officer, had hoped to ingratiate himself with the military by privately hiring a commercial aircraft to secretly overfly the corridor, in blatant contravention of a 1929 German-Polish Treaty, at high altitude and photograph what were believed to be Polish fortifications under construction.[36] Rowehl was a flyer of some experience, having made several reconnaissance flights over England in a Rhomberg C7 during the First World War. The mission was so successful that Rowehl, while remaining a civilian, was seconded to the Abwehr (German Military Intelligence) to form his own aerial photography company, the Hansa Luftbild GmbH.[37]

The company, theoretically independent but actual a tool of the Abwehr, soon began covert missions over the Soviet Union and western Europe using Junkers F13, and later Heinkel He111 aircraft. It grew in importance throughout the 1930s and eventually split into two new units now part of the Luftwaffe; the Versuchsstelle für Höhenflüg (Experimental High-Altitude Unit) and Fernaufklärungsgruppe ObdL (Long-range reconnaissance for the C-in-C of the Luftwaffe).[38]

This High-Altitude Flying Test Agency, as it was called in the early 1930s, was secretly set up as a civilian agency with three staff and a single chartered aircraft.[39] First World War cameras were modified in cooperation with the Zeiss Optical Works at Jena. In 1935, the agency moved to Berlin and increased its strength to five aircraft. When the new Luftwaffe command structure was formed in 1936, Rowehl's unit had matured sufficiently to be incorporated into the Intelligence Division of the Luftwaffe Operations Staff, as part of the 5th Abteiluing, in the Reich Ministry, giving it greater access to the latest aircraft and apparatus.

As early as 1930, despite being prohibited from operating military aircraft, the German air staff published *Principles for Employment of the Air Force*, which set out protocols for reconnaissance aircraft operating in support of the Army.[40] There was little expectation, at that time, of seeing an independent German Air Force and all operational air units were designated as extensions of the land forces Luftsreitkräfte. With international opposition weakening against German military resurgence, ambition within the country pointed to the creation of a greatly expanded Air Force, but it was still assumed that the bulk would remain under the control of the Army with a small part going to the Navy and no more than a token force assigned to an independent air arm. In 1932, a young, ambitious General Staff officer, Hans Jeschonnek, put down a marker for future ambitions by opposing this idea, preferring instead to have all aviation units under a single independent office, a brand-new German Air Force. When this eventually materialised in 1936, the new Luftwaffe commander Hermann Göring rewarded Jeschonnek with preferment culminating eventually, by 1939, with his elevation to Chief of the Luftwaffe General Staff.

When Air Fleets, Luftfotte, were established as the highest operational command units, almost a quarter of all their aircraft were devoted to reconnaissance work, with many of them seconded to the Army and Navy. A senior Luftwaffe officer, General der Luftwaffe beim Oberkommando des Heeres, was permanently assigned to the Army General Staff as liaison with others working closely with Army corps and Panzer divisions to report back on localised combat situations. Before Germany began enacting its expansionist policies, its ground-based military operations were limited to within its national boundaries and so long-range reconnaissance became a vital source of intelligence about circumstances in the wider world. These units, formed in 1935, were designated *Fernaufklärungsstaffeln*. Some were under Army control and others remained with the Luftwaffe. The essential role of these units was to collect photographic evidence of the military, communication and industrial resources of potential enemy states.

Although a short-range reconnaissance arm was also created, it was the long-range units which were most involved in the Battle of Britain, During the early months of the war, reconnaissance flights over Britain were increased. Aircraft flew at up to 20,000ft, often leaving vapour trails to advertise their presence, but interceptions by British fighters were infrequent. Radio silence would be observed except when a target such as enemy shipping was encountered, when its location would be immediately reported. As well as aerial photography, these long-range aircraft, such as the Focke Wulf Fw200 Condor, collected vital weather data which played an important part in the timing of the 'Adlerangriff' (Eagle Attack) offensive of August 1940. Early in the war the Luftwaffe had noticed that their losses were significantly higher for Reconnaissance aircraft flying at 20,000ft than for those aircraft skimming the waves on mine-laying missions. Had they questioned why these low-flying aircraft had been relatively unmolested in enemy air space relative to high-flying aircraft that regularly attracted fighter attention, they might have uncovered a clue about the British radar shield which was blind to low-flying aircraft.

Unfortunately, the reconnaissance aircraft such as the Fw200 'Condor', for security reasons flew at great height and were at the mercy of weather conditions, meaning that their photographs were often of poor quality and low resolution. The most popular German cameras fitted to the Aufklärungsgruppe reconnaissance units were the electrically driven Zeiss Rb/30 (Reihenbildapparat) automatic range with over 200ft of film. Little use was made of stereoscopic viewers on these cameras with more emphasis put on the acquisition of large-scale images.[41] It was bad enough that the photographic images often showed little detail, but allied to this was the dearth of information available from ground-based intelligence which might have helped in the interpretation of images. While large buildings were seen, their uses could generally only be surmised unless other sources of intelligence could provide more detail.

Other branches of German Intelligence had much less access to the leadership than the 5th Abteiliung and were considered to be more or less adjuncts of the lower levels of strategic decision-making. Boetzel's Cipher Department was tasked with monitoring diplomatic exchanges and radio broadcasts and had, serendipitously, captured three RAF Typex (Type 10 or Type-X) cipher machines at Dunkirk. The Typex had been developed on the same principles as the German Enigma cipher machine, one of which had fallen into British hands as early as 1934. When Boetzel examined the machine, he found that it exhibited sufficient similarities to the Enigma machines, whose codes were believed to unbreakable, that it was pointless to pursue a detailed investigation. It is indicative of the attitude to intelligence gathering at that time that Boetzel, knowing full well the contempt in which he and his department were held by OKL, never even tried to advise Göring of his discovery shedding light on Britain's encoding capabilities. Boetzel's reaction may also have been conditioned by the fact that both he and his deputy, Major Andrea, were, at the time, passing information to the British 'Lucy' spy ring in Switzerland, as was General Erich Fellgiebel, head of OKW communications and his deputy Generalleutnant Fritz Thiele.[42] Boetzel survived the war but Thiele and Fellgiebel, who were both involved with the failed Oster Conspiracy of 1939, were later executed in 1944 for their part in Operation Valkyrie, the failed July plot to kill Hitler.

The German Army Cryptanalytic Agency, OKH/In 7/VI, which did a great deal of work trying to break the Typex codes, were only told much later that the German Army had captured three Typex units at Dunkirk, albeit minus the rotors. Had they been given immediate access to the machines, even without the rotor, they could have learned a great deal. German codebreaker Otto Buggisch later recalled that some Typex-related documents found at Dunkirk mentioned 'an English cipher security officer pointing out that he has noticed frequent breaches of the strict regulation that wheels should be turned on at random after a message has been enciphered'. It appears that Britain started the war with cipher practices that were essentially no better or worse than Germany's. British cipher clerks were making the same sorts of mistakes as the German clerks did. According to a British Intelligence memo dated 20 January 1941, the RAF actually had little faith in the security of its Typex communications, and it is believed that Typex coded messages were, in fact, being intercepted and broken by the Germans in North Africa in 1942.

The 8th Abteilung of the Luftwaffe General Staff was created to inform OKL from a historical perspective. While the 5th Abteilung was concerned primarily with collating and interpreting immediate intelligence, the 8th was tasked with making studies of previous combats as a basis for formulating current strategies. Copies of all orders and wartime reports, as well as all unit war diaries were archived there. This department, like all the others, suffered from a shortage of qualified personnel.[43]

Strange to say that another avenue of intelligence which fleetingly gained approval but quickly proved unproductive (according to Schmid), was Göring's exploration of the occult. An elderly mystic and fortune teller in Kassel, called Hermann, was reputed to have supernatural powers. Göring seemed to trust this man implicitly and briefly allocated a sizeable staff to examine ways in which Hermann's 'powers' could be exploited both for him personally and militarily. This staff consumed an impressive budget before the complete lack of usable intelligence brought the project to a halt after a few short months.[44]

On a more practical level, a special unit was set up at Rechlin air base to examine and analyse captured enemy material and draw conclusions which would inform operational efficiency. Technical experts were seconded to examine captured enemy aircraft, for instance, to see if any components might be adopted for use on Luftwaffe aircraft.[45] The reports emanating from analysis of captured material was a major contribution to the intelligence coverage of the enemy aircraft industry and they began to fill the many gaps in their intelligence. This seemingly minor aspect of intelligence had a considerable effect in a wider context during the early years of the war by depriving British bombers of the most efficient bomb-aiming devices. The Norden Mk XV bombsight had been developed by the United States military to an unprecedented level of accuracy. Its secrets were requested by the British, through the Tizard mission of mid-1940 in exchange for details of British technological developments in radar, but the US refused to give up the details of the device for fear that it would be deployed in British aircraft which might subsequently be shot down over German-controlled territory, giving the Germans direct access to what was a major US military secret.[46] Furthermore, they could then be manufactured in Germany in breach of US patents, which was a major consideration while the US remained neutral. At the Nuremberg War Trials Göring was questioned about patents and replied, 'Patents never bothered me, whether they were German or foreign.'[47]

At Oberursel in the Taunus mountains of central Germany, a transit camp (Dulag Luft) was set up in December 1939, under the command of Major Rumpel, for the purpose of interrogating captured British airmen.[48] It had

200 individual sound-proofed cells to prevent prisoners from communicating with each other.[49] At first, intelligence techniques were benign, relying on simple questionnaires, which did not go down too well in Berlin and Rumpel was soon replaced. Intelligence officers from the Luftwaffe High Command staff were tasked with trying to elicit useful information during the early stages of imprisonment by exploiting the initial state of shock and disorientation. Their interrogations, however, were compromised by the lack of wider knowledge of the overall military situation, and poor coordination between sections which meant that, in essence, the questioners, during the early months of the war, did not really know what questions might be more productive than others. During May and June 1940, many French airmen who had flown alongside British squadrons had been captured and could have provided much valuable information about British organisation and operations. The retreat and flight of the British Expeditionary Force through Dunkirk, not to mention the blunt refusal of the British government to sanction the sending of extra Hurricane squadrons, had not exactly endeared them to 'perfidious Albion'. It seems to have been an egregious error, under the circumstances, that these French fliers were not prioritised as sources of intelligence about the RAF. The French Armée de l'Aire had been routed and so information about French forces was no longer a priority, but it did not seem to occur to the Germans that some French airmen would willingly cooperate in sharing their experiences and knowledge of RAF structure, morale and operational efficiency. The overwhelming majority of British airmen captured and interrogated at Oberursel during 1940 were bomber crews, and while information garnered from them might prove of some use in developing air defence strategy, it was of little help to the Luftwaffe in its operations against Fighter Command.

One other notable, but ultimately unproductive, source of intelligence with regard to British capabilities was a sizeable element of Nazi sympathisers in Britain who worked assiduously to undermine British efforts and assist the Germans. Many worked within the political sphere fomenting popular unrest and trying to undermine the government. For instance, William Francis Forbes-Sempill, the 19th Lord Sempill, had been selling British military secrets to Japan for more than fifteen years.[50] He was also a member of 'The Link', a pro-Nazi propaganda organisation, and while his nefarious activities were known to British Intelligence, he was allowed to work in the procurement and logistical section of the Ministry of Aviation throughout the war – despite strenuous efforts by Churchill to have him removed.

Some Nazi sympathisers worked clandestinely but others, such as Sir Edward Mosley's British Union of Fascists and National Socialists, which had been formed as early as 1932, were openly subversive and soon had accumulated 40,000 members. There were others who sat with Sempill on the red leather benches of the House of Lords who, like him, were unashamed apologists for Nazi Germany. Hugh Richard Arthur Grosvenor, the 2nd Duke of Westminster, held virulent anti-Semetic views and advocated appeasement during the early war years, while Walter John Montagu Douglas Scott, the 8th Duke of Buccleuch, had hosted Joachim von Ribbentrop, later to become German Minister of Foreign Affairs, at his Scottish estate at a time when Ribbentrop, with enthusiastic support from Hitler, was running an independent foreign policy intelligence gathering unit in Berlin.[51]

Both Grosvenor and Scott were enthusiastic members of the Rights Club, a 'patriotic', anti-Semitic organisation whose motto was 'Perish Judah', which had been formed by the Conservative MP for South Midlothian and Peebles, Archibald Henry Maule Ramsay. Ramsay had gained access to sensitive material and to prevent him publishing it under parliamentary privilege, he was interned in Brixton Prison on 23 May 1940 under Defence Regulation 18B, but allowed to retain his seat in the House of Commons, which he briefly took up again upon his release in 1945. There is no evidence that the Rights Club was actively involved in espionage, but it was its very existence – giving vocal and financial support to pro-German movements – that encouraged Hitler and Göring to believe that there was the real chance of a negotiated peace in July 1940 and gave them pause for thought about making hasty plans for invasion.

This issue of high-level support for appeasement within the British Establishment is important for the way in which it influenced German thinking about Britain in 1940. As early as February of that year, Hastings William Sackville Russell, Lord Tavistock, an avowed pacifist with deep religious convictions and a wealthy financier of pro-Nazi organisations in Britain, had travelled to Dublin, with the tacit blessing of the British Foreign Secretary, Lord Halifax, to meet a German legation to discuss what peace terms the Germans might offer. It could be said that these pro-German activists ironically, in a small way, influenced events and gave Britain a modicum of breathing space in the days immediately after the Dunkirk evacuation when Hitler's prevarication over invasion may well have been influenced by his hope that well-placed British pro-Nazi sympathisers might unseat Churchill. When Churchill had come to power after the

German attack on France on 10 May 1940, the British MI5 asked for the most prominent 500 of Moseley's British Fascists to be incarcerated, but the Home Office restricted the order to only twenty-five, including Moseley himself. Many prominent members of the Establishment were left free to openly express the kind of pro-German opinions for which other 'lesser mortals' had been interned under Regulation 18B of the Emergency Powers Act. The writer Cyril Connolly was briefly detained on suspicion of spying but released immediately when it was known that he had been educated at Eton.[52]

Espionage was not restricted to the aristocracy, but the extent to which pro-Nazi subversive activities were orchestrated by German Intelligence is unclear. There was clearly contact in the immediate pre-war years between high-ranking Britons and German leaders, and the open support this gave to pro-Nazi organisations in Britain was undoubtedly influential in encouraging the activities of others, such as a young clerk in the Admiralty Charts depot, Reginald Smith, who was arrested in June 1940 in possession of top secret documents showing the location of all RAF airfields in England. Thomas Hubert Becket, a BUF activist who worked in the Air Ministry, was caught with similar material in his possession. Becket, it was discovered, had been in touch with the German propaganda ministry. He was caught making maps of aerodromes and was sentenced to three years penal servitude

Meanwhile, the large numbers of refugees continuing to enter Britain from occupied Europe meant that the security services were terribly overburdened when assessing the risk of enemy agent infiltration. One such refugee, Mitzi Round (Smythe), the German-born wife of a British soldier, had settled in Ramsgate and set about trying to find out information about the Fighter Command station at Manston at the same time as infiltrating subversive pamphlets into the mess there. Round was interned for the duration of the war.[53]

There had been many opportunities for Germany to infiltrate agents into Britain, both before the start of the war and up to May 1940 during the 'Phoney War' or 'Sitzkrieg', when traffic between Britain and the Continent was pretty much unrestricted. The agency within the Abwehr responsible for air espionage against Britain and the US was run by Nikolaus Ritter (aka Dr Randzau), who operated from the headquarters of Military District X in Hamburg. One of Ritter's first British agents was an English-speaking former seaman called Walter Simon who was sent to England in March 1938. Ritter had trained Simon to scout for information about RAF airfields and factories using local newspapers and to learn more by engaging local workers in casual conversation. He duly reported back giving details of five airfields previously unknown to Ritter. Simon's mission was deemed a great success and he was sent again some weeks later to a different area. A third trip alerted immigration officials, who took the opportunity to arrest and interrogate him in February 1939 after he had failed to register correctly as an alien in a hotel in Tonbridge at which he was staying. Simon had been reconnoitring airfields in the area. He was convicted of illegal entry and imprisoned for three months in Wandsworth prison before being deported. When war broke out, Simon was obviously unable to return to England again and instead was infiltrated into Eire by submarine in June 1940. On land his behaviour alerted the suspicions of the local police who tracked him to Dublin, where he was arrested and found to be carrying a very large sum of British currency. His true identity was revealed by means of a fingerprint check with British police. He was convicted of illegal entry and sentenced to three years in Mountjoy Prison.[54]

Arthur Graham Owens (White) was a Welsh electrical engineer with strong anti-English sentiments who had frequent business contacts with the Kriegsmarine in Kiel shipyards. Despite his nationalistic views, he had been recruited by the British Admiralty, who codenamed him 'Snow', to report any interesting technical information he stumbled across on his travels. While abroad, he made no secret of his antipathy for all things English and when he was introduced by his German girlfriend, Lily Bade, to a London club with a predominantly German clientele, he persisted with the charade. The manager of the club turned out to be a recruiting agent for the Abwehr and, taking Owens at his word, introduced him to his German spymasters who recruited him in 1936. When he was passed along to Ritter's department in 1938, he was designated as agent 3504 (some sources say 3054) and given the codename 'Johnny' (aka Colonel Johnny). On a visit to Hamburg in August 1939, Owens and his girlfriend were trained in morse code and given a radio. On his return to Britain, however, Owens' estranged wife reported him to the police as a German spy. Owens admitted as much but agreed to act as a double agent after being imprisoned in Wandsworth under Defence Regulation 18B. While there he began, under supervision, to send radio messages, primarily weather reports, to his German handlers. He was subsequently released and allowed to travel to Brussels in December 1939 for a meeting with Ritter. Owens was treading a fine line because although Ritter considered him to be 'of the greatest value for Germany',[55] British Intelligence did not trust him and held over him the prospect of trial and execution if he proved false. Later, in 1940, Owens gave Ritter a list of false names and ration book numbers which could be used as cover for German agents infiltrated into Britain during the summer of 1940. These were subsequently used to identify the agents who were rounded up and forced to send back false information.[56]

Because of Hitler's desire to avoid conflict with Britain and reach a peaceful understanding instead, no great effort or cost was expended on embedding high-value deep-cover agents who could be activated at a crucial moment. Hitler was anxious to stabilise his Western flank before launching his great 'Lebensraum' offensive in the East and this meant first eliminating the military threat from France, and second, reaching a non-aggression pact with Britain. Overt spying, Hitler thought, would prejudice negotiations with Britain. Although this strategy was modified in 1937 when Ritter was given a free hand, too much time had been lost.

The strategy backfired as British intransigence grew to the point where the prospect of a negotiated peace rapidly evaporated. Suddenly there was an urgent need for up-to-date intelligence about all aspects of British military targets and preparedness to resist invasion. Ritter started an immediate search to find suitable candidates and two volunteers came forward: Wulf Dietrich Christian Schmidt (aka Hans Hansen, aka Bjorn Björnson; agent 3725) and Gösta Caroli. Schmidt was a fervent pro-Nazi Danish national who had been born in Prussia in 1911. When he was recruited by Ritter he was given the codename 'Leonhardt'. Caroli was a Swede who had worked as an Abwehr agent in Birmingham before the war posing as a journalist. In September 1940, Schmidt and Caroli flew from Rennes in a black Heinkel He111, were dropped by parachute over southern England and told to contact agent 'Johnny' Arthur Owens. Hansen had landed safely but was quickly rounded up by British Intelligence who told him that they had captured Caroli. Facing execution, Schmidt was given the codename 'Tate' and agreed to send fake reports back to Ritter, which he continued to do for the rest of the war. He moved to north London and set up a radio transmitter sending back intelligence about airfields such as Brize Norton, but mostly weather reports and information about bomb damage in London. He was allowed to travel freely throughout England reporting to Ritter on troop movements (British and American), some accurate some false, but all under the strict control of British Intelligence.[57] Information that could be verified by other means, such as aerial surveillance, was always accurate, but troop movements that could not be corroborated were easily falsified. He was awarded 'in absentia' the German Iron Cross First and Second Class. After the war he remained in England and changed his name to Harry Williamson.

In fact, Schmidt had been betrayed by Owens who, in the meantime, had made contact with Caroli. Caroli, fearing losing contact with his equipment which had been scheduled to be dropped independently, had insisted on jumping with it strapped to him. As a result, he landed heavily, injuring his ankle, and was rendered unconscious on a farm, The Elms, in the area of Denton in Northampton. He was discovered and arrested. Also facing execution, Caroli agreed to cooperate, was given the codename 'Summer' and reported back to Ritter that his aircraft had veered off its intended route and he had fallen into a tree to the north of Oxford sustaining injuries, and was in hiding being looked after by Owens. For a while he continued to send false information back to Ritter from his location in Hinxton but became increasingly unstable mentally, attempting to murder his 'minder' and escape to Holland by canoe on one occasion. Thereafter he was 'retired' and held in custody at Huntercombe near Oxford for the duration of the war. He returned to Sweden after the war.

While Schmidt was probably the longest serving German spy in Britain, a Dane, Vera de Schallberg (Eriksen), was undoubtedly the shortest. She, along with two men, a Swiss named Werner Heinrich Walti and Theodore Druecke, travelled from Stavanger by seaplane and dinghy to make landfall at Portgordon between Banff and Inverness. Druecke and de Schallberg aroused suspicion and were arrested immediately as they tried to board a train and Walti was picked up soon afterwards in Edinburgh. Druecke and Walti were executed. De Schallberg was released and her subsequent fate is unknown. It is known, however, that she had spent some time in England in the 1930s in London as a guest of Anna Sonia de Château-Thierry, who was subsequently also found to be an agent of German Intelligence and interned for the duration of the war.

The infiltration of German spies into Britain immediately before and during the war was fraught with difficulties, not least because of the 'spy hysteria' conjured up by the press which made everyone suspicious of strangers. Restriction on movement of the whole population made travel and observation difficult, especially in sensitive areas. The ease with which the police could detain suspects under wartime regulations also compromised anyone acting in even mildly unusual ways or with strange accents. This, of course, was allied to the dearth of preparations made by the Germans for espionage, a failing that could not be rectified quickly given the lack of expertise and training facilities. It meant that people like Ritter were forced to employ agents who were not properly vetted or supervised during their operations abroad where there were no secondary support agencies. All in all, this was an 'overwhelming failure of German espionage'. [58]

There were other British-born agents apart from Owens. William Gutheridge made maps of ammunition and aircraft factories, as well as aerodromes in the London area with the intention of getting the information to Germany. He also set out on a rampage of disabling telephone boxes to obstruct air-raid wardens. He was arrested and imprisoned for seven years. While there was a significant number of people from all ranks of society who were discovered to be active in this way, the bulk of the evidence suggests that they were mostly working on their own initiative in a very amateurish, although seriously motivated, way and had no contact with German Intelligence. The inference, therefore, is that their actions were of no consequence in terms of the conduct of the war.

Up until 1938, the Luftwaffe Intelligence operations against Western European countries had been somewhat desultory, but that changed in February of that year when the tensions which were growing over the situation in Austria prompted the Chief of the Luftwaffe General Staff, General Hans-Jürgen Stumpff, to order a comprehensive survey of Britain's preparedness for war. He called on General Helmuth Felmy, Commander of Luftflotte 2 to prepare an operational plan for such an eventuality with emphasis on targeting industrial areas of London and the south-east ports, but if Felmy carried out the instruction there is no record of his report ever being presented. The Sudetenland crisis in August of the same year saw Stumpff repeat his instruction, stressing again the importance of London as a target, and this time Felmy replied but with distinctly negative conclusions. He was clearly frustrated at having his attention and resources diverted from preparations for the defence of German borders both in the east and down along the border with France. He dismissed the whole idea by indicating that the vast majority of airfields capable of handling heavy bombers with their fuel and armament stores were well away from the Channel coast. At such ranges, the bomb loads of his aircraft, allowing for full fuel tanks, would be far too low to deliver a crushing blow. As far as waging war against naval assets, Felmy bluntly told his leader that his bomber crews had no training for operations over water or attacks on shipping. It would take many months, perhaps years, before his bomber fleets were ready for war with Britain, a war of destruction against England with the resources on hand is ruled out, he told Göring. Much that was wrong, such as the types of aircraft at his disposal, could not be quickly righted. The best that his air crews could hope for was to turn the screw on Britain's maritime trade by attacks on convoys and by laying minefields around the major ports.

While acknowledging the truth of Felmy's assertions, Göring was ever mindful that such negative attitudes would play badly in Berlin and threaten both his status and his relationship with Hitler. He furiously rounded on Felmy, 'I have not asked for a memo on our strengths and weaknesses which are well known to me. I wanted you to tell me how you would deploy your forces to achieve maximum effect.'[59] This effectively put an end to Felmy's career prospects in the short term and ensured that air operations against England were not a sensible topic of discussion within earshot of the Luftwaffe High Command for many months thereafter, but a number of smaller studies were made to determine technical requirements in the event of hostilities over Britain. The conclusions of all such exercises were not encouraging. When German plans for the invasion of France were compromised during the Mechelen Incident of January 1940, Felmy was scapegoated and Göring threatened to have him removed from office, which he eventually did, but not before Jeschonnek, who had raised the issue of war with Britain again as war with France loomed, asked Felmy to review his report, which he did but, to his credit, did not diverge in any degree from his earlier conclusions. In the meantime, Schmid had, somewhat unwisely, penned a memo which substantially supported Felmy's views, which may have further honed his survival instincts and encouraged a more carefully considered approach in the future. Even Hitler was pessimistic about the outcome of any war with Britain. On 23 May in Berlin, he told his military chiefs that Britain could never be defeated by air power alone, but only by a prolonged conflict employing all available resources.[60]

In the immediate pre-war months, Schmid had reorganised his tiny department into four sections tasked with gathering information on foreign air forces and aircraft types. With the advent of hostilities, the scope of their research was widened to included information about potential bombing targets. Given the department's woefully inadequate intellectual and financial resources, there were precious few intelligence sources embedded within foreign countries and they had to rely on whatever came in from sympathisers, alongside actual published works of reference and current media reports. The only substantial addition to this less-than-impressive collection of sources was data supplied by Luftwaffe and civilian aerial photographic reconnaissance and records of intercepts of radio traffic most of which had to be begged, borrowed or filched from rival intelligence units.

One major function of military intelligence during time of war is to identify potential tactical and strategic enemy targets. A Target Research Section had been set up in 1935 which published a magazine *Die Luftwacht* (*The Air Guard*), giving information about the organisation and efficiency of foreign air forces, but this agency was severely hampered by lack of resources and relied heavily on secondary sources such as foreign publications and newspaper articles.[61] Staff in this section were mostly reactivated First World War veterans who had little knowledge or understanding of recent developments in aviation. In January 1938, the section was ordered to update all its data on potential enemy targets. The selection of these targets was governed by the German Air Field Manual[62] which identified legitimate targets as:

- Manufacturing industries
- Food supplies and food sources
- Import activities and installations
- Electricity supplies
- Rail and road routes
- Military centres
- Centres of government or administration

The manual goes on to reject the idea of attacks against civilian populations for the purpose of terrorising the inhabitants. Article 25 of the Hague Convention stated: 'It is forbidden to attack or fire upon, with any means whatsoever, undefended, towns, villages, dwellings or buildings.'[63] But the manual assumes that the rule applies only to land warfare and that 'any means whatsoever' did not cover aerial warfare and, furthermore, did not apply to attacks on military installations within civilian areas. This was academic, however, since Germany had not signed up to the Convention anyway. Göring, speaking at the Nuremberg War Trials said, 'In my personal opinion the convention known as the Hague Rules of Land Warfare is not an instrument that can be applied to modern warfare.'[64]

At the outbreak of war, the special photoreconnaissance Staffel formerly subordinated to OKW was put under the control of the 5th Abteilung and became the ObdL Gruppe. Schmid was very supportive of its reconnaissance work with its pioneering technical achievements in high-altitude flying. A photographic survey was carried out by high-flying He111C aircraft, augmented by rather low-level intelligence gathering, which formed the basis of a strategic assessment of Britain's capabilities. On 1 June 1939, the German Air Ministry had issued a document entitled Orientation Book Great Britain[65] which contained an assessment of British air power alongside details of potential British targets in the event of war.

A series of 'target files' was created which allocated each target a code (e.g. GB10 for Airfields; GB50 for power stations; GB45 for docks; GB45 3 for Millwall Dock). The document, however, failed to recognise the extent to which British industry had moved onto a war footing after the Munich Crisis. Somewhat unenthusiastically, it offered the gloomy assessment that the British Isles presented 'very difficult meteorological flying conditions'.

When a thorough aerial survey of Britain had been completed, a target folder was compiled for each location comprising:

- a 1:250,000 scale map to determine aircraft approach
- proximity of enemy airfields
- navigational aids such as railway lines
- a 1:5000 scale map of the target

Other details which might be included were:

- the most important parts of the installation
- the most advantageous time to attack
- the best type of bomb for the installation

The number of British targets identified far outweighed the strike capacity of the Luftwaffe bomber fleets so it was necessary to prioritise targets. In order to do so it was necessary to determine:

- what category of goods was of most importance to the enemy's military?
- what level of stockpiling existed?
- the means of disrupting supplies of essential materials
- the main dockland areas
- the main inland transport routes
- the vulnerable points along internal transport routes
- the location and generating capacity of power stations
- the main electricity power supply lines

It was the job of Luftwaffe Intelligence to determine:

- when and under what circumstances a target might be attacked to offer the best prospect of success?
- what might be the consequences to the enemy of a successful attack?
- how might the success of an attack be assessed?

The document made clear the necessity for continuous reassessment of the results obtained through analysis of the surveys. In a fast-changing political and industrial landscape, it was essential to keep track of new (or diminished) sources of raw materials and development of new industrial processes and factories. With a clear directive to concentrate on the 'centre of gravity' of the enemy, the manual states 'operate only against the currently most important elements.'[66] The 'importance' factor was the vital consideration and this could change quite quickly, requiring a nimble response.

Throughout 1938, the Luftwaffe High Command, heavily influenced by the opinions of Göring, viewed a war with the British as both undesirable and unnecessary and in consequence had not developed any serious plans for an air war with them. By the start of 1939, however, Europe was being transformed as events presaged war, prompting Studie Blau, Schmid's first detailed 94-page assessment of British military strength in response to Göring'sorders to prepare an analysis of Britain's vulnerability to air attack.[67] Schmid convened weekly conferences attended by specialists in foreign affairs, counter-intelligence officers, economists, technical and scientific experts, industrial leaders, professors of geopolitics and the Air Attaché from London. It even had Milch, Jeschonnek and Ernst Udet, Luftwaffe Director General of Equipment, as permanent members. While the report covered all potential enemies it was the discussion of British life; government, constitution, trade, agriculture, power, rail communications and industry with special attention to air vulnerability, which dominated proceedings. Much information came from existing, freely available, publications, journals and especially British newspapers. Jeschonnek anticipated that the assessment would be 'of decisive importance for the success of aerial operations', particularly against Britain. The final report was presented in July to Göring who described it as 'exemplary', but in reality, it was less than comprehensive and the haste in which it had been prepared was evident in its lack of detail.

The report was augmented by photographic material derived from aerial reconnaissance of major British ports and airfields. Some information about armament production and deployment of RAF squadrons came from interception of radio traffic. Generalfeldmarschall Albert Kesselring, commander of Luftflotte 2 in 1940, later described Studie Blau as 'an integrated plan that constituted a really useful basis for the air battle against Britain and might well have served as a useful document in planning for an invasion'.[68]

The study contained analysis of all aspects of British life, from its political landscape through industrial strength to the level of British 'shadow factories' (buildings which could be rapidly converted to boost military production in the event of war). It included aerial photographs of the ports of London, south coast ports, aircraft factories and aerodromes.

Its conclusions were as follows:

- Britain had a very secure and firmly anchored form of government.
- Britain was in an extremely strong position economically.
- Its military power was built on its Navy, which had already begun mobilisation, and which was far superior to its German counterpart.
- The Royal Air Force was being rapidly modernised and might rival the Luftwaffe by the end of 1940.
- Defence against air attack is well-prepared and constantly improved.
- The British Army is small and efficient but is only of any significance in combination with the French.
- Stockpiling had begun in all spheres of British industry.
- The British economy relied heavily on imports and overseas communications, making its seaports the most critical organ of the British economy. Overall, Britain imported far more than three quarters of all its agricultural, industrial and oil requirements. While the country might be able to reduce its reliance on imported foodstuffs during time of war, its demand for mineral oil would increase substantially.
- The USA is capable of supplying more than 90 per cent of Britain's wartime import requirements. This means that Atlantic convoys in time of war would be the single most important means of British survival.
- In any war, the neutralisation of the British naval and commercial ports, together with defeat of the Air Force and elimination of the aircraft industry that sustains it, are essential prerequisites for success.
- To achieve this the Luftwaffe must be very strong to counter the British capacity for improvisation and its high levels of morale.
- It is doubtful that the British can be defeated militarily through the sole use of air power.

Although competition is weak, it is widely believed that Studie Blau, given the wide range of military, economic, diplomatic and technical input, was the best study ever made in the field of Luftwaffe Intelligence evaluation, interpretation and analysis. While its conclusions were sound, the intelligence upon which they were based was short on detail, which at the time was not thought too much of a weakness but which, once the Battle of Britain had begun, proved impossible to fill out or update. It is obvious that it did not make comfortable reading for Schmid's masters and possibly as a consequence of that was given scant attention, which is unfortunate given that its conclusion might have better prepared the Luftwaffe for the robust British resistance it subsequently faced. Anyway, at the time, an air war with Britain was not a prominent item on the Luftwaffe agenda.

The momentous achievements such as the Anschluss and occupation of Czechoslovakia had shown that military power was best employed in a supporting role to political manoeuvring and within the armed services, at least, there was little appetite for an aggressive war and a, perhaps hopeful, expectation that none would erupt for several years. Even the military build-up against Poland, many hoped, would see further territorial gain without interference from either France or Britain, and supine acceptance of yet another redrawing of the political map. By the time that Studie Blau was relevant to Luftwaffe strategists in the summer of 1940, it already had about it an air of redundancy offering little in the way of up-to-date analysis. Schmid later observed, however, that if his Studie Blau had been given more attention both at the time it was submitted, and later during the Battle of Britain, the course of the war could have taken a very different turn.[69] Robert Forczyk in his analysis disagrees and claims that even if Studie Blau had been used to plan Adlerangriff, it 'was well out of date' by July 1940.[70]

Once the invasion of Poland began, Schmid's department was tasked with a new and extremely important responsibility: to provide OKL with a daily resumé of the military situation all across Europe, drawn up from situation reports from Army, Navy and Air Force headquarters with special attention given to radio intercepts. The German B-Dienst Naval codebreakers had broken the Royal Navy Cypher No. 2 and were regularly reading many of the naval communications, while OKL Chi-Stelle, under its chief, Ferdinand Voegele, was listening in on traffic from British air attachés in neutral countries such as Switzerland.[71] These daily resumés were digested at OKL High Command close to Potsdam, but when German attention focused on France, it was soon apparent that Potsdam was too far from the Western theatre of operations, so the command was now split with the intelligence staff, headed by Schmid, moving with the highest echelon in a mobile headquarters and other units embedded in active units from where they were required to submit daily situation reports.

Schmid's next major report, entitled 'Proposal for the Conduct of Air Warfare Against Britain', came out in November 1939, after the occupation of Poland.[72] It would undoubtedly have been influenced by Hitler's Directive No. 6 for the Conduct of the War issued on 9 October which began:

1. Should it become evident in the near future that England, and, under her influence, France also, are not disposed to bring the war to an end, I have decided, without further loss of time, to go over to the offensive.
2. Any further delay will not only entail the end of Belgian and perhaps of Dutch neutrality, to the advantage of the Allies; it will also increasingly strengthen the military power of the enemy, reduce the confidence of neutral nations in Germany's final victory, and make it more difficult to bring Italy into the war on our side as a full ally.
3. I therefore issue the following orders for the further conduct of military operations:
   (a) An offensive will be planned on the northern flank of the western front, through Luxembourg, Belgium, and Holland. This offensive must be launched at the earliest possible moment and in greatest possible strength.
   (b) The purpose of this offensive will be to defeat as much as possible of the French Army and of the forces of the Allies fighting on their side, and at the same time to win as much territory as possible in Holland, Belgium, and Northern France, to serve as a base for the successful prosecution of the air and sea war against England and as a wide protective area for the economically vital Ruhr Basin.

Clearly Hitler now realised that a successful attack against France would alter the strategic landscape in relation to an attack against Britain especially with airfields closer to the target impacting on the fuel to bomb-load ratio of the bomber fleets. He sounded an optimistic note in a memo accompanying his directive in which he wrote 'The brutal employment of the Luftwaffe against the heart of the British will to resist can and will follow at the proper time.'

Schmid wrote his report on 22 November. It concentrated on the means of crippling British maritime commerce through an extensive bombing campaign of ports and the harassment of merchant convoys. In pursuit of this aim it was considered of vital importance that operations against the

British should begin soon and in as great a strength as possible. The most important ports must be attacked without exception, and as far as possible, simultaneously. The proximity of residential areas to port facilities should not be a deterrent. Raids must be repeated by day and night. Warships under repair and under construction were also worthy of attention. However, the report simply overlooked the obvious truth that the Luftwaffe lacked sufficient long-range bombers with the capability to find the convoys at sea, or the types of weapons, such as air-launched torpedoes, required to inflict significant damage thereafter. At the time, the attention of the German military was focused on preparations for Fall Gelb, the attack against France, and the report, like Studie Blau, was all but ignored. It was not a time to be bothering Göring with detail, which he eschewed at the best of times.

Hitler followed Directive 6 with a flurry of other directives, including Directive No. 9 issued on 29 November stating:

> In our fight against the Western Powers, England has shown herself to be the animator of the fighting spirit of the enemy and the leading enemy power. The defeat of England is essential to final victory.
>
> The most effective means of ensuring this is to cripple the English economy by attacking it at decisive points.
>
> 1. Attacks on the principal English ports by mining and blockading of sea lanes leading to them, and by the destruction of important port installations and locks. In this connection, aircraft are extremely valuable in minelaying, particularly outside English west coast ports, in narrow waterways and in estuaries.
> 2. Attacks on English merchant shipping and on enemy warships protecting it.
> 3. Destruction of English depots, oil storage plants, food in cold storage and grain stores.
> 4. Interruption of the transport of English troops and supplies to the French mainland.
> 5. The destruction of industrial plant whose loss would be of decisive significance for the military conduct of war, in particular key points of the aircraft industry and factories producing heavy artillery, anti-aircraft guns, munitions and explosives.

The most important English ports, which handle 95% of foreign trade and which could not be adequately replaced by other harbours are:

- London, Liverpool and Manchester – for the import of foodstuffs, timber and oil. These three ports account for 58% of the total imports in peacetime and are of decisive importance.
- Newcastle, Swansea, Blyth, Cardiff, Sunderland, Barry and Hull – for the export of coal.
- Alternative ports of limited capacity, and for certain types of cargo only, are: Grangemouth, Holyhead, Leith, Bristol, Middlesbrough, Belfast, Grimsby, Newport, Southampton. Goole, Glasgow and Dundee.

Schmid had sensed the change of emphasis in Berlin. The situation required something more and he was eager to supply it. With the focus now shifted to France, Schmid's small section had little time to give any thought to Britain, especially as it was not possible to foresee what might be the consequences once an attack had been launched. Schmid commented on his performance up to 10 May 1940 as having 'produced a tremendous amount of work', but he was always 'pressed for time' and there were still 'gaps in the information concerning [the RAF]'.[73] After the lightning German victories of May and June 1940, notwithstanding the failure of the Luftwaffe at Dunkirk, Schmid revisited his earlier assessments of RAF inadequacies in another attempt to gain attention by issuing a 'Comparative Study of RAF and Luftwaffe Striking Power' on 16 July 1940. While Allied forces were being bottled up at Dunkirk, Hitler's attention had been diverted by the first British bombing raids over Germany. He furiously and impulsively issued Directive No. 13 on 24 May. In stark contrast to Directive 9, which had identified blockade as the primary weapon against Britain, it significantly raised the stakes by authorising large-scale retaliatory air attacks on Britain which went much further than just economic blockade.

Apart from operations in France, the Luftwaffe is authorised to attack the English homeland in the fullest manner as soon as sufficient forces are available. This attack will be opened by an annihilating reprisal for English attacks on the Ruhr.

Oberfehlshaber, Luftwaffe will designate targets in accordance with principles laid down in Directive 9 and further orders to be issued by the Oberkommando der Wehrmacht. The time and plan for this attack are to be reported to me.

Hitler's change of tone after May alerted Göring to the prospect of the Luftwaffe now assuming the leading role in the war. He had been content to parade his brand new Luftwaffe across the European stage with pomp and pride and had nervously resisted the descent into war where it might have to be used in anger, but now that the conflagration was underway he saw only an opportunity to exploit it for personal aggrandisement. The Luftwaffe had acquitted itself well during the first months of war but had paid a high price in casualties which, Göring felt, had not been sufficiently appreciated when the Panzers had grabbed all the headlines. Now was the time to right that wrong. He quickly understood that the mood was changing now that France was beaten and he was keen to ensure that he would be on the right side of history when the Luftwaffe was catapulted into the vanguard of the war effort and poised to remove the thorn of Britain from the Führer's flesh.

RAF fighters, Schmid's report claimed, were inferior to the German Bf109, and even the Bf110 was normally considered to be a match for the Spitfire, but it was grudgingly admitted that the very best British pilots might give it a hard time. Fighter Command was said to have an adequate supply of trained pilots but, especially after Dunkirk, was struggling to maintain its aircraft numbers. Schmid's report failed, almost completely, to understand the sophisticated and integrated Dowding System of fighter control, believing instead that Fighter Command squadrons operated essentially as individual units controlled entirely from their home base independently of other squadrons in the same area but operating from a different airfield.

The following are extracts from Schmid's paper:

> ...there are about 900 first-line fighters (ca. 550 Hurricanes and 350 Spitfires) of which only 75% are serviceable at any one time. They are not equipped with cannon and should be considered inferior to the Bf109.
>
> ...there are about 1,150 first-line bombers of which the Hampden (ca.400) is considered to be the best. There are also a large number of Blenheims but these are not considered to be first-line aircraft. All bombers have poor armour and bomb-aiming devices, but are generally well armed.

33

…fighter crews are generally well trained but bomber crews are mostly inexperienced and inefficient.

…the RAF is entirely dependent on home production of aircraft (200–300 fighters and 140 bombers every month).This level of production is likely to decrease in light of maritime blockade of essential raw materials. Any intensification of the air war will further reduce production. Any aircraft supplied by the US are not expected to make a contribution before 1941.

…there are substantial stocks of fuel.

…production of bombs is adequate for several weeks of operations.

…the number of heavy and light anti-aircraft guns available is by no means adequate to ensure protection of the whole island ground defences, but there is a large number of searchlights.

…there are many airstrips throughout the country but only a few can be considered to be operational with modern facilities and supply installations. There is little strategic flexibility in operations.

…the command at high level is inflexible in its organisation and strategy. As formations are rigidly attached to their home bases, command at medium levels suffers mainly from operations being controlled by officers no longer accustomed to flying. Command at low levels lacks tactical skill.

…bomber formations, even with fighter escort, are not capable of carrying out effective daylight attacks regularly, particularly as escort operations are in any case limited by the lack of long-range single-engine or heavy fighters. The RAF will therefore be obliged to limit its activity to night operations even in the event of intensified air warfare. These operations will undoubtedly achieve a nuisance value but will in no way be decisive. In contrast, the Luftwaffe is in a position to go over to decisive daylight operations owing to the inadequate air defences of the island.

…the Luftwaffe is clearly superior to the RAF as regards strength, equipment, training, command and location of bases. In the event of an intensification of the air war the Luftwaffe, unlike the RAF, will be in a position in every respect to achieve a decisive effect this year if the time for the start of large-scale operations is set early enough to allow advantages to be taken of the months with relatively favourable weather conditions.[74]

Since so much reliance was placed upon this report by the Luftwaffe High Command, it is worth noting in detail the flaws in Schmid's assessment, which were many:

- The inferiority of British fighters to the Bf109 was exaggerated; in reality the differences were small in terms of performance but certainly the Bf109's cannon were significant. The Bf110 proved to be highly vulnerable when employed as an escort fighter. Its main tactic was the formation of a defensive circle, 'Abwehrkreis', which was very effective in certain situations but when exposed in single combat, the Bf110 was quite unable to compete with the more manoeuvrable British fighters.
- The number of British anti-aircraft guns was slightly underestimated.
- Emphasis was placed on aircraft production but Dowding's real problem was in the inadequate number of qualified pilots coming through the flying schools. After its losses in the Battle of France, Fighter Command was beginning to suffer from a serious shortage of experienced, combat-hardened pilots. Aircraft production was never a problem during the Battle of Britain with more than 450 machines coming off the production lines each month. This confounded Luftwaffe analysts whose estimates of British strength were based on 'victories' from the combat reports and Schmid's low production figure.
- The analysis of British command and control was completely wrong. Schmid believed that each squadron was inflexibly tied to a particular base, but actually squadrons could move from one base to another at a moment's notice. The assessment of commanders who had lost touch with the realities of flying and combat was graphically contradicted by those, like Sir Keith Park, AOC 11 Group, who flew regularly – sometimes even in combat. This was in sharp contrast to many in the Luftwaffe middle-ranks who could not fly at all.
- Little note was taken of the repair and maintenance facilities available to squadrons especially as damaged aircraft would be landed on home ground, whereas damaged Luftwaffe aircraft had to land in enemy territory or face a long haul back across the Channel during which they would be at the mercy of pursuers.

Perhaps the most egregious error of all was that there was no mention of the British radar operations and radio communications network. The report's assessment of Luftwaffe capabilities, which Schmid was not particularly commissioned to make, by contrast, glossed over its obvious shortcomings in a way that ensured he did not disturb the mood of elation and superiority engendered in its ranks by recent successes. The limitations of this report were exacerbated by the fragmentation, rivalry and petty jealousy rampant within the German Intelligence Services. The report reiterated his assessment made months earlier:

> From Germany's point of view Britain is the most dangerous of all possible enemies. The war cannot be ended in a way favourable to us as long as Britain has not been mastered. Germany's war aim must therefore be to strike at Britain with all available weapons.[75]

Schmid had quickly recognised the new mood in Berlin and responded in a way that he thought was most advantageous for himself. The tone he adopted in his June report was totally at odds with the conclusions of Studie Blau and seems to have been clearly influenced by the stunning victories in France. It was more of a celebration of recent triumphs rather than a cold assessment of future challenges. Schmid later claimed that Studie Blau would have provided a realistic basis for preparing an aerial war with Britain, but he had comprehensively overwritten it with his report of June 1940. With Luftwaffe morale now riding high and Britain on the point of capitulation, he judged that it was not a time for him to be pessimistic. He had predicted the collapse of the French Armée de l'Aire, which boosted his confidence and elevated his department somewhat in the eyes of his superiors, prompting him to make similar forecasts regarding the RAF. Investigations had shown that his intelligence about French military and industrial centres had been particularly sound. Cursory interrogation of French officers seemed to confirm his belief in the weakness of Fighter Command, but in reality, these vanquished flyers had little interest in lauding their erstwhile allies after the retreat and evacuation of the British Expeditionary Force and, as they saw it, the abandonment of their French allies in their greatest hour of need. In this regard it was a case of Schmid hearing what he wanted to hear without questioning the motives of the speaker. It was, perhaps, a telling exposé of his general approach to intelligence.

As a result of over-optimism and misguided intentions, Schmid's paper, which the Luftwaffe High Command offered up as its contribution to invasion plans of Britain, contained many inaccuracies. In this hour of euphoric self-congratulations which permeated OKW at the time, Udet's ministry waded in with a report deprecating the fighting qualities of the Spitfire and Hurricane. In intelligence terms the situation was deteriorating by the day. Put simply, German Intelligence saw no urgent need to step up and maintain a high level of activity against Britain because Schmid believed that invasion plans were a bluff by Hitler, and many in OKW believed that British resistance was little more than belligerent rhetoric which would very quickly evaporate when the military situation was fully appreciated.[76] The sight of dishevelled and dispirited soldiers returning from Dunkirk would accelerate the decline of morale.

When Göring read Schmid's report, with its unequivocal triumphalist assertion of German aerial superiority over all other European states, it cemented Schmid's position as a close and trusted adviser. It concluded that British war production was well below that of Germany and showed little potential for expansion, and such military industrial resources as existed were extremely vulnerable to aerial attack. It failed to address, or even recognise, the existence of British radar or the nature of Fighter Command control systems set up under Air Marshal Dowding. General Halder, the German Army Chief of Staff was equally dazzled by the study and believed that the conditions were favourable for a quick demolition of the British Air Force if the need arose.

During the early part of 1940, the III./Luftnachrichten-Regiment 2, part of Martini's 3rd Abteilung, was stationed at Wissant constantly monitoring British radio traffic, and consequently gained a great deal of information about subjects such as Fighter Command Order of Battle and deployment as well as convoy movements through the English Channel.[77] There was direct contact between Wissant and all the Luftwaffe forward airfields on the Channel coast which were informed whenever a British bomber or reconnaissance aircraft had taken off and was heading their way. This close cooperation was also of vital importance in coordinating attacks on Channel convoys where RAF deployment of escort fighters informed the timing of raids. Göring had been a frequent visitor to Wissant and declared himself 'impressed'[78] with its work, but is reported to have called Martini 'a fool' on one occasion for exaggerating the importance of his work, which may account for why Martini's intelligence was low on Göring's, admittedly short, list of priorities, and why he was not listened to more closely during the Battle of Britain.

All intelligence from Wissant was handled through Luftflotte 2 headquarters, from where Kesselring sent his comments direct to Göring. The constant monitoring of British radio traffic meant that conversations between pilots and ground controllers were overheard at times when microphones were left on accidentally. Experience taught the eavesdroppers to differentiate between genuine intelligence and fake radio traffic designed to simulate non-existent ground-to-air contacts which might give the impression that more aircraft had been deployed in an engagement than was actually the case. During September, Wissant reported that a lessening of radio traffic picked up from British fighters suggested that their numbers had decreased considerably.[79] This may have encouraged both Schmid and Kesselring, whose headquarters were also at Wissant and who visited it every other day, to believe that Fighter Command strength had indeed fallen away significantly but Generalfeldmarschall Hugo Sperrle in Luftflotte 3 HQ in Paris, who did not have the same close relationship with Martini, and daily counted the heavy cost to his bomber missions, was not convinced. It was the case that Park had ordered his 11 Group squadrons to reduce radio contact between aircraft to keep airways clear for ground control transmissions, and this may have been a contributing factor in persuading Wissant that the number of British fighters was diminishing, but the empirical evidence of actual numbers encountered daily should have been a warning not to rely too much on Martini's reports.

In the early stages of the war, Schmid's 5th Abteilung had been responsible for producing a synthesis of reports coming in from all Luftflotte headquarters and Wissant, and creating situation reports concerning air attacks, air defence and the current sea and land situation.[80] This task, given the volume of intelligence coming through in twice-daily reports and the limited capabilities of Schmid's staff, was inevitably selective, both in the reports it chose to prioritise, and the conclusions drawn from them. Such conclusions were often at variance with others reaching Göring through his own operational channels. This inevitably left him wondering which of the intelligence sources was most reliable. Schmid's department was somewhat compromised by intelligence reports reaching Göring through Udet's technical officer, Oberst Ing, who appeared to consider that its task was to prove that all foreign equipment was inferior to German. His reports on the excellence of German Intelligence, bombs, and weapons were much appreciated by Göring, who placed great importance on them after the French campaign.

Since the Luftwaffe's strategic approach to the Battle of Britain was formulated according to intelligence reports emanating primarily from

Schmid's 5th Abteilung, which were, in turn, heavily influenced by Göring's over-optimistic and under-evaluated opinions, it had only a moderate chance of success right from the start. And then, disastrously, as the battle progressed, Schmid's malign influence continued to hold sway over German strategy – even when his assessment of RAF losses was seemingly contradicted by pilots' own reports of the number of British fighters and the losses of their own *geschwader* over southern England. Schmid had no direct links with the *geschwader*, which he may have been at no great pains to rectify given the bleak assessments that he was likely to hear from them. Unlike at Fighter Command, there were no specialist intelligence officers at unit level to debrief crews on a daily basis for an up-to-date picture of the battle.

Intelligence reports had been hastily produced in June to take account of the situation after Dunkirk. For the previous weeks, all attention had been focused on France, but now there were discussions in OKW about continuing the fight across the English Channel and questions needed answering. The first assessment was that the final victory over France was imminent and the British Expeditionary Force, which had been quick to give up its positions along the Dyle and had, improbably, scuttled home from Dunkirk, was demoralised and stripped of huge quantities of heavy armour and transport. The whole British effort in France was seen as evidence of weak morale and an unwillingness to engage. The loss of so much armour and equipment after their evacuation convinced German Intelligence that Britain had no possible chance of continuing the war by themselves. This sat comfortably alongside Hitler's well-known disinclination to pick a fight with Britain, the outcome of which, he believed, would be detrimental to both their interests. The majority opinion within the higher levels of military and political leadership was that Britain would sue for peace. What German Intelligence had failed to appreciate in all this, however, was the stubborn will of the new British Prime Minister, Churchill, and the growing mood of resistance that his belligerent rhetoric was engendering in the British population.

On 30 June, Göring issued such a wide-ranging list of objectives for his commanders that in pursuing them all, the accomplishment of any one of them was almost impossible. Military doctrine demanded that Luftwaffe Intelligence should have, from the start, identified the British 'centre of gravity', the main source of its military power and capabilities, and concentrated all its efforts unceasingly on its destruction. Instead, the Luftwaffe was commanded to attack RAF ground-based organisations, harass shipping and harbour facilities and, at the same time, deal crushing blows to British industrial centres. Göring's directive exemplifies the way in which his approach to leadership, evident throughout the Battle of Britain, owed everything to exhortation and wild optimism and almost nothing to deliberation and detailed analysis or indeed to sound military practice.

Schmid, meanwhile, was required to furnish the Luftflotte commanders with details of potential bombing targets, but all he had to go on was his Sudie Blau appraisal which had not been updated for months. A cursory perusal of the Luftwaffe Air Field Manual would have alerted him to the possibility that 'the results of combat action can be exceptionally important in the political field and in the field of International Law. Attacks carried out at the wrong time can produce results diametrically opposed to those intended.' It was clear that the caveat, 'the Supreme Command directing the whole war [Hitler] must retain the possibility of exercising a strong influence on the conduct of air warfare,' would have had Schmid looking over his shoulder at every turn of events and trying hard not to suggest actions that might prove to be out of step with the volatile political decision-making elite.[81]

Once the battle had started in earnest after 10 July, there was no indication that Luftwaffe operations were driven by intelligence-based decisions. Operations were desultory and without any clear objective. Political directive on an operational level was nebulous and it was left to Luftflotte commanders to carry out whatever operations they judged to be within the broad confines of the vague aspirations that had been expressed. Initially, an order to attack convoys as a means of disrupting maritime commerce and acquiring dominance of the air space over the English Channel seemed to be no more than a holding operation giving crews experience of combat in a new environment, while newly acquired airfields in northern France were occupied and made combat-ready. While these attacks were successful in causing Atlantic convoys to be rerouted north of the British Isles and disrupting coal shipments to south-west England, they were hardly a significant blow to British maritime trade.

By the end of July, however, as the Luftwaffe were completing the relocation of Luftflotten 2 and 3 to French airfields, Göring instructed his commanders to prepare for Adlerangriff (Eagle Attack), a massive four-day onslaught on Fighter Command infrastructure in south-east England the success of which would force Britain to the negotiating table. The tone of Göring's instructions prior to Adlertag (Eagle Day) was set at his Hague Conference on 1 August. The flawed intelligence upon which he based his plans was exposed but suppressed, as illustrated by an exchange with the Jagdfliegerführer Commander Generalmajor Theodor Osterkamp. Osterkamp had flown missions over Britain and assured Göring that in his estimation, based on observation of squadron markings on British aircraft, there were between 500 and 700 British fighters operating in the south of England, which was about 50 per cent more than the figure on which Göring had based his plans but also, incidentally, rather more than was actually the case since there were never more than twenty-two squadrons in 11 Group at any one time. Göring angrily refuted Osterkamp's claim and declared that his own intelligence was 'excellent', and anyway the Bf109 was much superior to the British fighters which, evidence showed, assiduously avoided engagement with Luftwaffe fighters. Furthermore, Göring was dismissive of Sperrle and Kesselring's objections to the deployment of daytime bombers over the British mainland before the fighter defences had been eliminated, quoting Schmid's figures for British fighter losses in the previous weeks as evidence that the bombers would face weak resistance.

On 7 August, Schmid circulated a memo to all commanders which was factually inaccurate and strategically misleading. He was reluctant to revise his earlier opinion that British fighters were controlled directly from their home station and confidently denied that there was a wider communications web. He wrote:

> As the British fighters are controlled on the ground by R/T, the forces are tied to their respective ground stations and thereby restricted in ability, even taking into consideration the probability that the ground stations are partly mobile. Consequently, the assembly of strong fighter forces at seven points and at short notice is not to be expected. A mass German attack on a target area can therefore count on the same conditions of light fighter opposition as in attacks on widely scattered targets. It can, indeed, be assumed that considerable confusion in the defensive networks will be unavoidable during mass attacks, and that the effectiveness of the defences can thereby be reduced.[82]

Adlerangriff was some recognition of the need for focus, but a combination of poor weather, muddled operations and stout British resistance denied the Luftwaffe a clear success. The operation was repeatedly delayed owing to unsuitable weather, eventually starting on 13 August, but even then, it started with a shambolic episode where a bombing raid was launched without fighter escort, resulting in severe losses. Göring, reacting in panic to a sudden change in the weather, had ordered a last-minute pause; being so far from the action on his estates near the Polish border, however, his message failed to reach all units in time. Later in the day, when operations were given the green light, far from delivering the decisive blow to Fighter Command, the *geschwader* laboured repeatedly under the burden of inadequate intelligence about targets. Göring had boasted that four days would be time enough to finish the job, but instead of identifying the 'centre of gravity' and concentrating all effort on its destruction, the Luftwaffe dissipated its energy over a wide range of targets, many of which were Coastal Command stations and no part of Fighter Command operations. Göring had failed to take seriously Martini's warnings about radar and while dive-bombers did make some attempts to knock out coastal radar stations, their importance was short-lived when Göring quickly reverted to his default position of scepticism and removed them from the target list on which he had only reluctantly agreed to put them in the first place.

When the British radar stations were attacked and apparently hit during Adlerangriff, Martini's 3rd Abteilung reported that they were continuing to operate as normal. It was clear that the radar towers had not been destroyed, relatively immune as they were to bomb blast due to their open structure, but the fact that they continued to emit signals led Luftwaffe Intelligence to erroneously conclude that the Operations Rooms were underground and undamaged. In fact, where a station had ceased to operate through bomb damage, as at Ventnor, mobile units were drafted in to continue emitting signals which gave the impression that the station was undamaged. The critical importance of radar and the way in which it underpinned British defensive strategy was still not appreciated by the Luftwaffe and under the circumstances attacks on the towers, while not entirely abandoned, were given a lower priority.

All of Göring's hopes for a swift resolution to the conflict were shattered by his failure to deliver the coup de grace through Adlerangriff, which brought about a hiatus in Luftwaffe activity as it struggled to redefine its objectives. Adlerangriff had failed in part because of Schmid's misunderstanding of Fighter Command control systems which operated through a hierarchy of control centres from Sector through Group up to Bentley Priory, and a stubborn resistance on Göring's part to recognise and address Martini's concerns over radar. Luftwaffe plans, such as they were, required urgent modification. Hastily concocted plans based on simplistic assumptions about Fighter Command strength would no longer do.

The attacks on airfields, in August, once again illustrated a lack of clear strategy which can be attributed to the Luftwaffe Intelligence failing to study carefully and analyse the difference between Luftwaffe attacks on airfields during the French campaign and those now under way against the British. In France, the air raids were part of a cohesive Blitzkrieg strategy in which they would be closely followed up by ground assault. This meant that follow-up air raids were not required and the defenders, who were mostly in retreat, were not motivated to repair the bomb damage. As German forces overran the airfields, they found them damaged and initially unusable due to having only manual labour on hand to fill the craters. This experience encouraged Luftwaffe Intelligence to believe that single, heavy and successful strikes would have the same effect in Britain, but they completely failed to understand how quickly bomb craters in grass runways could be filled when there was an urgent requirement and heavy machinery available to do the work. The result was that they believed airfields they had attacked would be unusable for many days, and so not requiring follow-up raids, whereas the reality was that in the vast majority of cases, the airfields were fully operational again within hours. The exception to this was Manston, which was repeatedly attacked from 12 to 24 August, eventually being put out of action, except for emergency landings, for almost a week while unexploded bombs were defused. While Manston had been an important forward base for Fighter Command thus far it was clear to Fighter Command that its exposed location meant that it might have to be abandoned but that would, in no way, affect the control and command structure that underpinned their defence strategy.

Erprobungsgruppe 210 was a specialist low-level bombing unit specially trained to approach the target undetected and carry out accurate bombing raids. These skills were particularly useful in attacking airfields and it was in this role that the gruppe was often employed. Their deployment to attack Southend airfield on 13 August, and Ramsgate airfield the following day, neither of which were any part of Fighter Command operations, however, is a damning indictment of Luftwaffe Intelligence. At the end of August, Schmid reported that the following airfields had been made inoperable: Eastchurch, Gosport, Lee-on-Solent, Lympne, Manston, Tangmere, Hawkinge, Portsmouth, Rochester, Driffield and Martlesham Heath. Nothing better illustrates Schmid's ineptitude than the fact that so few of these airfields were used by Fighter Command and, even then, only Manston was actually put out of action for any length of time.[83]

At a conference in early September, Luftflotte commanders Kesselring and Sperrle disagreed wildly on RAF strength, indicating that intelligence was seriously flawed. Schmid had put the number of British aircraft downed as more than 600 during the latter part of Adlerangriff. Sperrle treated such assessments with contempt, knowing what a price the bomber fleets were still paying. Göring and Kesselring, however, seemed eager to accept Schmid's figures, probably less because they believed them and more because they supported their own views, which were gaining favour with Führer headquarters, that the time had come to begin the 'terror-bombing' of London to finally force Britain to submit. The resulting policy change, based in part on Schmid's opinion that RAF Fighter Command was no longer a threat, meant that hard-pressed and suffering RAF airfields and communications hubs were no longer prioritised as targets and focus shifted to the destruction of Britain's industrial and economic centres. This change was made at a time when Fighter Command was, in fact, reaching a critical point where further pressure could quite easily have tipped it over the edge into a downward spiral of exhausted disintegration.

The motivation for this new strategic initiative is not clear. There are reasons to suppose that Fighter Command's ability to continue meeting raids in undiminished strength was eroding confidence in the current strategy, especially in the bomber *geschwader*, who demanded more and more protection from their fighters, a cry that could hardly support the view that the British were beaten. Facts were piling up uncomfortably against supposition and threatening to expose the hollowness of Göring's earlier boasts. When evidence appeared showing that the mood in Berlin was becoming more belligerent after the RAF bombings there, and pressure was building from invasion headquarters for resolution to the RAF problem, as a precursor to implementation the way opened up to disguise failure as a reasoned and logical strategic shift which they now knew would find little opposition at OKW. Oberst Kurt Gottschling, who was on the Luftwaffe Intelligence staff in 1940, later claimed that his section could not be blamed for the change to terror bombing of London, which was a 'strategic error' made by Göring personally.[84]

In the event, it was this change that allowed the British, stretched now almost to breaking point, just enough breathing space to avoid collapse of their command and control systems and make enough of a recovery to continue their resistance. It was not the numbers of aircraft lost that had brought Fighter Command to this juncture, but the degradation of its control and command centres at places such as Biggin Hill. Luftwaffe Intelligence had completely failed to appreciate the way in which Lord Beaverbrook had galvanised British aircraft manufacturing to the point where aircraft numbers were actually increasing rather than diminishing, and how British aircraft losses were not reflected in pilot losses since they could abandon damaged aircraft and bale out to land safely and rejoin their squadrons.[85] It is therefore instructive to note that the Luftwaffe policy change was wrong for two reasons: first, it placed emphasis on British fighter numbers, which in itself was wildly inaccurate; and second, it failed to appreciate that it had gained the upper hand by seriously damaging a command and control system, the importance of which it had little understanding. This may well be considered to have been the crucial point of the Battle, and the moment when their failure of intelligence was most pronounced. Had the Luftwaffe continued its strategy, then Fighter Command may well have been forced to abandon most of their aerodromes in 11 Group and operate out of 10 and 12 Group Sectors, and may possibly have given the Luftwaffe just enough control of airspace above the Channel and ports such as Dover to tempt Hitler into giving the green light to invasion plans.

When, in September, Hitler authorised the bombing of London's dockland, the Luftwaffe was again presented with a new mission – and one which was not universally agreed upon. Superficially, the new strategy did not specify civilian targets, but it was obvious that London docks could not be bombed without substantial collateral damage. However, the appearance of restraint had to be maintained even though some influential German voices were urging blatant targeting of the working-class population in the hope of fomenting revolt against the British government. Although throughout September and October, when all restraints were removed, extensive damage was done, it failed to achieve its objectives due in part to the inability of the bomber fleet to deliver a sufficiently high tonnage of bombs.

It was at about this time that Hitler was presented with a memorandum from the Chief of War Economy, Fritz Siebel, which was copied to Göring, Jeschonnek and Udet, expressing the clear opinion that air power was the key to victory in the war but that the Luftwaffe was insufficiently resourced, especially in terms of aircraft production. Siebel had seen the level of production and plans for expansion of the US Air Force and knew for certain that if the US was drawn into the war, Germany was beaten. Hitler was quite unmoved and as an example of the way he refused to allow unwelcome advice to divert him from preconceived plans, commented as an aside to Udet that 'this is all very interesting and may even be correct but I have almost won the war already'. He ordered that the memorandum be withheld from wider distribution. Udet relayed the message to his staff. 'The war is over,' he told them.[86]

Göring embarked upon his campaign to destroy Fighter Command by wielding a blunt instrument of massive force against, as he had been advised by Schmid, a weak and under-resourced enemy. Strategy had been built on weak intelligence. Overwhelming power was expected to overcome whatever resistance was offered. The effort needed to acquire detailed intelligence either before or during the Battle seemed unnecessary and might even be seen as a lack of confidence in the Luftwaffe capabilities, an attitude that nobody within Göring's entourage would want to convey. The successes of Poland and France had engendered within the Luftwaffe command a sense of pride and omnipotence which would not serve them well when faced with an entirely different sort of foe.

Schmid later refuted claims, no doubt in a bid for justification of his role, that the Luftwaffe failure emanated from its underestimation of enemy strength. He referred instead to the failure of the Luftwaffe High Command to take note of his Studie Blau, which had warned of Britain's strong military position, albeit by overestimation, and the need, if Germany chose to attack, to do so with every means at their disposal or refrain from doing so at all.

In September, the Luftwaffe campaign adopted an entirely new objective since the threat of invasion had been removed and Fighter Command was still a potent force. It is not clear, even now, what that objective actually was, but any analysis of that must consider Hitler's growing enthusiasm for advancing into Eastern Europe and confronting his bête noir, the Soviet Union. Continuing military pressure on Britain during the winter of 1940/41, he believed, was essential to ensure that when he launched Operation Barbarossa, the British would be in no position to threaten his Western flank.

The purpose of the intelligence agencies is to provide the political and military leaders with information drawn from all possible sources, and while OKW was assiduous in collecting intelligence, its efforts to utilise it were severely hampered by a lack of clear political leadership which dissipated over time.[87] After the end of the First World War, Germany had no serious intelligence gathering capability until the mid-1930s, when the resurgence of militarism created an urgent requirement for information about the military capabilities of potential enemies. Hitler, however, was inclined to see situations in a way that suited his purpose. He was inclined to obtain information from a variety of sources and select the version he liked best.[88]

While his military intelligence agencies submitted realistic assessments, the non-military diplomatic and political agencies were more inclined to filter and manage intelligence to make it more palatable and it was this attitude that began to prevail throughout the intelligence community, especially where personal advancement depended less on competence and more on compliance.

The inability of the Luftwaffe to defeat Fighter Command in 1940 can be attributed in great part to the failure of intelligence, but also to the lack of preparedness for the battle they found themselves facing. There had been a general acceptance in OKW that the fate of Britain was inexorably tied to that of France, and the decisive battles would be fought on continental soil. When France fell, few believed that Britain would hold out for long after it had shown an unwillingness to send aircraft reinforcements in May and performed a rapid retreat to Dunkirk, where it lost the bulk of its transport and heavy armour leaving an Army with no weapons. Hitler's oft stated view that German interests were best served by preservation of the British Empire further reinforced the feeling that, if not peace, a stalemate might be reached. The slow realisation that Prime Minister Churchill was not going to allow this to happen in June 1940 exposed the dearth of German intelligence about British military capabilities, and when Hitler ordered the Luftwaffe to clear southern British skies of Fighter Command aircraft a strategy was concocted 'on the hoof', with little solid intelligence to inform it. Such intelligence that was forthcoming was channelled through the 5th Abteilung, whose efficiency had been seriously compromised by Schmid's clear unwillingness to report the true facts. His Studie Blau of 1939 had been 'a composite effort of all military, technical, economic and other civilian agencies'. It was the best ever produced in the field of intelligence evaluation, interpretation and analysis.[89] It had, however, been assigned to the waste bin a few months later for no other reason than that it no longer conformed to the mood of the times.

It is clear also that throughout the summer months of 1940, Schmid made exaggerated claims of Fighter Command losses based on the 'victory' claims of Luftwaffe pilots and this has often been quoted as one of the, if not the single, most egregious errors of the Luftwaffe campaign. He misreported the aircraft production capabilities of British industry recently galvanised under the control of Lord Beaverbrook.[90] His estimates of Fighter Command strength were as low as 100 at the end of August.[91] He claimed that the British were even using the antiquated Gloster Gladiator biplanes as substitute fighters (in fact these aircraft were used, but only as convoy and dockyard patrol reconnaissance aircraft). It is unlikely that Schmid actually believed his own claims. His Studie Blau shows that he was fully capable of making well-reasoned and responsible intelligence assessments, but it was made at a time when neither his chief, Göring, nor *his* chief, Hitler, showed any appetite for war with Britain. Poland was clearly in their sights, but the experiences of Austria and Czechoslovakia led them to believe that they could advance their immediate agenda without major conflagration. In the longer term, of course, Germany was gearing its economy for a major war, but a war focused on 'Lebensraum', expansion in the East. Göring, fully aware that Hitler's worldview included leaving the British Empire intact in exchange for a free hand in Europe, was actively reaching out to British sympathisers hoping to persuade them that Germany posed no threat to the British Empire. Schmid, still fairly new in post and feeling his way, saw no reason not to give a true picture of British strength in 1939, but the scant attention paid to it might have started him thinking that his profile and career prospects could benefit from a more nuanced approach to intelligence.

Even when he revisited Studie Blau a few months later when Britain declared itself at war with Germany, the uncertainty and anxiety over Hitler's plans for an attack against France, which ran hot and cold for months, ensured that once again he was virtually ignored, but in the spring of 1940 there was a clear belief among the more aggressive German generals such as Heinz Guderian that the French military, so formidable on paper, was actually lacking morale and leadership. Schmid picked up on this mood and began feeding Göring reports of weakness and vulnerability in the French Armeé de l'Aire; reports which were partly vindicated by its precipitous collapse under the German onslaught. The stunning victory over France and its effect on German morale was the high point of German military achievements but, ironically, it blinded them to its shortcomings and this wilful refusal to see the victory had more to do with French failure than German success was the root of all future failures.

Schmid, however, saw his reputation somewhat enhanced as he surfed the victory wave alongside everyone else. Neither he nor Göring was prepared for Britain's sudden, stubborn rebuff of German overtures to peaceful negotiation, and the mood became one of anger and frustration that Germany was forced to forego its summer of glorious celebration, dealing instead with the extremely annoying 'British bulldog'. No longer would it profit Schmid to laud the British, whom Hitler had been ready to tolerate as a co-manager of the world order, but whom he now found to be a bit of a nuisance. Göring exuded confidence in the ability of his Luftwaffe, despite grievous losses suffered against the French, to squash British intransigence, and Schmid was eager, once again, to show that he was on the right side of history by fully supporting his chief's ambitions for glory. The Luftwaffe, already Hitler's favourite service, would destroy British resistance and take a step up in the German military hierarchy. Who knows where this might take Schmid?

As the Battle of Britain progressed, Göring's confidence seemed unshakeable in the face of repeated setbacks, but it was a bravado that could tolerate no criticism. Based as it was on false optimism, his whole position was fragile and, like a dam that springs a tiny leak, vulnerable to rapid erosion and catastrophic collapse. If Göring was wilfully blind to the flaws in his approach, there seemed little benefit to Schmid in pointing them out. Whether or not Schmid believed everything he reported to Göring, he certainly believed that it was in his interests to appear to do so. Negative assessments would be ignored or, worse, punished. When the final victory came, if it came, the glory would be his also. Schmid may be condemned for giving poor advice, but he appeared to have little choice other than to feed his chief exactly the 'facts' that supported whatever strategy he was following at the time. It is equally true to say that even Kesselring ignored his intelligence when it came to supporting his personal view that the bombing of London should be the prime strategic imperative. The shifting sands of Luftwaffe strategy during the summer of 1940 were due to winds that blew from several directions, and it is probably fair to say that Schmid was as much buffeted and driven by those winds as he was an instigator of them.

The following charts show the discrepancy between claims of enemy aircraft destroyed and actual losses. The loss figures themselves include aircraft lost through accident, whether or not that aircraft was returning from combat. (The Ju88 was notoriously prone to landing accidents due to its weak undercarriage.) Luftwaffe claims of Spitfires destroyed are particularly exaggerated, due possibly to its iconic status and the desire of Luftwaffe pilots to claim a scalp. On the RAF side, claims of Bf110s destroyed are most noticeable in those engagements involving large numbers of aircraft (4, 11, & 27 September) where a Bf110 might have been attacked and hit by a number of different RAF fighters before going down. It was the case that the Bf110 and other Luftwaffe bombers could take a great deal of punishment, given that British fighters were only using .303 ammunition, and continue flying as long as no vital areas, such as the cockpit, were hit.

THE ROLE OF INTELLIGENCE IN THE BATTLE OF BRITAIN

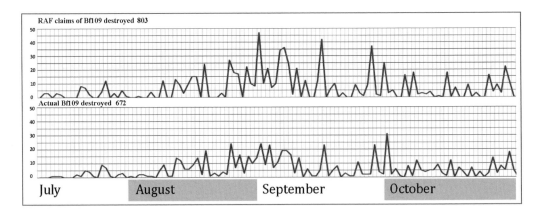

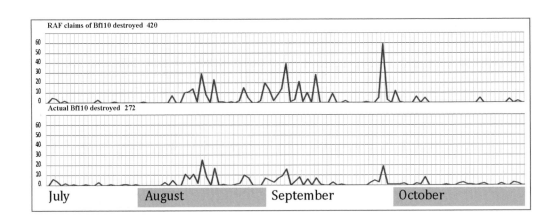

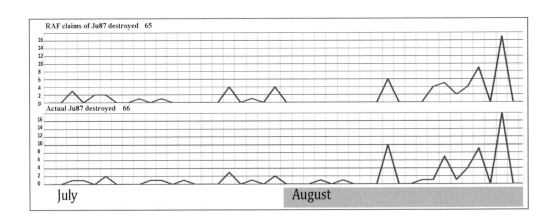

LUFTWAFFE INTELLIGENCE

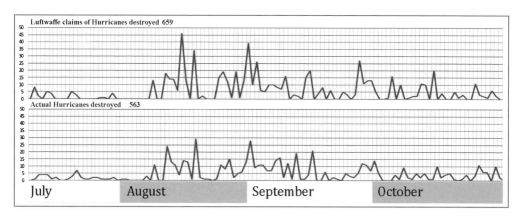

Luftwaffe claims of Hurricanes destroyed 659

Actual Hurricanes destroyed 563

July | August | September | October

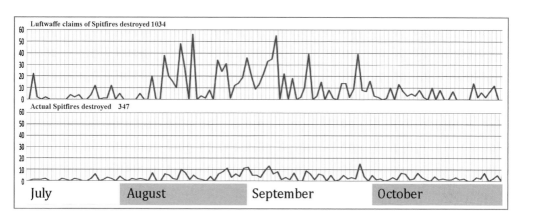

Luftwaffe claims of Spitfires destroyed 1034

Actual Spitfires destroyed 347

July | August | September | October

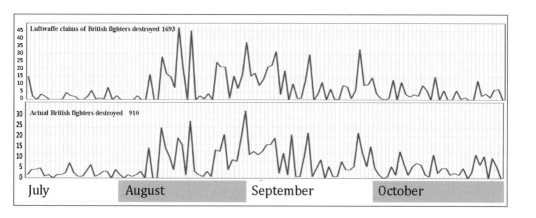

Luftwaffe claims of British fighters destroyed 1693

Actual British fighters destroyed 910

July | August | September | October

Luftwaffe estimates of the number of Fighter Command aircraft available to Dowding failed to take sufficient account of the numbers of new aircraft coming off the production lines under Beaverbrook's management of the aircraft industry. The following charts show that numbers produced were, in fact, greater than numbers lost. (production figures according to R.J. Overy, *The Battle of Britain Myth and Reality*; losses according to author)

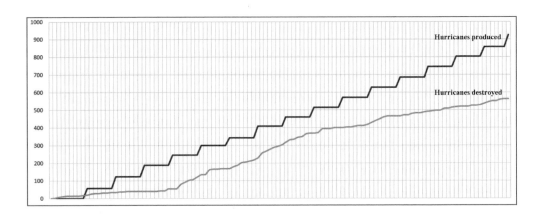

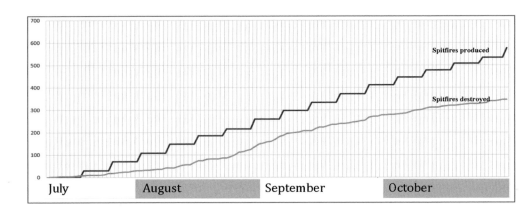

Chapter 2

Reichsmarschall Hermann Wilhelm Göring

> The question arises … why a man like Göring, … should
> have sinned against [the Luftwaffe] so gravely by inadequate
> leadership on the one hand and by overbearing decisions on
> the other.[1]

The historian R.J. Overy thought Hermann Göring 'a curiously neglected figure in historical writing'.[2] It has been a common thread of historical accounts of the Battle of Britain to heap criticism, and almost ridicule, upon the person of the Reichsmarschall for the failure to deliver on his promise to destroy Fighter Command which was, in no small measure, derived from his lack of understanding of strategic air warfare but also, most damningly, from his wilful disdain for intelligence-based analysis of the battle day by day. History has shown that Göring was ill-equipped mentally and psychologically to lead the Luftwaffe into a battle for which it was ill-prepared and during which he, personally, appeared content to be ill-advised. Having said that, it is instructive to examine the trajectory of his rise to powers which will, in part, explain why he was the wrong man in the wrong place at the wrong time.

Göring had not achieved his status as 'der Zweite', second-in-command of the Nazi Party, by being bumbling and incompetent.[3] He seemed to have succeeded in everything to which he turned his hand in the years 1933–36, as the National Socialists tightened their grip on German politics. His status and authority within the party were second only to Hitler's, and in the wider population he had a reputation of being a down-to-earth and 'the best of family men',[4] albeit one given to ostentation and luxurious living. Unfortunately, his boundless energy and enthusiasm to take on more and more responsibility was at odds with the side of his character that craved luxury and relaxation, and it was this conflict of interests that gradually robbed him of the will to engage with the repercussions of Hitler's military and expansionist ambitions. His image of himself as a classical Teutonic warrior-statesman came under attack and eventually failed to survive his country's nightmare as political theatre collapsed into the reality of war. No longer would he be able to take refuge in his vast country estates far from the centres of power and command, where it was still possible to see the world in his own terms, buoyed by optimistic reports from the battlefront and unsullied by unwelcome contradictory details. As events turned against Germany, after the disasters of the Russian campaign, Göring fell into what became a slow, drug-fuelled decline of energy and faculties briefly rekindled at the Nuremberg War Trials when incarceration had facilitated withdrawal from his addictions. For a short while, it was apparent why he had achieved such power and status in Germany during the 1930s. Dispassionate observers commented on his 'mental dexterity and eloquence' when giving evidence, and his authority over, and in many cases contempt for, his fellow defendants was clear for all to see.

Göring was born to wealth and privilege. His father had been a Governor of German South-West Africa and the family-owned 'ancient and rambling' castles and estates at Veldenstein in upper Franconia and Mautendorf in the Salzburgian Lungau.[5] The young Göring is said to have been 'strong-minded', with 'great determination and energy', but 'seems to have been virtually unaffected by [the discipline of]' schools at Fiirth and Ansbach, which he attended only rarely and which left him with a 'contempt for all that was intellectual'.[6] It was in these estates that he acquired a fascination for the pageantry and chivalry of Teutonic Knights, such as the sixteenth-century Gotz von Berlichingen, that was to colour his personal life as he rose to power in his own right. As a youth he was also an intrepid and tough-minded alpinist, narrowly avoiding death on one occasion when he lost his footing 2,000ft above the Glockner-Kars glacier and was only saved from plunging to his death by his brother-in-law who was roped to him. On another occasion, when he was only 15, he reset a dislocated shoulder in mid-climb on the Mont Blanc range.[7]

He was hugely popular with his fellow cadets when he joined the Royal Prussian Cadet Korps at the Lichterfelde Cadet School, from which he graduated with the highest honours (des Kaisers Belobigung). As an infantry officer, he was considered to be a natural leader and his enthusiasm spurred him on to be among the first German officers to make contact with the enemy at the outset of the First World War at Muehlhausen in Alsace. After taking an unauthorised spin as observer in his friend Bruno Lörzer's aircraft one day, Göring was severely bitten by the flying bug and was quickly able to transfer to a field reconnaissance squadron and become their star trainee. His dare-devil strategy to overcome the fuselage obstructions that impeded his ability to take photographs was to lean the whole of his upper body out of the aircraft and hold himself in by wedging his legs across the cockpit.[8] For their service, Göring and Lörtzer were both awarded the Iron Cross First Class.[9] His commander commented, 'Goring's reports excelled all others on that sector. Everything that he carried through was marked by a thoroughness par excellence and attacks were built up, speedily, based on his observations. He had a complete understanding of essentials and gained a mastery of them to the elimination of all minor material.'[10]

In 1915 he applied for pilot training and was duly accepted to fly the new breed of twin-engine fighters with Jagdstaffel 5. These aircraft were superior to their British counterparts and aerial dominance was quickly achieved, but they were not always victorious in air-to-air combat. In one encounter, Göring suffered multiple leg wounds when his machine was riddled with sixty British bullets. Fleeing for home, he got lost in fog and almost crashed, but landed in a cemetery before losing consciousness. Sometime later it was a French aircraft that caught him napping and almost repeated the damage, but a timely intervention by Lörzer saved him.

By 1917, Göring had risen to command the mediocre Jagdgruppe 27, which he very quickly whipped into shape to become a crack outfit. His exploits earned him the highest honours, 'pour le Merite', and he was given command of Richthofen's *geschwader* when that German ace was killed. It was through his First World War experiences that he embellished his ideas of personal heroism (the loyal, daring and honourable warrior) and his rejection of bourgeoise values giving rise to 'an unspeakable force'[11] which was a substitute for his 'lack of intellect'. He was devastated by demobilisation after the Armistice, and after disbandment of the German Air Force under the terms of the Treaty of Versailles he swore allegiance to new political forces (National Socialism) in Germany that promised revenge for these humiliations.

He was drawn to political rallies and made no bones about expressing his frustration. In December 1918, he had attended a rally of the German Officers' Society in the Berlin Philharmonic Hall and interrupted a speech by the Minister of War, General Walther Reinhardt, to denounce those who had betrayed Germany in 1918 and swore that the 'criminals' would see their day of reckoning.[12] The audience responded to Göring's tirade with 'great enthusiasm'. He replied by saying to them: 'I preach to you the deepest hatred against these criminals who are attacking the German people. The day will come, and this I know, when these "gentlemen" are finished and when we can hunt them down and out of our Germany! For that you must work – you must be armed. That day will surely come.'[13]

Göring still owned property, but his capital had evaporated during the war, so he was forced to look for paid employment. He began work as a commercial pilot with a Swedish airline, Svenska Lufttrafik. On one occasion, flying his aircraft through a raging blizzard, he was just able to land at Lake Baven, close to Rockelstadt Castle, the home of his passenger, Count Eric von Rosen. Inside the castle, Göring was transfixed by its 'panoply of ancient nobility', and even more impressed by the count's elegant sister-in-law, Carin von Ganzow (née von Fock). The two met occasionally thereafter and it is no wonder, given the circumstances of their introduction, that they became close. Carin was a woman of 'great spiritual strength', but suffered from a near-permanent invalidity. Her unhappy marriage was ended and she married Göring in whom she found someone ready to 'strike a blow for the rebirth of the Nordic spirits of Europe'.[14] In 1922 his political activism brought him into contact with Hitler, whose rhetoric impressed him and seemed to speak to his own ambitions for retribution. He was quick to declare an oath of allegiance and stood on stage behind Hitler in the Burgerbrau Keller in Munich on the night of 8 November 1923 when the Nazis launched their first bid for power. When demonstrators marched towards Odeon Platz the next day, Reichswehr soldiers opened up on them with machine guns; Göring was hit in the stomach and taken to Garmisch hospital. After treatment he was spirited away over the Austrian border to avoid arrest. Hitler was thrown into Landsberg Prison. Göring, tried in absentia, had his estates confiscated and he fled Austria to avoid extradition, later crossing over into Italy and, finally, Sweden.[15] His painful injury trapped him into a morphine addiction which bedevilled him for the rest of his life.

Göring was given an amnesty and returned, impoverished, to Germany in 1927 where he was reacquainted with Hitler and once again became active in the movement, winning a seat in the Reichstag for the National Socialist Party. He became a hugely popular speaker for the cause.[16] His First World War reputation gave him prestige and he rose quickly through the ranks. In 1930 he was appointed as Hitler's 'political commissar' in Berlin but suffered a personal tragedy when his wife Carin, to whom he had been devoted, died in October 1931 after a long illness.[17] When the Nazi Party eventually gained control of the political apparatus after 1933, Göring was at the very heart of power and poised to evolve into the kind of folk-hero he had so admired in his youth. Hitler appointed him as State Aviation Commissioner (Reichskommisar für die Luftfahrt), and later that year as State Minister for Aviation.

For him to have achieved such a high status within the Nazi Party is indicative of a ruthlessly ambitious character profile. He had a 'vast appetite for political power' and fully understood the potentially dangerous feelings of animosity and jealousy generated towards him within the party. In consequence, he surrounded himself with bodyguards and travelled in bullet-proof cars. His obsession with costume and all accoutrements of an almost medieval court was well documented as was his passion for acquiring great art, but this did not necessarily detract from his abilities and performance as a political and military leader. His relationship with Hitler is crucial to understanding how Göring fitted into the political structure of Nazi Germany. He was fanatically loyal to Hitler and sufficiently ruthless to act as a protective shield against opposition or rivals. Unlike Hitler, he was born into the conservative upper classes and could move effortlessly in their circles. He became a vital ambassador between the party and entrenched conservatism in the country. It was this socialising that Göring prized above all else, but it left insufficient time or energy for the increasing number of administrative and leadership roles that he willingly accepted without due regard for the burden of responsibility that came with them. He eschewed detailed discussion about anything and refused to read lengthy reports leaving policy detail to his subordinates.[18]

Having acquired for himself a range of high-powered offices, as a result of his standing within the party and with Hitler personally, the problem was that he failed to immerse himself in the detailed management of his various responsibilities. His prodigious energy, which had propelled him to such heights, could only go so far. Leadership of the Luftwaffe and responsibility for the German economy allowed him to bestride the European stage which was all well and good until the attack against Poland in September 1939, which he had vigorously opposed, threw everything into turmoil. The massively increased demands of a Luftwaffe now at war swamped Göring and his immediate staff which had hitherto paraded the service as more of a propaganda tool than a fighting force. To lead the Luftwaffe was now a very different prospect and 'shattered his pretences and revealed his inner weakness and lack of force.'[19]

During the early part of the Second World War, Göring was allowed a great deal of autonomy in his leadership of the Luftwaffe. This may be because Hitler had little understanding of, or interest in, aerial warfare per se, and possibly because of the high regard in which he seemed to hold Göring, the nature of whose military leadership, of all the High Command, most closely resembled the political tenets of the Nazi regime. This relationship between Göring's military, economic and especially political power gave him immunity from criticism within the German leadership at this time. It also placed him in a unique position in relation to other military chiefs who, by and large, were wary of his authority and whom he treated with a measure of contempt as a result. His great wealth and many political connections gave him enormous power. Even Hitler recognised Göring's reputation and popularity within the Nazi Party and was a little in thrall to him. He was everything that Hitler was not: down-to-earth, affable, ostentatious, cultured, optimistic, outwardly 'jolly' and a dedicated family man. Even his portly figure, which gave rise to his popular nickname 'der Dicke' (the fat one) was admired, not least by Göring himself who had 'a sense of humour which enabled him to laugh at himself as well as others'.[20] All this, of course, disguised a darker side which was brutal, vindictive and insatiably greedy, giving rise to a less friendly nickname, 'der Eiserne' (the iron man)[21] and, like Hitler, he was ambitious, ruthless and egocentric as well as being, as his personal physician, Dr Ramon von Ondarza, said, 'remarkably cunning'.[22] His close involvement with the 'Night of the Long Knives' on the 30 June 1934, when his great rival Ernst Rohm was murdered, eloquently illustrates this dark side of his character. The writer, and member of the American prosecution team, Telford Taylor, who saw Göring at close quarters during the Nuremberg Trials of 1947, found him 'lucid and impressive', but said that 'reliance on undertakings made by Göring would have been about as sensible as entering into a no-first-strike treaty with a cobra'.[23] Also, like Hitler, Göring believed that he could succeed in whatever task he set himself by sheer force of will and an indomitable desire to win, a characteristic that was to prove both irresistible and damning during the Dunkirk evacuation and the Battle of Britain, when his arrogant boasts were exposed by subsequent failure.

He was a political power in his own right, and this was recognised by Hitler, who, despite being suspicious of Göring's popularity, was nevertheless appreciative of his many contributions to his own rise as Führer, and to the successes of the Nazi Party. The two men never had a close personal relationship, given Hitler's asceticism and Göring's hedonism, but throughout 1930s and the early war years, in matters pertaining to the Luftwaffe, Hitler trusted Göring implicitly – although would not support his bid to become Minister of War after von Blomberg's dismissal in 1938, considering Göring 'too lazy'.[24] In the early years of their relationship Göring had considered himself superior to Hitler, but became increasingly less confident in his presence as his failures mounted, knowing that Hitler's patience was apt to snap without warning.[25] He protected himself by refusing to give Hitler honest reports that might reflect poorly on him; reports which had already been edited by subordinates to omit the most damaging and unpleasant details. Like many leaders who lacked intellectual depth, he preferred simple answers to complex questions, and both requested and relayed information in compliance with this requirement.

On a personal level, it was recorded by some who met him that Göring suffered from halitosis and appeared pompous, with a disturbing penchant for touching those to whom he was speaking. Others found him 'alert and interesting' and always keen to spend time with pilots to hear about their combat experiences and regale them with stories of his own. He also had a tendency to rant against real, and imagined, enemies. His vicious rages often included threats to have the recipient shot, as was the case later in the war when he upbraided his Chief of Supply and Procurement, Ernst Udet. Although the threat was never carried through, it undoubtedly contributed to Udet's suicide in 1941. One-time Chief of the Luftwaffe General Staff, Karl Koller, said that Göring 'was hopelessly under the influence of his none too reliable intimates and his totally incompetent friends who had absolutely no idea of the functioning of the Luftwaffe'.[26]

In the matter of relations with his General Staff (ObdL), he tended to fill posts with young officers from flying units who had limited experience of action or administration. These young officers tended to be in thrall to him, making it easy for him to dominate discussions but denied him mature and considered argument in return. When left to their own devices, many of these young officers, flushed with pride at their rapid promotion and afforded influence far beyond their abilities, became arrogant and were despised by officers of other services. ObdL was organised and operated more like Göring's personal staff in much the same way that OKW was treated as Hitler's personal staff rather than like, for instance, the General Staff of OKH (Oberkommando der Heer), which operated along traditional military lines. ObdL did not handle operational strategy which was left to the Luftflotte and Fliegerkorps commanders. Right up until the fall of France these subordinate commands had been assigned to work alongside OKH in combined operations and the Battle of Britain was the first where they were called on to develop an independent strategy for which they had no training or guidance. Once Göring had thrust his Luftwaffe into the forefront of German plans to deal with Britain, overall strategy was developed 'on the hoof' by means of conferences and directives. Göring, however, 'was determined that he, and he alone, should receive credit for [the Luftwaffe's] successes; he had no intention of sharing this credit with anyone else.'[27]

As head of the Luftwaffe, Göring had seen the service grow into a formidable fighting force, but his other commitments left him insufficient time to keep abreast of technical developments. He was essentially a man of action and not deliberation. His place was on the bigger stage and not in detailed briefing rooms. At an air show in Rechlin in 1938, Hitler was subjected to what amounted to a wholly exaggerated propagandised display of Luftwaffe capabilities which included, among other things, a report on jet-engine aircraft that were apparently almost ready to go into production.[28] Göring was as surprised as Hitler by this revelation but, though sceptical, chose not to disabuse his leader of such fanciful notions. While the hugely optimistic atmosphere of the Rechlin Air Show may have had the effect of enhancing Göring's prestige, which he would have welcomed, it is possible that it also projected an unrealistic picture of German air power which may have encouraged Hitler to pursue an increasingly reckless political agenda in Europe.[29]

All during the 1930s, despite his aversion to detail, Göring was renowned for his common-sense approach to problems, his enthusiasm, energy and ability to perform effectively under pressure. Kesselring said of him, 'when the rest of us were completely exhausted [he] was still able to go on'.[30] With the growth of his power there also emerged opportunities to indulge his personal passion for pageant and luxury, which began to reduce his appetite for work. All this, allied to a huge desire for popular acclaim, glory and obsession with pomp and spectacle created a complex, self-assured and very dangerous man. Although a close confidant and adviser to Hitler, Göring proved to be a liability in foreign affairs. Mussolini called him an 'ex-inmate of a lunatic asylum',[31] which was little better than his own opinion of Il Duce. He was, however, active and more successful with internal economic management and was allowed to acquire power and influence in military affairs through involvement with the nascent Luftwaffe.

Up until the early 1930s, military aircraft had come under the control of the Army, who fought hard to prevent the formation of a separate service, but in May 1933, Hitler, having less than total faith in the support of the Army politically, established the Air Office under Göring's control in the first stage of creating a third service which would have allegiance to the party rather than to OKW. Göring's swashbuckling style and disdain for military protocols was viewed as a positive qualification for leadership of this new organisation with ambition to challenge the conservative approach of OKW, which seemed to frustrate Hitler at every turn. It was Hitler's aim to create a third independent military arm which would create an important power base for Göring, who would have the freedom to develop a doctrine for the Luftwaffe outside the influence of the OKH or Kriegsmarine. Göring's habit of working from his Prussian State Ministry offices, however, meant that he spent little time at Luftwaffe headquarters and consequently did not develop a close relationship with staff there, or an intimate appreciation of its operations. That is not to say he was without influence in creating a modern air force, but his contribution was more in his ability to represent it with prestige at the highest level and to manipulate the German economy in ways which favoured investment. His failing was that he showed scant interest in how the Luftwaffe actually worked, what its strengths and weaknesses were on an operational level, and what his responsibilities would actually be in the event of war. Nevertheless, it is true to say that under his leadership, Germany rebuilt its air force from a position of near invisibility to the most combat-ready air force in the world in 1939.

From that moment on, the Luftwaffe emerged as an independent force which merely paid lip-service to OKW, and sowed the seeds of division which would undermine future military planning. Having been proscribed by the Treaty of Versailles, the emergent Luftwaffe had no history or tradition on which to build an ethos. Göring's first appointment was the highly efficient Erhard Milch, Director of the State airline Lufthansa, as State Secretary for Aviation, and his deputy. A colonel and ex-Army man, Walter Wever, was the next important addition. Wever and Albert Kesselring, another soldier, together with Milch, laid the foundations upon which the Luftwaffe was built, but could not have done so without Göring using his political clout to overcome bureaucratic hurdles and his influence within the wider German economy to channel the necessary funds, often by direct appeal to Hitler. Göring's demands for expansion of the Luftwaffe required vast resources which were only realised by the exploitation of his many industrial contacts and by using his great political influence, not least with Hitler himself, to face down opposition from the Reich's War Minister, Werner von Blomberg, a man to whom Göring was theoretically subordinate militarily.

The highest-ranking officers were, almost to a man, ex-Army. One such, Albert Kesselring, who was drafted in as Chief of Staff, was conscious of the limitations this placed upon the character of the service but said that 'in my long years as a soldier, I have never been so free of outside influence and so able to act independently as during this early period of Luftwaffe development'.[32] However, he felt that these constraints upon the Luftwaffe were greatly ameliorated, and the new Luftwaffe given a measure of respectability within the OKW by having a First World War ex-fighter pilot as Commander in Chief. The reticence of men like Kesselring to become involved in politics gave Göring the opportunity to make his own personal office the conduit for relations between the Luftwaffe and the National Socialist political leadership.

As the Luftwaffe grew, more and more of its ranks were filled with Nazi Party members and it was only in 1936, when Göring calculated that Army influence had been sufficiently reduced, that he appointed Milch and Wever to run the service. With that, the whole policy shifted in such a way as to conform with Göring's personal preconceptions, prejudices and ambitions. For him, the strength of the Luftwaffe was not its supposed superiority of numbers or methods, but the quality of its airmen. He based his strategic thinking on his experiences as a pilot in the First World War, where personal heroism had been the main guarantee of success. The men on the front line would always be the ones he admired while having little time for the views of administrators and technicians. When in discussion with pilots he would want to know every little detail of their combats in an effort to relive his own First World War memories. Blinkered by nostalgia, however, he failed to even try to understand modern warfare which, when almost dictatorial power was in his hands, proved to be a serious drawback. Any failures in the early phases of the Battle of Britain would be attributed to poor leadership or inefficient, if not treasonous, support staff, and never to the actual flyers themselves. They, like him, would be, initially at least, the victims of incompetence elsewhere. However, this faith in his fighter pilots turned to criticism as the failures of the Luftwaffe strategy began to sink in.

Wever's untimely accidental death in June 1936 left Göring shaken. Wever had been a restraining influence, bringing a measure of realism and practicality into some of Göring's more fanciful ambitions. His replacement as Chief of Staff, 'smiling' Albert Kesselring, proved effective but the two men never had the same close personal affinity. Milch and Kesselring, between them, had gathered together an elite staff of officers, mostly ex-flyers, to build a service allied to the exacting standards demanded by Göring, but were unceasingly antagonistic towards each other. Kesselring objected to Milch, as Secretary of Aviation, having authority over him and demanded parity. Göring had a propensity for playing one man against another, either to favour the stronger who prevailed, or perhaps for mischievous purposes. In this case he humiliated Milch by giving Kesselring parity. Kesselring had shown disinclination to become involved in politics which might have persuaded Göring to give him elevated status. This slap in the face for Milch contributed to his waning enthusiasm and fall in authority, exposing a serious power vacuum which in turn encouraged factionalism to take root in the Luftwaffe General Staff. Such a state of affairs seems not to have bothered Göring to any great extent and may well have been one reason for his decision.

Despite the feverish activity, there was little planning for a comprehensive strategy that addressed the real issues inherent in a modern large-scale aerial conflict such as an assessment of enemy strength, organisation and capabilities, as well as a detailed understanding of enemy vulnerabilities. Göring held very few conferences where experts could compare notes and discuss options, and some of those that were called were peremptorily curtailed when he became tired or bored. Individual Air Force leaders were obliged to develop their own strategic priorities, ones which often put them at odds with their peers. Crucially, the issue of aircraft production and maintenance was not addressed which, once war started, very quickly exposed a weakness in supply and repair facilities as well as a slow depletion of experienced crews. Rearmament accelerated and plans were laid to create a modern air force. In 1938, the German economy was put on a war-footing, in which the Luftwaffe would take pride of place, but not until 1943 or 1944 would the armed forces be sufficiently modernised and expanded to meet its ambitions, but of course, by then it was too late.

The Luftwaffe was tasked with two major objectives; to develop a close-support capability for the Army and build up a strategic bomber force. The first was non-contentious and readily embraced by OKW, but the second was met with strong opposition which was faced down by Göring who prioritised it over the first. The long time-span between design and production meant that decisions were urgently required about the size and composition of the Luftwaffe going into the 1940s. In the meantime, production of existing models would have to suffice; models whose capabilities had been exaggerated and which were rapidly becoming obsolete. When Hitler's ambitions and impatience precipitated war earlier than planned, the Luftwaffe was unprepared both in aircraft and armaments, having based its plans on no war breaking out before 1942. Göring was acutely aware of the Luftwaffe's unpreparedness for the extended war that would be inevitable if Poland was invaded and Britain stepped in with 'mutual assistance' as specified in the Anglo-Polish military alliance. He was active, both before and after September 1939, in trying to avert war with Britain. In many public announcements he had claimed, in relation to the balance of power in Europe, that the Luftwaffe was 'a major contributor to world peace'. He tempered this, however, with a warning that 'if the Luftwaffe gets the order to strike … [it will] … be the terror of the aggressors and nothing shall hold it back.'

Göring's Forschungsamt Intelligence assessment of relations between Britain and Poland led him to believe that Britain could be persuaded to 'see sense' and concede that 'German claims [over Danzig], one way or another, had to be fulfilled.'[33] Göring had many friends and admirers in Britain, both political and industrial, and it was to them that he turned to persuade them of Germany's lack of animosity towards the British Empire, a stance which he maintained even after the invasion of Poland in September 1939. He had a special envoy, a Swedish engineer called Birger Dahlerus who conveyed to Chamberlain and Halifax, personally, Göring's wish for a meeting that would 'be of the greatest value', but the signing of the Nazi-Soviet Pact put paid to any chance of developments.[34] A last desperate attempt by Dahlerus to arrange a meeting with General Ironside met with a similar fate.[35] Alongside the diplomatic appeals to Britain came the threat of facing the victorious German forces, especially the Luftwaffe, which had achieved stunning propaganda victories way beyond its actual contribution, albeit against an antiquated and unprepared foe. His efforts at diplomacy failed, however, and he was quick to shift the blame for that onto the German Foreign Minister, Ribbentrop.

On 7 February 1940 Göring, in optimistic anticipation of the short, sharp war that Hitler had promised him, signed a decree abandoning development of any aircraft that would not be available for service by the end of the year. This included secret work on the development of the jet-propelled aircraft which had made such an impact on Hitler at Rechlin in 1938. Some manufacturers ignored the decree and continued their research, but were hampered by a lack of funding and skilled manpower which delayed the introduction of jet fighters, for instance, until very late in the war.

Problems to do with moving the economy onto a war-footing in the early months of the Second World War were threatening to derail the whole military venture. Göring dealt with them in a typically high-handed and brutal way, although hampered by a lack of means to implement his decrees. Having been called upon to produce in excess of 20,000 aircraft a year, only half that number came off the production lines in 1940. The consequences of this would be that the Luftwaffe would have less aircraft in 1941 when it launched Barbarossa, the attack on the Soviet Union, than it had in 1939 when it had attacked Poland. Luftwaffe efficiency was further seriously hampered by Göring's policy of separating key departments such as strategic planning and aircraft development, and making them each directly responsible to him alone. Direct cooperation between the two was discouraged.

The early and somewhat unexpectedly easy victories over Poland and, especially, France had papered over the cracks in Germany's military machine. Göring was not enthusiastic about facing a continuation of the war with Britain, but Hitler's confidence in the capacity of his armed forces to wage war had grown, although he would prefer a peaceful conclusion to his Western campaign before turning East. Göring advocated hitting the British Empire in the Mediterranean, possibly Gibraltar, rather than tackling them head-on, but because of his long and close relationship with Hitler, he knew that such a long-winded approach would not find favour with his leader, so he did not press his case with any great enthusiasm. Neither did he make much effort to reopen covert negotiations with British Nazi-sympathisers, having seen them fail in 1939. The best solution, to his mind, was to apply pressure to force Britain to the negotiating table by a short intense aerial bombardment of its critical military and industrial infrastructure.

During July, when peace initiatives were rebuffed and there was little visible weakening of British resolve, OKW plans for invasion and Göring's boastful predictions of what his Luftwaffe could achieve inadvertently spawned the air campaign against Britain. He had always been a fervent believer in Douhetist philosophy, which he now applied to the task in hand.[36] The Luftwaffe had quickly moved up to, mostly makeshift, airfields in northern France and the Army was flushed with its successes in France. There was, however, no explicit directive about how the armed forces would combine to bring about the desired outcome of British capitulation, preferably achieved at minimum cost.

The Austrian historian Richard Suchenwirth, in his *Command and Leadership in the German Air Force* believes that there were three aspects of Goering's character which contributed to the Luftwaffe's failure in 1940 and its eventual collapse.

- First, Göring felt compelled to take everything personally and judged every situation on the basis of how it might be manipulated to his own advantage. The Luftwaffe was seen as essentially a vehicle for his own political advancement, almost a personal possession, rather than as an independent arm of the military establishment. He also avoided facing up to unpalatable truths when results failed to live up to his expectations.

• Second, he demanded total loyalty from his subordinates which severely restricted the possibility of negative reports or comment reaching him.

• Finally, it was his waning enthusiasm and energy, resulting from his growing passion for luxury, relaxation and 'country-living', which he indulged at Carinhall and Veldenstein Castle, and often kept him far from the centre of events at Luftwaffe headquarters at Potsdam-Werder. He spent more and more time seeking out and acquiring art treasures, designing outrageous costumes and taking 'afternoon naps'. Even though he was acutely aware of the consequences of military failure both for himself and for Germany, he seemed unable to rekindle his old drive and enthusiasm for action and involvement in political, military or economic affairs.[37] During the Battle of Britain, many Luftwaffe conferences and discussions took place at Carinhall or Rominton, where the temptations of good living and stag-hunting in the vast estates were a constant distraction. General Koller remarked on 'the frequency with which conferences were simply broken off before a decision had been reached. … Göring was very receptive to remarks of the often irresponsible men making up his circle of associates, most of whom were totally incompetent.'[38] Sperrle, in particular, was dismayed by the lack of application and concentration exhibited by the Luftwaffe commander, which placed a heavy burden on his subordinates, both at headquarters and in the field, who often disagreed on strategy and looked for leadership which was rarely forthcoming. The suicide of Udet has been alluded to and a similar fate awaited Göring's second-in-command, Jeschonnek, later in the war. Both men can be seen as the victims of Göring's abandonment of responsibility within the Luftwaffe and his increasing propensity to blame subordinates for his own failures.

It is not possible to understand the part Göring played in the Battle of Britain without looking at the broader political landscape in Germany at that time and in the years leading up to it. During 1935, the German economy was being drawn inexorably under the control of the National Socialist party, with Göring taking on ever more responsibility as head of the Raw Materials and Foreign Exchange Office. Up until 1936 the German economy had been managed in such a way as to create domestic affluence and wellbeing designed to cement the party's popularity with the wider population. Business and military leaders, too, had been seduced into an unwritten contract with the political leadership which allowed Hitler to acquire total control in return for political and economic stability. Government took on a 'top down' approach where all major decisions were made by the individual at the head of a department and all lower-level sections, discouraged from lateral communication, reported directly to the top man. Göring flourished under this regime proving to be a 'cunning and determined' politician.[39]

The economic landscape in Germany was about to change, however, with the introduction of the second Four-Year Plan, designed to divert massive resources into armament production and put the country on a war footing. The new plan required a new approach and all such necessary powers as were required were invested in the person of Göring, who acquired total control over the economy with his 'massive energy and organisational effort',[40] despite asking 'how can I be expected to understand these complicated problems of economics?'[41]

This was a huge achievement for Göring whose ambition knew no bounds, but which made a right decision 'a matter of pure luck',[42] his having been chosen purely for his National Socialist credentials and absolute loyalty to the Führer. This was a clear indication that the country would now be totally controlled by the Nazi Party. Threats to ideological purity or the personal status of Göring himself would not be tolerated as evinced by the demotion and side-lining of Göring's own expert economic adviser Wilhelm Keppler, and the banker Hjalmar Schacht, which, at a stroke, stripped him of the sort of expert opinion he would require to have any serious capability of managing the economy. He insisted on making all major decisions himself and, for a time, occupied himself totally with 'an unceasing round of interviews, meetings, receptions and speeches', as well as regular meetings with Hitler and inspections of his front-line troops.[43] This management style and overload of responsibility resulted in his appointment of a coterie of subordinates who offered no resistance to his instructions and who, in consequence, failed to give balance to his judgements.

As well as his responsibility for the economy, Göring was, at the same time, Minister for Air, allowing him to channel investment into aircraft production, which tripled between 1936 and 1939. His military status was further enhanced in October 1937 when he orchestrated the resignation of Blomberg, but his further ambition to replace him at that time was blunted by Hitler's refusal to sanction the appointment. Göring, however, was mollified by being promoted to the rank of Feldmarschall making him the highest-ranking officer in the armed services. In terms of actual power, there is no doubt that Hitler was the supreme leader of Germany by this time, but his involvement in the details of government was minimal, preferring instead to paint bold political strokes on a wider canvas thus allowing his subordinates to fill in the details. As Hitler's trusted confidante and, to some extent, inspiration, Göring found himself at the centre of a web of control spreading out through the whole economy, and free to impose party discipline and policy. He was also popular with the general public and the rank-and-file military establishment, being held in contempt only by those who openly opposed or threatened him (and suffered as a consequence). Now acting out the role of warrior-statesman, after the fashion of Charlemagne and Napoleon,[44] with almost unlimited power he had become the personification of his own ambition. Having so much power concentrated in his own hands, however, would prove to be a significant factor in the failure of this ambition, both economically and militarily. The administrative structures under his control, especially those in the Air Ministry, became notorious for 'intense compartmentalisation' and a penchant for defending their independence, which encouraged 'bureaucratic inertia and the stifling of co-operation and initiative'.[45]

At the Nuremberg trials after the war, Göring claimed, in his defence, that he had been a 'man of peace',[46] drawn unwillingly into preparing for war; the policies he pursued as part of the Four-Year Plan, however show that he not only supported the war aims, but was a strong advocate of 'total war'. His popularity meant that his personal contribution to bridging the gap between party ambitions and public acceptance was an essential part of preparing the country for war.

The main objectives of the Four-Year Plan, which was time-constrained in name only, were initially to create an industrial landscape which supported large-scale weapons production in a 'gigantic programme compared with which previous achievements are insignificant', which, it was envisaged, would not be completed until 1944–5.[47] By that time, Göring anticipated that the Luftwaffe would have 2,000 heavy bombers of the He177 type supported by 5,000 medium bombers. The Army was to acquire twenty motorised divisions. This could only be achieved by greatly expanding the money supply and increasing the national debt, neither of which policies gave Göring pause for thought, but a greater obstacle was converting manufacturing output that satisfied domestic demand for consumer goods to producing military hardware. It was also the case that the arms industry was a notoriously inefficient user of resources. For instance, aircraft were commissioned and developed by officers who assumed the right to incorporate the very best materials and equipment in their designs, which resulted in machines of the highest standards but whose production consumed vast amounts of capital and skilled labour, which was in especially short supply. During 1940, Germany spent almost twice as much on weapons than Britain but produced only half as many aircraft.[48]

In the event, war came much earlier than had been anticipated. When the Austrian and Czechoslovakian issues were settled without intervention by other European governments, it came as a shock to Hitler that Britain and France confirmed guarantees of military assistance to Poland in 1939. Göring played a major role in trying to achieve a compromise with Britain whereby the 'Danzig Question' could be resolved by diplomatic means, but Hitler was impatient and, spurred on by his Foreign Minister Ribbentrop, gambled that Britain would not intervene when he invaded Poland on 1 September 1939. Göring was privately furious that his efforts had been undermined but, in true opportunistic style, gave total support to the invasion and claimed, against the weight of evidence, that his much-vaunted Luftwaffe had been instrumental in making the decisive contribution to victory. The effect of the early victories was actually to disguise the true weakness of the Luftwaffe, which became apparent when it elected to act independently of the Heer and Kriegsmarine. In accepting intelligence reports about the inferiority of foreign aircraft and production capacity, the Luftwaffe failed to prepare for a strategic air campaign, both in the range and types of aircraft required and in planning how such a campaign should be conducted.

The absence of British or French military action in response to the German invasion of Poland persuaded Göring to accelerate his efforts to reach a compromise with Britain allowing Germany a free hand in eastern Europe, but British intransigence hardened Hitler's attitude and Göring was quick to fall in line with a new, more belligerent approach.

While Göring had central control over the whole war economy, he lacked, at all levels, the administrative infrastructure to implement his policies. It should be noted here that Hitler relied almost totally on Göring to run the economy and it was reported that Hitler made no important political or military decisions without previous discussion with Göring. It was clear to Göring that, despite his best efforts, the war economy was under-performing against targets, but because of his immediate access to and influence over Hitler, he was able to greatly exaggerate his achievements and conceal the worst aspects of failure, at the same time as boasting of the prowess and capabilities of the Luftwaffe, in particular, to the point where Hitler came to believe that his Air Force was the most effective strategic weapon in his armoury.

When the invasion of France and the Low Countries was discussed in the aftermath of the stunning victory over Poland, the armed service chiefs rapidly had to prepare for an extended war for which they had little enthusiasm. It was the unequalled qualities of the German officer corps rather than strategic planning which proved decisive in the management of chaotic and unexpected situations and made possible the stunning victories of May and June 1940. As the French Army disintegrated and the British Expeditionary Force retreated under the assault, following the rapid destruction of Dutch and Belgian resistance, German military strategy was modified almost on a daily basis, and when the Panzers surrounded Dunkirk on 24 May there was no clear idea of how to deliver the 'coup de grace'. The Panzers alone, faced with a waterlogged terrain, were wary of advancing without infantry support, which was still some days behind them. Hitler approved the Halt Order issued by Army Group commander Generaloberst von Rundstedt.

For two days the German Army hesitated; two days during which Operation Dynamo, the British evacuation plan, was inaugurated. By the time the Halt Order was rescinded, British and French troops had already begun their evacuation. Realising what was going on, Göring ordered his bombers to render Dunkirk harbour unusable and assured Hitler that this would curtail the evacuation and force the Allied armies to surrender. Hitler, clearly influenced by the Army's reluctance to press home the attack on land in view of their over-stretched supply lines, accepted Göring's assurances without demur. In the event Göring failed conspicuously, as most Allied troops fled the city and spread out along the beaches from where they were evacuated under cover of RAF fighters. The success of the Allied evacuation, however, was not allowed to detract from the military victories of May, and the massive amount of military hardware abandoned by the evacuating forces reinforced the German belief that the British were broken and incapable of further resistance. This encouraged the hope that they might be amenable to discussing peace terms. The precipitate action against France and the Low Countries, following on directly from Hitler's miscalculation over Allied commitments to Poland, had propelled Germany into a war for which it was ill-prepared. That the British and French were no less ready was little consolation now that Germany had an implacably hostile Western front as it planned its main objective of a drive east into the Soviet Union.

REICHSMARSCHALL HERMANN WILHELM GÖRING

Nothing in German military planning had prepared them for a situation where the Blitzkrieg strategy, which had brought such swift victories, was entirely inappropriate to deal with an enemy entrenched behind a defensive line twenty miles wide and several fathoms deep. Göring, however, saw this as another opportunity to promote the status of his Luftwaffe by using air power alone to force Britain into submission. Unfortunately for him, his hunger for military glory far exceeded his willingness to apply himself to its realisation. He relied on propaganda, coercion and an appeal to nationalistic aspirations rather than detailed planning and management, and this was amply reflected in his approach to the task now facing him: namely to defeat a foe whose capabilities were only vaguely known to him and do it with resources that were less than ideal. The failure at Dunkirk was conveniently ascribed to circumstances beyond Göring's control, such as the weather, and little attention was given to the effectiveness of British fighters in confronting and disrupting Luftwaffe bombers. This was a moment that required sound intelligence, critical evaluation, careful in-depth study and total concentration of minds. Intelligence estimates of British aircraft production put it at around 180 a month, which would drop as industrial capacity was diminished through bombing of factories. Too little importance was given to Luftwaffe losses sustained during the French campaign, which amounted to more than 2,000 aircraft with factories failing to make up all shortfall. When the Luftwaffe subsequently failed to deliver a quick 'knock-out' blow to Britain in August, owing to the lack of long-range strategic bombers, attrition on both sides, but especially on the German side, started to play a decisive part in the battle and it was then that the flawed intelligence adversely affected Göring's decisions.

At the same time as planning his action against Britain, however, Göring was still the principal controller of the German economy and had begun to get involved in another project: the setting up of an Economic Commission to deal with the French economy now under German control. Either task might have been sufficiently daunting to any man whose personal attributes and suitability far exceeded those of Göring, so it is little wonder that he performed neither role effectively. His strategy was not unlike that of his leader. He made bold, broad assertions and outlined strategic objectives, but then left subordinates to work out the details of how they would be achieved. His third persona, as art collector, bon viveur and country squire, also consumed rather more of his time than was appropriate for a man of his responsibilities.

THE ROLE OF INTELLIGENCE IN THE BATTLE OF BRITAIN

When it came to air strategy, Göring was not entirely at a loss, having been a decorated pilot in the First World War, but his attitude had not progressed in line with developments in machines and air power. He still saw personal courage and determination of the individual crewmen as the driving force behind his policies. Ironically, it was these very attributes which Air Marshal Dowding found in his crews of Fighter Command, which eventually succeeded in thwarting Göring's ambition. Strategically there was nothing wrong with Göring's aims of drawing Fighter Command into a war of attrition, thereby opening up either the opportunity for an invasion of the British mainland or British capitulation. The flaw was in his inability to translate that objective into a cohesive strategy. He was initially hampered by inaccurate intelligence reports. Again, irony played a part: the way in which Oberst Josef Schmid edited and distorted assessments of British strength and capabilities exactly reflected the way Göring edited and distorted the information and advice he gave to Hitler. He may well have been only too willing to accept Schmid's distorted reports and funnel them directly up to his leader. It is clear that he failed to treat them with the scrutiny that a competent commander would have demanded.

He was further hamstrung by not having under his control aircraft that were suitable for the roles allotted to them. The Bf109 fighters had too limited a range; the medium bombers were too slow and the Ju87 dive-bombers were sitting targets for British fighters. Even when Göring belatedly demanded a 3:1 ratio of fighter protection to the Ju87s, they suffered catastrophic losses and were withdrawn temporarily from the battle. The fundamental problems which arose from the different tactical priorities of the bomber and fighter crews were never properly addressed. While there is only limited evidence upon which to base a judgement, it seems from what is available that Göring, rather than providing an opportunity for detailed discussions between the Luftflotte and Fliegerkorps commanders to hammer out a policy, chose instead to issue operational directives based on flawed intelligence fed through to him from Schmid's 5th Abteilung.

One of the few aspects of the Luftwaffe campaign which seemed to afford them a significant advantage, namely their ability to wear down the defenders with diversionary and feint attacks and so choose the most propitious moment of attack, was undermined by the RAF's, albeit not totally reliable, use of radar to anticipate attacks and vector defending aircraft onto paths of interception. It may be confidently stated that this ability of Fighter Command to employ its resources in such an efficient way was the single most important factor in the failure of the Luftwaffe to defeat it, and since it was the use of radar which underpinned the whole of Dowding's strategy, it is a damning indictment that the Luftwaffe, and Göring in particular, failed to understand the importance of radar and did not incorporate into their strategy a concerted effort to destroy the radar chain.

While the importance of radar was never fully appreciated by Schmid and Göring, other intelligence agencies such as Martini's and operational commanders would have been only too well aware of the way in which Fighter Command was able to meet their attacks with un-nerving promptness and precision and conclude that radar was the key. Too often, however, when conferences were called, disagreements were allowed to erupt without resolution of the underlying issues. Rather than applying cold, hard scepticism of Luftwaffe claims of RAF casualties to assess progress in the war of attrition, Schmid's wildly optimistic reports, although brusquely challenged by Sperrle, were too easily accepted as fact. When considering the failure of fighters to protect the bomber streams, Göring reduced the argument to one about the fighter pilots' lack of courage and resolve, instead of trying to understand their frustration at the restrictions being placed upon them by close escort deployment. There is little evidence that Göring made any great efforts to face up to the growing catalogue of failures as the battle progressed, relying instead on inspirational conferences and meetings at his Carinhall estate. During these conferences, whether through boredom or fear of embarrassment at his poor grasp of technicalities, he showed a reluctance to engage in detailed discussion of strategy, often breaking off the discussions to indulge in a stag hunt or a tour of his art collection.

All in all, Göring's varied and onerous responsibilities and preoccupations made it unlikely that he ever had a commanding grip on the issues surrounding the Battle of Britain. He failed to elicit the opinion of more technically gifted subordinates when making strategic judgements. He failed to seek balanced understanding through regular conferences where priorities and alternatives could be discussed. Such technical and developmental issues as might have been pertinent to evaluation of strategy often failed to penetrate Schmid's censorship screen, and those that did were not given sufficient attention. Historical analysis usually points to 7 September as the pivotal moment in the Battle of Britain, when the whole focus of Luftwaffe attacks turned from RAF airfields to London itself. At the very moment when Fighter Command was reaching its limits of endurance by the degradation of their Control and Command system, they were thrown a lifeline which allowed them to take a breath and spend a few days of relative quiet to repair the damage and return to a higher state of operational efficiency. Nothing could better illustrate the failure of Luftwaffe Intelligence and competence to prosecute the assault on the RAF than this decision made by Göring, with the full support of Hitler, which blatantly flew in the face of Luftwaffe doctrine as laid out in the Luftwaffe Air Field Manual: 'If emphasis is shifted to a new target or target complex it might prove necessary to continue attacks against the former targets in order not to forfeit the advantage of successes already achieved.'

Chapter 3

German Radar

Now gentlemen, let us all be frank. How are you getting on with
your experiments in the detection by radio of aircraft off your
shores? We've known for some time that you are developing a
system … So are we, and we think we are a jump ahead of you.

Gereral Erhard Milch
inspecting Hornchurch fighter station
in October 1937.[1]

Radar was a near perfect intelligence tool in that it yielded real-time
information about enemy intentions without the enemy knowing exactly
to what extent their operations had been compromised and, crucially,
it denied the enemy the advantage of surprise. In view of the pivotal
contribution made by radar to the British effort during the summer of
1940, it is fundamentally important, when comparing German and British
efforts, to look closely at the German attitude towards radar and the way
in which their strategy was influenced by it. The Germans had done a
great deal of work on radar technology since as early as 1929, but their
priorities had been conditioned by strategic ambitions. For most of the
1930s, and especially after rearmament had begun, Germany had pursued
its territorial ambitions through political brinkmanship underpinned by the
threat of war. Its military forces, whose strength was often exaggerated
for effect, were, nevertheless, becoming formidable, and since there
was little risk of either France or the Soviet Union launching unilateral
attacks against them, felt no need to concentrate over much on defensive
capabilities. German military philosophy at this time was one of attack,
strike and destroy.[2] Large, fixed radar stations, in this context, played
no role and any work done on radar was confined to short-range mobile
systems that could follow an advancing army and be employed as close
support in battlefield scenarios. This much was understandable, but the

weakness in this approach was that the Germans failed to investigate other ways in which the technology could be developed.

It is universally accepted that the first successful demonstration of electric waves being reflected back to a receiver was conducted in Cologne by the prolific German inventor Johan Cristel (Christian) Hülsmeyer as early as 10 May 1904.[3] He formed a company, Telemobiloskop–Gesellschaft Hülsmeyer & Mannheim, and was granted a British patent (DE 165546) for a Telemobiloskop, which was a 'Hertzian-wave projecting and receiving apparatus ... to give warning of the presence of a metallic body such as a ship or a train.'[4] He tried to interest shipping companies but, despite successful trials of his equipment in Rotterdam, found it an uphill struggle because few took the time to try and understand the significance or usefulness of such a system at a time when radio itself was new and poorly understood by non-technicians. As a consequence, ship-owners were at the mercy of the radio giant, Marconi, who provided most of their radio equipment and protected their monopoly position with restrictive contracts that ship-owners were unwilling to challenge at a time when the shipping industry was in recession. Rejection from all quarters forced Hülsmeyer to find more lucrative work, even though his patent drawings show ideas which were incorporated into radar research some thirty years later by engineers who had never heard of his invention.[5]

During the First World War and the 1920s a number of ideas were floated around the idea of detection by reflected radio waves. In the US, Taylor and Young had some success but the US Navy, for whom they worked, filed their work and forgot about it. The work of Butement and Pollard at the British Signals Experimental Station at Woolwich had similar success and an identical fate. In Germany, in 1929, Dr Rudolf Kühnhold at Kiel's German Navy Research Establishment explored the idea of the 13.5cm waveband for radar but was discouraged by the realisation that the generation of a transmission in this region required enormous amounts of energy. Radar research in Germany was primarily conducted by the Navy in such departments as the Torpedo Research Establishment, but limited funds meant slow progress, especially since they lacked the technical skills and were unwilling to make the sort of investment that might encourage civilian researchers to work with them. It was a time of innovation in many fields of electronics and the attention of the small number of firms with expertise was focused on 'other urgent and ... more lucrative pursuits'.[6]

That is not to say that radar research was abandoned. The clear superiority of the Royal Navy over the Kriegsmarine was of great concern;

naval research was given extra resources to look at radar and it developed several of the best pre-war radar systems.[7] Having been effectively rebuffed by the military, Kühnhold formed the Gema Company with Dr Willisen and raised enough finance to continue developing his ideas, which repeated the work of Hülsmeyer without being aware of it. This bore fruit in October 1934 when successful trials this time convinced the Navy to make available 70,000 Reichsmarks (£10,000) for further work in the 50cm waveband, work which henceforth would be conducted under strict military secrecy. Progress was rapid and the next year further trials produced 'outstanding' results using an ultra-low frequency of 2,000 Hz, but still the range of detection was low. There were two schools of thought about how to proceed and Willisen decided to support both low frequency transmission in the 48cm wavelength and very high frequency in the 125 Mhz band. Low frequency experiments were first to show promise sufficient to attract further funds from the Navy which now demanded that all research be disguised under the working name of Dezimeter Telegraphie, abbreviated to De-Te (in much the same way that British radar research was undertaken under the guise of 'ionospheric research').[8] Transmission frequency was increased to 82cm and was now the standard built into the new naval Seetakt radar systems.

Meanwhile, research in the 125 Mhz field had also borne fruit, but here the emphasis shifted from detection of ships in open sea to early warning against aircraft which led to the development of the Freya system. These advances sparked the interest of other firms who were encouraged to work on improving the efficiency of components of the system rather than the system itself. The Lorenz Company developed excellent antenna systems, while Telefunken worked on delivering high-power transmitting valves. Lorenz were considered a security risk due to their international connections (they supplied the RAF, under licence, with a blind landing system) but their work was vital to the cause. General Martini, head of the Luftwaffe 3rd (Signals) Abteilung, took a keen interest in the work and tried to ameliorate the risk by drawing Lorenz into a closer, 'unofficial' relationship with the military which resulted in the development of anti-aircraft gunnery radar A2-Gerät.[9]

In 1936 the German High Command was sufficiently interested in radar to make specifications for future development in order to guide the direction of research. Within a few months Gema were ready to show off their first A1 Gerät Freya system. This was markedly different from the British CH and CHL systems in that it operated on a much higher frequency giving greater accuracy, but consequently sent out a narrower beam which meant that more stations were needed to cover the same area. Telefunken, meanwhile, had developed the Würtzburg rotational device operating on a 53cm wavelength which had also shown remarkable results in detection of aircraft, but was found to be more suited to close-range detection and became an essential component of flak defensive systems. Telefunken, at the same time, was developing small airborne radar sets which were being installed on Junkers 52 transport aircraft for testing.[10] The combination of the Freya and Würzburg radar allowed both a system of ground-based search radar giving long-range early warning, and an integrated, defensive system.

At the beginning of 1939, Martini had demanded and got control of Freya research. The underlying philosophy in the German military as a whole, which embraced the concept of mobile warfare, was instrumental in determining the character of Freya, which was compact and easily moveable. The first indication to the British that the Germans had advanced radar was the Oslo Report in November 1939 which gave some details of a system that had been instrumental in the interception of bombers over Wilhelmshaven a few weeks earlier.

Like the British, the Germans began creating a coastal chain of radar stations for air defence, which proved their effectiveness on 18 November 1939 when a British force of twenty-four Wellington bombers of 9, 37 and 149 Squadrons was detected off Wilhelmshaven by a Freya radar station on Wangerooge island. Thirty-four Bf109 and sixteen Bf110 Fighter aircraft at the nearby Jever airfield were sent up to intercept them, which they did as the Wellingtons turned for home. Half of the aircraft were shot down and six more were battle damaged and crashed on landing back at base. It was a major victory for Luftwaffe defences and a catastrophe for Bomber Command, who were taught a salutary lesson in the folly of deploying massed bombers without fighter protection.[11]

By this time, radar had also been adapted for use in aircraft for night interception of enemy bombers. The Luftwaffe, however, saw radar as being a component of localised defence of vital industrial and military installations, and while radar stations were still under direct control of the Luftwaffe, they were for the most part deployed along the border with France. The small size and mobile nature of Freya systems meant that they could be very quickly deployed when the Germans occupied the Channel coast in June 1940. 'It appeared to us,' said British scientist R.V. Jones, 'that at the beginning of the war the Germans had not thought nearly so much about the use of radar as [the British] had.' The inference being that the Germans 'were giving priority to offensive action'.[12]

The Luftwaffe, especially, with its National Socialist, anti-intellectual philosophy did not place great emphasis on scientific research, but it was not ignored completely. They had actually realised the need for an adequate air defence capability as early as 1936 but this had relied heavily on anti-aircraft artillery. Nonetheless, they had made great strides in radar technology and, as early as 1936, had tested a prototype radar with a detection range of fifty miles. They even built a chain of coastal radar defences in 1937–39, over the same period as the British deployed the Chain Home (CH) radar system. The German system, however, was not integrated into a coherent defensive strategy to augment the flak batteries. German air defence was essentially decentralised and based on the defence of individual targets in vital industrial areas. 'Luftwaffe planners fought any project that would threaten the build-up of offensive air power. This strategy fit well with Germany's military tradition of the offensive being the best defence.'[13]

The main problem with development of radar as an integrated component of the German military was the poor coordination between the military and the scientific community. While radar technology progressed with impressive speed and efficiency, creating devices of great stability and precision and outstripping British achievements at the time, its practical application was left to the military, who chose to apply it as an adjunct to its observer corps. This corps operated in a localised fashion with little sophisticated communication between areas and when radar systems were deployed, they were isolated and did not form any coordinated pattern. It was also noted by Professor Wilhelm Runge, head of development at Telefunken, especially in the case of the Luftwaffe, that they 'never seemed to know what they wanted. One department said one thing, and this was usually countermanded by another.'[14]

When a series of tall structures started appearing along Britain's coastline their purpose was misconstrued. Their construction was quite unlike either Freya or Würzburg systems which did not encourage the idea that they were part of radar detection systems. Clearly they were transmitters of some kind, but thought most likely to be part of a communications network. It was known that Britain was working on radar, but the Germans had no idea what form their research was taking. Martini was of the opinion that, given Britain's reputation for scientific achievement at the time, and their vulnerability to air attack, they would have made significant investment of time and money in radar. He had a strong suspicion that the towers could well be part of an early warning system and he set out to test his hypothesis by investigating the signal emanating from these towers.

On 17 May 1939, before the outbreak of war, he despatched the airship LZ127 Graf Zeppelin, now retired from commercial service and serving as a long-range surveillance craft, loaded with various types of radio receivers to drift up the British east coast and listen to any signals emanating from the towers. Despite flying over Bawdsey and Canewdon radar stations and inland up the Humber Estuary, Martini's technicians were unable to draw any conclusions from the signals they picked up in the ten to thirteen metre band.[15] The wavelength of the signals was unlike any that they, themselves, were using in their own radar research. While not ruling out radar as the purpose of the towers, the team had insufficient evidence to convince the sceptics. Unwilling to let the matter lie, Martini repeated the operation on 3 August, but again all they picked up was what they perceived to be high-frequency noise in the same frequency band as before which, because of their failure to investigate the potential role of VHF and UHF in their own research, they could not prove was anything other than meaningless static rather than radar beams. The airship was picked up by British radar off Dundee and initially, generating such a large echo, was taken to be a large formation of aircraft.[16] When the radar signal indicated that the intruder was moving south and not approaching the shore, it was allowed to proceed unhindered, but radar stations tracked it all the way down the coast and even let it drift some nine miles inland at one point.[17]

There the matter rested, with Martini unable to make further investigations after the declaration of war on 3 September. British radar was not high on the German military agenda while all attention turned to France, and did not raise its profile when a crude British mobile radar unit was discovered among the debris left behind by the fleeing troops at Dunkirk, which seemed to confirm that the British level and direction of radar development was well below that of Germany.

Even when Martini's listeners intercepted British radio traffic in July, confirming that Fighter Command was getting early warning of Luftwaffe raids he found it hard to make his voice heard but Luftwaffe Chief of Staff, Jeschonnek, thought it prudent to take note and eventually agreed that evidence supported the idea that the British towers had a significant part to play in Fighter Command early warning operations. On 3 August, Jeschonnek sent out a directive to Sperrle and Kesselring with the instruction to use special forces, Erprobungsgruppe 210, to strike at the British radar masts along the south coast as a precursor to the main Adlerangriff assault. A sceptical Göring initially supported the move but still held that the towers were linked to communications rather than early warning. This view was generally accepted by pilots themselves as evidenced by Helmut Malke, who flew in a Ju87 dive-bomber with III./StG 3 during the Battle of Britain and described Ventnor radar station, which they were instructed to attack during Adlerangriff, as 'British Fighter Control HQ'.[18] A number of direct attacks on Ventnor, Pevensey, Rye, Dunkirk and Dover radar stations were made on 14 August. The masts did not seem to have suffered much damage despite accurate bomb strikes, and furthermore, Martini's men at Wissant continued to pick up transmissions from all the targeted radar sites after the raids had ended. The stations had proved to be 'remarkably resilient to bomb damage', with the towers especially 'capable of absorbing tremendous' blast effects.[19] Where stations were temporarily put out of action it was caused by damage to telephone and electricity supply lines. The obvious conclusion was that the control rooms were either underground, or sited some distance away and linked by land lines. In either case, Göring, in his directive of 15 August said, 'It is doubtful if there is any point in continuing the attacks on radar sites, in view of the fact that not one of those attacked has so far been put out of operation.'[20] Despite this, raids still continued. On the following day Ventnor was badly damaged and on the 18th Poling took ninety bombs, suggesting that Kesselring and Sperrle were much more concerned about the tall towers' contribution to Luftwaffe losses; but the damning fact remains that at no time was the degradation of Fighter Command radar systems a significant part of Luftwaffe strategy.

Chapter 4

RAF Intelligence

Can anyone tell me what the Germans are up to? For the past few days, Manston has been packed full of our aircraft flown back from France and presenting an ideal target; yet no German aircraft has attacked![1]

Deputy Chief of the Air Staff, Air Marshal William Sholto-Douglas to the Tizard Committee in early June 1940

From an RAF perspective, intelligence was all about trying to understand how and when the Luftwaffe would attack once they had established themselves in their newly acquired airfields across northern France and the Low Countries. The British armed forces as a whole had a wider consideration involving planning against the threat of invasion which, for all their reliance on the Royal Navy, meant essentially preventing the Luftwaffe from establishing control of the air above the invasion beaches. In this sense their intelligence priorities coincided with those of the RAF.

There were a number of traditional intelligence sources such as diplomatic missions and surveillance of industrial and military developments in peacetime, but Britain found these just as poorly exploited as the Germans did from their own side. Neither side had made any great effort to establish the sort of undercover networks that became such a staple of intelligence work after 1945, and neither had a reliable means of pursuing, with any great success, many of the old methods once hostilities broke out. The interception of enemy communications, which offered huge rewards, was greatly hampered by increased security and advances in encryption of radio transmissions and the other reliable source, aerial reconnaissance, was no longer tacitly tolerated but met, where possible, with extreme resistance. While it was essential to continue to improve the efficiency of these methods, it was also the case that counter-measures on both sides would have the effect of maintaining a kind of stalemate.

In order for intelligence to become a significant contributor to victory, this now required a strategic shift in emphasis towards new intelligence methods which might give an advantage to one side or the other. The essential requirements of any effective innovation were that it must give advance warning of enemy intentions and establish the means of countering any aggressive action. It will be seen that in this regard the intelligence facilities available to Fighter Command in the form of radar, command and communications, and the ways in which they were implemented, far outstripped those of the Luftwaffe and were a major contributing factor to its success in repelling both the aerial assault and, by doing that, invasion itself.

During the late 1930s a number of British Intelligence agencies had evolved along different lines and so were uncoordinated with no single controlling authority; the threat of war hastened their awareness that this would have to change, although it was neither easy nor quick to bring about the change.[2] In the Air Ministry, attention had been focused on the Middle East until 1935 when it became clear that there were pressing matters closer to hand and the Directorate of Operations and intelligence staff were steadily increased in line with the rise of international tensions in Europe. Intelligence was reorganised whereby gathering was carried out by the SIS (Secret Intelligence Service) and the GC & CS (Government Code and Cypher School), while the analysis of intelligence was in the hands of the ATB (Advisory Committee on Trade Questions in Time of War), the FCI (Industrial Intelligence in Foreign Countries Sub-Committee) and the IIC (Industrial Intelligence Centre). In 1936, the Chiefs of Staff were persuaded to create a new body, the JIC (Joint Intelligence Sub-Committee), through which information pertinent to all three armed services would be channelled.[3] This committee met regularly, but was forced to overcome hostility from the service chiefs who persisted in jealously hoarding intelligence within their own departments. It did, however, find champion in the Foreign Office, with which it began to work closely. By 1939, the JIC had grown to include the heads of intelligence of all three armed services as well as a counsellor from the Foreign Office. Its remit was:

I. the assessment and coordination of intelligence received from abroad with the object of ensuring that any Government action which might have to be taken should be based on the most suitable and carefully coordinated information available.
II. the coordination of any intelligence data which might be required by the Chiefs of Staff or the Joint Planning Committee for them.

III. the consideration of any further measures which might be thought necessary in order to improve the efficient working of the intelligence organisation of the country as a whole.

When the level of German rearmament became apparent in 1935, with the creation of the Luftwaffe, international reaction was ambivalent. Some saw it as the realisation of legitimate aspirations to rekindle national pride in a country that was seen as a bulwark against Soviet power, while others feared a resurgence of a German authoritarian, militaristic state and a settling of old debts. Whichever was the case, the need to monitor developments was of paramount importance to Britain and her allies in Europe. Few avenues for surveillance existed outside the usual diplomatic and economic exchanges and, indeed, few agencies were capable of extending the range. It became an urgent requirement of such intelligence agencies as there were to find new, or at least improved, ways of collecting and analysing information that might shed light on German capabilities and intentions.

British Intelligence had exhibited similar weaknesses to those of the Luftwaffe, namely dissipation of resources, jealousy between departments and a general lack of cooperation which diminished the end product of such departments in the eyes of military and political leaders. The intelligence agencies were seen as consisting mostly of a certain type of unreliable, gung-ho, upper-class adventurer and were kept at arm's length by the military establishment. It became a self-fulfilling prophesy whereby intelligence became a professional backwater where those considered surplus to requirements were swept to further its reputation for incompetence and irrelevance.[4]

As an example of why they might be viewed in this way, the incident involving Michael Golovine is instructive. Golovine, a member of the RAF Volunteer Reserve, had been born in Petrograd, the son of an Imperial Russian general who had moved to Britain, and was a fluent speaker of Russian. Before the war he had worked in the aero-engine department of Rolls Royce and had co-authored two books on Air Strategy and Air Defence. He was engaged in the evaluation of enemy aircraft and power plants as an officer working in the Administrative and Special Duties Branch of the RAF. His department was informed that a Messerschmitt Bf109 had crashed in an unspecified location and had been stripped of vital components before Luftwaffe engineers could get to it. One such component that was of a particular interest and offered to British Intelligence was its fuel-injection pump, important in giving the Bf109 a crucial advantage in dog-fighting against British aircraft in 1940. Golovine was sent to Belgrade where a meeting was arranged in a café with a fellow Russian-speaker who handed him the device wrapped up in a brown paper parcel. It was clearly impossible for Golovine to carry the parcel back to England himself through the many and various customs posts between Belgrade and London, so he took it to the Air Attaché at the British Embassy in Belgrade requesting that it be sent through diplomatic channels. The Air Attaché had no idea who Golovine was and initially refused to accept it before eventually agreeing. The fuel pump was never seen again. (Michael Golovine was made an MBE and awarded the US decoration, the Bronze Star Medal, in 1946.) On another occasion a complete handbook of the Bf109 was in the hands of intelligence operatives for twenty-four hours, during which time they meticulously photographed every page. Unfortunately, a subsequent search through department files later failed to find any trace of the copies.[5]

Things changed as war loomed after the Anschluss and Munich crisis when British Intelligence agencies saw the danger and were forced to adopt a more professional approach by the creation of the JIC; as an indication of how the status of intelligence had now been elevated, the RAF component, in stark contrast to the Luftwaffe organisation, was led by an Air Commodore. Resources were channelled into investigating German resources, intentions and capabilities as well as technological research, especially in the area of radio telecommunications. Development of British capabilities in communications went hand-in-hand with interception of German radio traffic which was analysed at Bletchley Park. The intelligence branch was required to work closely with a scientific officer to evaluate the information acquired. Photographic reconnaissance boosted the flow of intelligence, but the poor quality of camera lenses and the high level at which the reconnaissance aircraft were required to fly placed severe restrictions on the amount of information that could be derived.

The Air Ministry made a fundamental error in believing that the outbreak of hostilities would see an immediate strategic bombing offensive of British cities, despite informed opinion from within that German bombers could not carry a sufficient bomb-load given the high fuel requirements for the long track to targets.[6] The widely accepted theories of strategic bombing expounded by the Italian theorist Colonel Giulio Douhet, with the default assumption that in any future war 'the bomber would always get through', and the propaganda emanating from Germany had clouded the Air Ministry's deliberations resulting in a thoroughly pessimistic assessment of Britain's ability to withstand a major assault by the Luftwaffe bomber fleets.[7] Neither did the Air Ministry think that the German approach would differ from their own Douhetist interpretations of 'massed attack' strategic bombing theory, when all available evidence gleaned from radio intercepts indicated that there had been no special exercises carried out by the Luftwaffe to train crews for such missions.[8]

It is not surprising, therefore, that the difficulties in acquiring specific information that might have shed more light on Luftwaffe capabilities encouraged British Intelligence to overestimate Luftwaffe strength and exaggerated the effect of German bombing. Winston Churchill MP demanded an increase in the intelligence budget in 1935 to uncover more about German capabilities, but still intelligence failures led to simple, egregious errors such as overestimating the bomb-carrying capacity of the Heinkel He111 by not realising that the weight of full fuel tanks, necessitated by the distance from base to target without flying over Dutch airspace, would reduce it by half. The fear instilled by these gloomy assessments inevitably had considerable influence on political and military thinking in the immediate pre-war years. A more nuanced appreciation might have been easily arrived at by consideration of how British bombers would fare if required to attack the Ruhr, but there was no appetite to pursue such a move – possibly because that would have lowered the mood even more by showing how difficult it would be for Britain to retaliate.

The most obvious source of intelligence about Germany was the interception of enemy communications which was an old tradition, but which had changed in character with the advent of radio. The interception of electronic signals had continued, to some extent, since the First World War, but increasingly sophisticated encryption was a constant challenge to eavesdroppers. German expansion of its armed forces had, however, taken place with such speed that it had outstripped its ability to shield much of its communication network which meant that there was still a huge amount of radio traffic as opposed to transmission through fixed telephone wires. This may not have been such a weakness had operators adhered strictly to time-consuming and tedious operational protocols but, especially in peacetime, there was little incentive to shield navigation signals, weather reports and low-grade tactical transmissions. This signals intelligence was acquired through the Y-Service (WI, Wireless Intercept) radio interceptor station at Cheadle. F.R. Hinsley says that while it is not possible to make a detailed study of the ways in which Cheadle directly influenced Fighter Command operations, 'There can be little doubt that [the Y-Service] made an important contribution … during the crucial weeks.'[9]

The Y-Service was a network of listening posts set up all over the world to eavesdrop on radio traffic, but of crucial interest in the late 1930s were German radio communications. Y-Service personnel were highly skilled in languages and morse code and required particular qualities of concentration and precision. There were large listening stations at Beaumanor, Chatham and Whaddon Hall but the main RAF wireless intercept station was at Cheadle, which specialised in the interception of low-grade tactical communications using American HRO radio sets. A special listening station was even set up inside Wormwood Scrubs prison to listen for radio transmissions that might be sent by enemy agents inside Britain. In the early days, there was little haste as messages were transcribed (morse code translated and written down in plain text as the message was intercepted) and sent to Bletchley Park for decoding before going on to the Air Ministry. Later, cypher clerks moved to Cheadle and decoding was done on the spot despite vociferous complaints that this risked security breaches.[10] Intelligence from Cheadle, however, was limited since German strategic decisions were 'rarely spelled out in wireless signals'.[11] Furthermore, 'The organisation for handling operational intelligence [was] defective in one important direction.'[12] After 1939, a rift had opened up between GC and CS, that normally handled Enigma traffic, and Cheadle which was not staffed or equipped to handle it. The GC and CS decrypts of high-grade German operational traffic was channelled into a different section of Air Intelligence from the low-grade Cheadle decrypts meaning that, due to the intransigence of Air Intelligence to sanction close cooperation between the two, the two different intelligence streams were never properly integrated until towards the end of the Battle of Britain, and even then intelligence was not shared in real time, only after the event.[13] In one respect, however, both worked effectively towards an understanding of Luftwaffe organisation and order of battle. Cheadle had exploited the Luftwaffe's dependence on radio for navigation and weather reporting to break low-grade ciphers and this, together with interception of the increasing volume of radio telephone communications by German-speaking WAAF and WRNS staff at Home Defence Units in small stations along the south-east coast, housed in caravans or clifftop cottages, produced important intelligence.[14]

At the basis of all 'Boniface' intelligence (the codename for intelligence derived from Enigma decrypts) were the listeners. Without interception and recording of German signals there would no story to tell about Enigma or Bletchley Park. The listeners eavesdropped on both radio telephony (normal voice transmission) and wireless telephony (Morse code). Radio telephony was used mostly by fighter pilots communicating with ground control or with each other in the air (they had been ordered to maintain radio silence during operations, but this directive was frequently ignored), so obviously the listeners were required to have a sound knowledge of the German language. Normally this traffic was on very high-frequency wavelengths (VHF) and could only be picked up in close proximity to the source. Luftwaffe bomber crews, however, used mostly medium and high frequency communications which could be picked up from much further away. This meant that listeners could often eavesdrop on bomber crew chatter as the larger raids formed up over Pas de Calais, often beyond radar detection range, giving vital extra minutes of warning. Wireless telephony signals were transmitted on high or medium frequency and often in code, but GC & CS had broken these codes. Listeners, mostly women, sat 'glued to earphones at intercept stations', working in shifts of six hours 'spent twiddling knobs and hectically taking down in pencil what they could'.[15]

It cannot be overstated what intelligence, skill and concentration was necessary for the listeners to become proficient at recognising individual German operators, sometimes by their accents in the case of radio or, in the case of wireless, by their individual styles of tapping out Morse code (their 'fists') which helped to identify the units, especially since unit call signs were frequently changed. It was even the case that individual transmitters emitted a unique background noise that immediately identified them.[16] Tuned in to given wavelengths with receivers orientated in a particular direction, listeners would wait in silence until a message would suddenly erupt in their earphones and they would have to respond immediately to capture the first crucial letters and transcribe each subsequent letter with unerring accuracy in order for the analysts to make sense of the message. All of this was of critical importance, given that when a signal in Morse code was first intercepted there was really no way of telling where it had originated. It was simply a sequence of sounds. What was known was the frequency of transmission, the volume of traffic on that frequency and possibly a clue as to the direction from which it had emanated. If a message was picked up from the beginning it would also usually include a call sign. Identifying the unit involved and its operating altitude often gave clues about the type of aircraft and the intended target. All this fed into the Filter Room at Bentley Priory and added detail to the overall picture.

From this meagre intelligence, even when the signals remained undeciphered, it might be, over time, found that a certain unit at a certain location with a certain call sign was often in contact with another unit (or units) at another known location with a known call sign, and from the accumulation of such intelligence could be derived a growing understanding of the German order of battle and sometimes, simply by virtue of a sudden increase in volume of signals, forewarning of a major operation such as the movement of a unit from one location to another, or even a major offensive.[17] Knowledge of call signs was of paramount importance to breaking the codes. Fortunately, the British had two German code books, one captured in North Africa and the other captured by the Soviets and passed on to British Intelligence.

The reliance on medium frequency communications throughout the Luftwaffe bomber force allowed Cheadle to predict, with increasing frequency and certainty, the position, course, height and target of bombers and which units were involved.[18] Even before aircraft had appeared on radar screens listeners were sometimes able to detect bomber groups forming up in preparation for an attack and even pass on information, based on voice intercepts, of the composition of the formations in terms of fighter or bomber aircraft. In some cases, signals could be picked up as much as thirty minutes before aircraft had actually left the ground.[19] Furthermore, the overheard conversations, in plain language, might give information about what sort of reception the attackers were expecting, which in turn told of the extent to which they understood the British fighter control system, subsequently referred to as the 'Dowding System'. This exploitation of Luftwaffe low-grade traffic was a serious weakness indicating either a level of desperation on the part of the Luftwaffe, or sense of material superiority over waning British resistance since the Germans would have been quite certain that their traffic was being intercepted, yet felt that the advantages for themselves in using radio so profligately in this very insecure way overrode any advantage it might have given to Fighter Command. While there can be no detailed examination of the impact this had on Fighter Command operations, there is no doubt that this contribution could have been greater given that Luftwaffe units such as KG 100, known to be pathfinders for the bombers, made free use of wireless in flight, meaning that targets were sometimes identified ahead of the strike – but wireless was intercepted by GC and CS, not Cheadle, and GC and CS intelligence was channelled into the long-term research section meaning that little, if any, of this intelligence ever found its way to Fighter Command in time for them to use it.[20]

Codebreakers Hugh Alexander, Gordon Welchman and others were alarmed when, in August 1940, it was proposed to move staff monitoring Enigma traffic from the Army listening station at Chatham, important because of its proximity to France, to Chicksands Priory, near Bedford, with a new and expanded staff of listeners. Chatham had acquired a sound reputation for expertise and efficiency which was based on such subtleties as recognising the unique characteristics of particular German signallers, allowing the listeners to track them even when they changed transmission frequencies. This required 'a sensibility and delicacy of hearing that [could] only be gained by long experience'. Alexander warned that the whole intercept system 'hangs by a thread', and 'a reduction in the standards of interception might be fatal'.[21] The recording of intercepted messages and an understanding of the source of the signals, they said, required much more experience and precision than was generally accepted by higher authorities and the introduction of large numbers of new, inexperienced personnel would greatly jeopardise the whole operation. The move was necessitated, however, by the increased risk from bombing and by the need for more Army staff to move in to counter the threat of invasion.[22] The Chatham staff remained at Chicksands for a brief time before moving into permanent quarters at Beaumanor.

During the immediate pre-war years there was significant cooperation with French and Czech Intelligence, whose proximity to Germany gave them increased incentive to monitor their radio traffic and who were extremely diligent in acquiring intelligence, given their vulnerability to German expansionist ambitions. After the Munich Crisis, the British decided that signals intelligence from all sources should be channelled through a central hub at Bletchley, but the administrative problems of coordination and cooperation proved to be beyond the capabilities or even desires of the various agencies involved and the idea was abandoned. The outbreak of war, however, galvanised the government into a new effort to break down inter-departmental barriers and when Bletchley Park was again mobilised, previous lessons had been learned and the codebreakers got down to some serious work there.

The next most important source of strategic intelligence was aerial photography of enemy bases, harbours and industrial areas, but while its importance was acknowledged, all efforts to create an agency were opposed by an intransigence bordering on hostility on the part of the Air Ministry, which viewed specialised units as being anathema to RAF tradition. They initially failed to invest in the development of cameras, or to provide facilities for crew training, and refused to adapt aircraft to meet the requirements of high-altitude, long-distance flight. The imminence of war eventually broke down resistance and the development of the Spitfire, capable of avoiding interception by flying at high speed and altitude, was just the breakthrough that was needed to give the project a boost. Early photo-reconnaissance missions had relied on heavily armed bombers such as Blenheims, which were deemed capable of defending their air space, but heavy losses and unfruitful missions soon threatened to derail the whole strategy. A new unit, the Heston Special Flight, was set up under an ex-First World War pilot, Wing Commander Sydney Cotton.

Cotton started out somewhat modestly, with an American Lockheed twelve-passenger aircraft which he began fitting out with cameras in January 1939.[23] In the summer of that year, before hostilities broke out, Cotton made a number of trips over military installations in Mannheim, Germany, which highlighted the first problem: frosting of the camera lenses at 20,000ft. His unit was renamed the PRU (Photographic Reconnaissance Unit) and, on 18 November 1939, flew its first mission over Aachen with a Spitfire Mk 1 specially adapted with 5-inch focal length cameras in place of the Browning machine guns. Having seen Blenheims benefit in terms of performance by giving them an extreme high polish to reduce air resistance, the Spitfire was similarly groomed and painted duck-egg blue/green for camouflage against the sky.

Once the principle was established, Cotton got down to the business of making his new unit useful, which meant getting his Spitfire to fly faster, higher and further.[24] To this end, they became among the first British fighters to be converted to 100%-octane fuel. A new all-metal propeller was fitted which was balanced by an extra fuel tank under the tail. More fuel tanks were fitted into the wings, causing one of the pilots, Wing Commander Geoffrey W. Tuttle, to claim that it was impossible to fly straight and level for the first thirty minutes until the rear auxiliary tank had been emptied. Once stability was restored, however, the aircraft could remain airborne for five hours, giving it a remarkable range as far as Berlin. In January 1940 the unit had acquired a Mk 1B Spitfire with improved Type 24 8-inch focal length cameras, and then in April the camera was upgraded again to an F52 with 36-inch focal length. It was at this time that it suffered its first casualty when one of its aircraft was shot down by a Bf109 over Arnhem. The aircraft was now flying at 35,000ft, but the technique of actually taking the photograph required precision and judgement.[25] There was still the highly technical problem of analysing and interpreting the photographs before useful intelligence could be extracted, not to mention resolution of the scrap between the Ministry of Economic Warfare (MEW) and the Air Ministry over its use.[26] Eventually a new device was developed by the Swiss and put into play by the photo-interpreter Michael Spender, which made it possible to calculate the dimensions of structures in the photographs and this breakthrough resulted in creation of the Photographic Interpretation Unit (PIU), which henceforth handled all photo-reconnaissance intelligence. After Dunkirk, despite Cotton's achievements in setting up the PRU, he was considered too self-willed and independent for Air Ministry tastes and was replaced by Tuttle, who was seen as more reliable and professional.[27]

Bomber Command, which was the section most likely to benefit from PRU work, was rather dismissive of Tuttle and Spender, who they considered to be a 'nuisance'.[28] They had their own reconnaissance unit and were in no mood to be undermined by what they clearly saw as an upstart organisation. Despite this opposition, the PRU gained favour with the Air Ministry and moved to facilities at Wembley after it became the PIU. When Bomber Command eventually deigned to make use of the unit they, somewhat recklessly, sent their aircraft deep into Germany, which quickly resulted in a number of losses. The PRU was most effective during the summer of 1940 in its role of monitoring the build-up of invasion barges all along the French, Belgian and Dutch Channel ports.

The MEW had been created in an emergency efficiency drive in 1939 as a single entity to combine the functions of a number committees which had previously kept an eye on economic developments in Germany. The MEW had its own intelligence branch, the Economic Warfare Intelligence (EWI) which was required 'to keep under constant observation the enemy's economic potential for war with the object of assisting other branches of intelligence in detecting in advance his possible intentions, in estimating his strength and his weaknesses and in selecting points vulnerable to attack by any weapon that we could command ....'[29] While the work of the branch was seen as vital to the war effort, it was only with some difficulty that other government departments with a finger in the intelligence pie were persuaded to cooperate. It fell to the Minister of Co-ordination for Defence to knock a few heads together and elevate the MEW to a seat on the Joint Intelligence Committee – but as we have seen, this by no means resulted in seamless cooperation with the Air Ministry who had access to intelligence, denied to the MEW, over the assessment of intelligence about potential targets.

As it grew in confidence, Germany had been eager to influence international opinion with its economic and military progress, and had, up until 1938, allowed British officers and government officials almost unlimited access to its military establishments. Demonstrations at the

German aeronautical research establishment at Rechlin Air Base on 3 July 1939 were blatant attempts not only to impress and intimidate foreign visitors, but were also used as propaganda exercises to influence internal politics. To the amazement of both Göring and Hitler, a prototype jet-propelled aircraft, the Heinkel He176, was rolled out apparently in an advanced stage of development, but they did not enter service until the final months of the war.[30] Göring was later reported to have said that he had been 'deceived' and that Hitler 'made a number of exceedingly vital decisions' based on what he saw that day.[31] British engineers had been given access to the German aircraft industry establishments, but of course this was a reciprocal arrangement whereby intelligence gained was offset by intelligence acquired by the other side. Diplomatic sources still fed back intelligence, however, and to some extent the loss of direct access to German establishments was compensated for by a marked improvement in exchange of information with other European countries which began to feel threatened by German resurgence.

Where intelligence had scored some success was in the compilation of statistics surrounding German aircraft production, but this was becoming increasingly speculative as sources of information dried up. An estimate of German military aircraft production of 750 per month in 1939 was only slightly higher than the true figure, but their assumption that wartime production, which could increase as extra shifts were introduced in the factories, would double was wide of the mark when, for the next two years, there was little increase at all. However, it was noted that the difficulties resulting from a shortage of skilled labour (Germany in the 1930s was still evolving from a predominantly artisan industrial base), and the use of substitute materials that slowed the production of armaments in other areas were markedly less noticeable in aircraft production, due, no doubt, to the overarching influence of Göring as both head of the Luftwaffe and controller of the German Four Year Plan of industrial production. Economists rightly questioned whether the Nazi regime could simultaneously boost military production and maintain an adequate level of production of consumer goods to meet civilian expectations.

All in all, British Intelligence had few successes in its operations during the immediate pre-war years, primarily due to a lack of adequate funding together with a significant increase in security measures adopted by the totalitarian states, about which intelligence was most urgently needed. The information that came through from various sources was often contradictory and there was little solid evidence against which it could be tested. Criticism of the SIS was so acute in 1939 that Sir Alexander Cadogan, the Permanent Under-Secretary of the Foreign Office, who had assumed the chairmanship of the JIC in July 1939, was obliged to publicly defend it against accusations by the War Office that it was failing.[32] The intelligence agencies were viewed with great scepticism by the War Office, which repeatedly dismissed reports of advances in German armament as unrealistic based on the simple, but blinkered, assumption that Britain could not have made similar advances anywhere near as quickly. The SIS argued that it was given insufficient guidance as to the kind of intelligence the War Office required, and furthermore was side-tracked by Foreign Office demands for intelligence on such things as internal German political opposition groups.

The dismissive attitude towards the JIC was evident by the fact that up to May 1940, it had only once been called to attend meetings of the Joint Chiefs of Staff. It had failed to make an impact, having been burdened with administrative tasks which diverted its resources resulting in providing little intelligence that was not readily available through diplomatic sources. Too often they were forced to admit that their conclusions were based largely on inspired guesswork. It is not difficult to see why the Joint Planners treated the JIC with such disdain when a report on German intentions after the fall of Poland concluded, 'which of these courses Germany will select will depend less upon logical deduction than upon the personal and unpredictable decisions of the Führer.'[33] When they were further asked to comment on a speech in September 1939 where Hitler boasted of 'new and secret weapons', JIC were quite unable to confirm or deny the likelihood of their existence. It transpired that a review of the translation of the speech revealed that a better interpretation would have been,' we have a weapon with which we [ourselves] could not be attacked', referring to the Luftwaffe, which had no rival of equivalent capability in other countries.[34] As an example of how poor intelligence adversely affected the operations of the British military, the bulk of the British Home fleet was anchored at Scapa Flow in the Shetland Island, the Admiralty having been told that up to 800 German bombers were within range, when the true figure was closer to 300.

In direct contrast to the elaborate systems set up to collect and process intelligence, one of the most important documents, albeit one which was initially considered unreliable, to fall into British hands came through a much simpler route. At the end of 1939, the British Naval Attaché in Oslo, Hector Boyes, received an anonymous document purporting to contain information about German Military advances. It was one of many similar documents circulating through diplomatic channels at the time and was treated with some scepticism, but it turned out to be 'one of the most remarkable intelligence reports of the war'.[35] In the normal way, it was sent to London with the others and, because the original package had also contained what appeared to be a new type of proximity fuse for anti-aircraft shells, it ended up on the desk of the British Scientific Officer at the Air Ministry, Professor Jones, who had been brought in to assess the value of intelligence about both British and German scientific and technological developments that might have an effect on the conduct of the war. Having read the report he was impressed with its contents, but when attempting to interest higher authority in it, he was rebuked by the Deputy Director of Research at the Admiralty for his naivety in believing that it was anything other than an elaborate hoax, despite the accuracy of some details in the report being supported by other sources. Criticism was based on the assumption that no single man could have access to so much varied and top-secret information and it prevailed over evidence that the proximity fuse enclosed with the documents was of remarkable value to intelligence, being far in advance of anything comparable in the British armoury. Unable to pursue the matter further, Jones was sufficiently interested to keep his translation of the report but others were discarded or filed away without further examination.

The report was written by a German electronics expert, Hans Ferdinand Mayer, and contained information that turned out to be completely accurate. Indeed, one high-ranking member of British Intelligence claimed that, 'in the few dull moments of the war, we used to turn to the Oslo Report to see what should be coming along next.'[36] Mayer was a scientist working at the Siemens Research Laboratory. He held high rank within the company and had extensive contacts all over Europe. The outbreak of war convinced him that he had to act to bring down the Nazi regime in Germany and so, on a business trip to Oslo in October 1939, he surreptitiously made contact with British Intelligence through the Oslo Embassy and left the report signing it 'a German scientist, who is on your side'. Mayer's identity as the author remained a secret until after his death in 1980.

Inter-department wrangling, even after the outbreak of war, continued to burden British Intelligence. The Air Ministry took exception to sharing its signals traffic and aerial reconnaissance material with the Ministry of Economic Warfare and was only brought into line at the end of 1940 by the personal intervention of Prime Minister Churchill. British Intelligence suffered further blows to its relevance and morale by failing to predict the German invasion of Norway and Denmark on 9 April, despite several indications that operations there were imminent. This came on the back of another debacle, the Venlo Incident in November 1939, when two top British Intelligence agents were tricked into a clandestine meeting on the German border, kidnapped and interrogated.

One area which proved to be more productive, however, was the breaking of German military radio codes. The rapid rise of Luftwaffe administration had outstripped its capacity to contain the security of its low-grade communications. In its use of radio for navigation and weather reporting it used rudimentary encipherment, which it must have known would easily be broken by eavesdroppers, but thought it unimportant. That was a mistake, since it was through intercepts that the RAF was able to discover the location of important airfields and the units stationed there. High-level radio signals, however, were encoded using Enigma machines which were very sophisticated, and although much knowledge of the system was acquired from Polish Intelligence, it was not until January 1940 that the first British breakthrough came in decrypting Luftwaffe Enigma traffic. The groundwork for this had been laid by Polish codebreakers who had been working on the German Enigma codes since 1931. Early in 1940, a number of new recruits joined RAF Intelligence which had been galvanised to meet the imminent German threat and this had precipitated the introduction of new divisions within its organisation to concentrate on specific areas of interest. Many of the new recruits were highly trained technical specialists, which resulted in a marked improvement in intelligence gathering and analysis. All sectors and squadrons now had specialist intelligence officers attached to them to collect real-time information from active units and also disseminate instructions from above based on the latest intelligence assessments. Beyond this point, RAF Intelligence became much more efficient than its Luftwaffe counterpart. It was well coordinated and had multiple sources.

In June 1940, Britain was still reeling from the disaster of its full retreat during the Battle of France and its miraculous deliverance at Dunkirk. Many feared an imminent invasion. It was clear from analysis of German radio traffic that any invasion would be preceded by a campaign to gain aerial dominance over the south coast. This combined with the morbid fear of an all-out bombing strike on London meant that RAF Fighter Command would be at the very heart of Britain's defences, and any and all intelligence pertaining to invasion would be of crucial importance to the Air Ministry.

The PRU played a central role in monitoring German preparedness for invasion. By constant patrols over the Dutch, Belgian and French ports for signs of build-up of invasion craft, it gave 'the only immediate hope of guarding against surprise'.[37] JIC noted that reports were circulating in the British Press to the effect that Germany was planning armed landings in the Thames Estuary from fast boats, possibly coming in from the Baltic. At this stage such areas were well outside the range of PRU Spitfires, but when German troops were said to be massing in southern Norway, flights from Wick could just about confirm the lack of evidence for any such venture. Not until mid-July was the area around Bordeaux, another possible invasion embarkation port, surveyed by F-Type Spitfires to eliminate that also. The lack of evidence of preparations for invasion, however, did not dispel the fear that invasion was imminent. In June, Churchill had requested his Joint Chiefs to prepare a study of possible invasion scenarios. They came back with a 'British Strategy in a Certain Eventuality', including the means of carrying on the fight in the event of French capitulation. They saw coastal defences, food supplies and terror bombing as the three crucial issues. It was, however, a feature of British reaction to invasion scares that many of the more bizarre examples were given credence simply because the actual level of understanding of German intentions and capabilities was so low.

With the Royal Navy cowering in the Orkneys and the British Army in disarray after Dunkirk, it was the RAF which carried the burden of facing the enemy alone. Fortunately, the service had benefited greatly from the appointment of Air Chief Marshal Sir High Dowding. When Dowding took over at the newly formed Fighter Command in 1936, he had placed great importance on scientific research and innovative strategies as ways of countering the inadequacy of actual aircraft numbers. He saw Fighter Command's role as essentially one of fighter defence against bombing attack, which was in stark contrast to the Luftwaffe strategy of pure attack using fighters and bombers in combination.

Dowding's contribution to the success of Fighter Command's repulsion of the Luftwaffe assault in 1940 cannot be overstated. His support for radar development and his creation of a highly sophisticated command and control system to coordinate the actions of operational units was fundamental to the way that his acolyte, Sir Keith Park, AOC at 11 Group, was able to deploy his resources in opposing the superior numbers of enemy aircraft. Dowding had, since his appointment in 1936, championed the development of radar which, if made to work effectively, he believed could become an essential component of his planned fighter control system, the Dowding System, by giving early warning of approaching aircraft. This, however, was just one component of early warning. The Observer Corps, which he also eagerly supported, would become a vital second stage of aircraft detection and a vital addition to the RAF Intelligence network. It was clearly understood that neither radar, struggling with the intricacies of its emerging technology, and the Observer Corps, really only capable of making telling observations in clear weather, would be infallible when confronted with a Luftwaffe encamped only twenty miles across the English Channel and capable of attacking in massed formations at short notice, but it was all there was and it was hugely better than nothing at all.

The defensive strategy developed by Dowding was securely founded on intelligence gained through early detection of Luftwaffe attacks and effective control of his fighters when deployed to meet them. It perfectly fulfilled the three requirements of intelligence: acquisition of information, interpretation of information and efficient application of the conclusions. This approach was underlaid by a determination that, first of all, the enemy must be confronted at all times and never allowed free rein over British airspace, and second that Fighter Command must, at all costs, continue to exist, to whatever extent is possible, as a viable force until the threat of invasion had been removed by the passage of time. Radar provided essential, detailed information about the threat both on a strategic level (what were the enemy's strength, deployment and capabilities), and tactical level (how were his assets to be deployed on a daily, even hourly, basis).

The proximity of Luftwaffe bases to mainland Britain, especially in Luftflotte 2, meant that attacks could strike before British fighters could be alerted and made airborne. Even then they required up to twenty minutes to reach an effective combat height. For operations against Channel convoys in the Dover Straits this meant that attacks could be staged, completed, and Luftwaffe aircraft withdrawn before interception was possible. The only solution was to mount constant standing patrols over the convoys which was draining of Fighter Command energies and resources. When the Luftwaffe eventually made a serious effort to destroy a convoy, as on 8 August, there was little that Fighter Command could do to prevent it and convoys were thereafter temporarily suspended.

Later, as the combat zones crept northward over mainland Britain, and especially when raids approached up the Thames Estuary, there was more time for Fighter Command to respond and the nature of engagements changed with heavier deployment on both sides and attrition began to play a major role in the dynamics of the battle. Radar was instrumental in early detection and determining avenues of attack, but was much less useful in estimating aircraft numbers and their altitude. A miscalculation of either of these factors could put British fighters in murderously unforgiving situations. The Luftwaffe developed a respect for British radar, although perhaps not fully appreciating how it worked and was integrated into the Dowding System; they used it against Fighter Command by putting up large numbers of aircraft within the range of radar detection, which would prompt Fighter Command to scramble many aircraft in anticipation of attack. The Luftwaffe would then hold their aircraft in position while British fighters used up their fuel, then when their empty tanks forced them to land, fresh Luftwaffe aircraft would strike against a weakened defence. Later, in the next stage of this 'cat and mouse' scenario, British controllers would refuse to scramble their squadrons until they were convinced that an attack was actually in progress. There were numerous instances of these strategies failing on both sides as they both vied for the element of surprise, but as conflicts moved closer to London and further from the Luftwaffe airfields, the advantage shifted significantly in favour of the defending aircraft.

After Dunkirk, British Intelligence had to make rapid reassessments of Britain's perilous military predicament. Signals intelligence was severely truncated when the British Expeditionary Force was evacuated, leaving a skeleton liaison team embedded with French forces. Aerial reconnaissance and radio intercepts provided evidence of the rapid Luftwaffe occupation of its new airfields along the Channel coast by two whole Luftflotten with significant bomber *geschwader* component, but it provided only the big picture and was short of detail. What did emerge, which was of great significance, was intelligence that the German panzers which had surrounded Dunkirk were being redeployed to move south across the Seine in pursuit of French forces. This was taken as an indication that the Germans did not have plans for an immediate invasion, and it gave Fighter Command precious time to come to terms with the new situation and organise its defences.

With the imminent capitulation of the French, a crisis point was approaching. On 19 June, the British Chiefs of Staff reported that 'the struggle against Germany would almost certainly turn upon our ability to hold out during the next three months'. It was implicit, but not stated, that 'holding out' would hinge on the ability of Fighter Command to protect its airspace over southern England. While it was tentatively assumed that there would be no immediate invasion, the German Army's 'unexpected ability to carry out large-scale overseas operations', and mastery of 'secret preparations and rapid execution of plans', did not allow for the least measure of complacency.[38]

On 1 July, the JIC had admitted it could not determine German intentions but advised that German military superiority was such that it could move in any direction it chose with little or no warning, and the defeat of France had graphically illustrated the ability of German field commanders to 'think on their feet' and exploit situations with lightning speed. A few days later they reported that an invasion, given the British codename 'Smith', was possible by 15 July and was expected, at least in the absence of any concrete indications to the contrary, to be against the east coast of Lincolnshire, Norfolk or Suffolk. As early as 10 May, when news came through of the German attack against France, JIC had warned that 'the provision of adequate shipping and troops for an invasion would present Germany with no problems'.[39] By early June, despite the paucity of supporting evidence, General Edmund Ironside was convinced that 'vast preparations in the way of air and sea invasion are being made', but Churchill, possibly aware of the loss of so many German aircraft during May and early June, was sceptical and said that he had 'not seen any evidence' that the Germans would embark on such a 'hazardous and even suicidal operation'.[40]

While intelligence reported on 19 July that any preparations for invasion across the Channel should (not would) be detected by aerial reconnaissance, they could not rule out the possibility of an invasion using fast boats from ports in the Baltic, which were beyond the scope of aerial reconnaissance and therefore impossible to detect. Paranoia was rife and confidence in its own intelligence later faded to the point where it stated that it could not completely discount an invasion force being collected and despatched at short notice across the English Channel. The lack of evidence was not sufficient to deter speculation that the enemy might come at night or under cover of cloud and rapidly establish a bridgehead, then reinforce that bridgehead with troops from Holland and Belgium.

PRU aerial reconnaissance and intercepted Enigma signals had alerted JIC to the movement and refitting of many Luftwaffe gruppen. Newly acquired airfields in Belgium and northern France were being extended and fitted with permanent structures. Long-range guns were being installed at Cap Gris Nez. The evidence was clear that the Germans were preparing for some kind of offensive, but its true character could not be discerned. The strategy master-stroke of its advance through the Ardennes forest to Sedan, and the innovative techniques employed during Fall Gelb such as the glider attack on Eben Emael and the use of paratroopers in Holland, showed that the German military was very capable of springing strategic and tactical surprises.

Fear of invasion in Britain reached new levels of intensity when intelligence reports claimed that the enemy might get as many as 100,000 troops ashore with little or no warning. This report was given credence despite the fact that a cursory analysis would question the availability of naval resources needed for such an operation. Unbeknown to British Intelligence, OKH, had made its initial plans with not the slightest regard for how a large invasion force could be transported across the English Channel. These plans were fiercely opposed by the Kriegsmarine chief, Grossadmiral Raeder, who predicted that any confrontation between his fleet and the Royal Navy would simply show that his men could 'do no more than show that they know how to die gallantly'. It was a matter of some concern that the Royal Navy had not questioned the intelligence when it came to committee, in light of their own certain knowledge that such an operation could not be mounted without massive administration and logistical efforts that would take a considerable amount of time, and would be immediately detectable by surveillance at all stages of its preparation.[41]

Luftwaffe Enigma traffic was being regularly intercepted, but decryption techniques were at a very early stage and the amount of detailed intelligence that could be drawn from it varied. The most useful information concerned the Luftwaffe Order of Battle and the movement of units between airfields, which gave some indication of the number of different types (bomber or fighter) of aircraft in a given zone, which in turn gave some indication of the type of raids that could be expected from any given area. Dowding based his strategy on an over-estimation of Luftwaffe strength which was entirely in keeping with his cautious approach. Knowledge of Luftwaffe deployment in Luftflotten 2 and 3 convinced him that the main Luftwaffe attacks would fall on south-east England and so he, along with Park, prepared a strategy which placed 11 Group at the forefront of British defence; Fighter Command's other three Groups would be at the disposal of that strategy by supplying replacement squadrons as required and offering rest and recuperation to exhausted squadrons taken out of the battle front.

Tactics was a different matter altogether. Knowledge of enemy strength was most useful when allied with knowledge of enemy intentions. The Luftwaffe order of battle indicated broad avenues of attack and the type of aircraft that might be used, but the timing and strength of such attacks was vital to indicate the level of defence required to be deployed against them. For instance, intercepted signals giving clues about German losses in early August encouraged analysts to lower their estimates of the daily bomb load that could be dropped on southern England and thus allowed Fighter Command to modify strategy accordingly. Intercepts, however, were quite unable to give any indication on the crucial and growing issue of if, where, or when an invasion might be expected. All communications at command level between Luftflotte headquarters and Berlin were now by secure land line. All wireless intercepts could achieve was an indication that a strategic shift may be expected, but gave no information of what it might be. Even where Enigma traffic containing information about targets, timing and levels of raids was intercepted, it was only after the event that decryption revealed the details, by which time the information was of little use operationally. Furthermore, because of the way that signals intelligence had been developed with high-level Enigma traffic and low-grade intercepts going through different analytical channels, it was often the case that opportunities were lost to combine both sources to reveal more results than could be arrived at separately.

A third source of intelligence about Luftwaffe movements was acquired through intercepts by German-speaking operatives of plain-language, high-frequency radio traffic between aircraft and ground controllers at airfields. The listening station at Cheadle had, over several months, acquired sufficient expertise to be able to identify Luftwaffe units from certain characteristic of their signals traffic. Once identified, these units' home bases could be guessed and while this might not identify the target, it would indicate the likely flight path of the aircraft as they returned to base after an attack and this would give British fighters a better chance of intercepting them. German crews were supposed to maintain radio silence during missions but there was a myriad of circumstances under which this instruction was disregarded, which allowed for a further opportunity of acquiring information about the units. During September and October, the German crews became increasingly undisciplined in their use of radio communications and this, together with the increasing efficiency of radar data, was instrumental in adjusting the balance of forces during the great air battles over London and south-east England.

A major requirement of the intelligence agencies during the Battle of Britain was the continuous assessment of the invasion threat. The first alarm was raised in early July, more on the basis that an invasion 'could not be ruled out', rather than because it was actually expected. On the 14th, the threat was played down due to intelligence that many Luftwaffe units were still in the process of redeployment to airfields in France, some of which were merely open fields, which, in many cases, required much work to bring them up to operational efficiency. This assessment was repeated on the 27th, but carried the caveat that German bombers were now forbidden to bomb harbours along the British south coast, presumably to preserve them for use by invasion troops. By mid-August intelligence confidently reported that no invasion would be considered by the German forces until air superiority was established, and because deployment of troops to the embarkation ports, which had not yet commenced, would take up to three weeks. When Enigma intercepts in early September indicated that bomber units were being transferred from Norway to France and dive-bombers were being deployed in the Pas de Calais. Coupled with aerial reconnaissance beginning to report significant accumulations of barges and other small ships at major ports along the French and Belgian coast, JIC began to change its tune. Other reports said that all leave of German troops had been cancelled, which prompted Britain to transmit the codeword 'Cromwell', calling all home defence forces to immediate action stations.

Pressed for information as the invasion threat grew, JIC was quite unable to give any information about Luftwaffe air transport deployment which, in itself, was a negative indication, but such units could be brought up at the last minute. There was still a lingering fear that at least part of any invasion would emanate from the Baltic, which was still beyond the range of PRU Spitfires. Late September saw an increase in radio traffic concerning the grouping of German Army units into 'waves', but not before a German naval signal had been sent out simultaneously on all frequencies, an unprecedented occurrence, which was followed by a marked decrease in traffic.[42] It is now clear that this was the signal from Hitler himself, to postpone the invasion until the following spring; the Admiralty, whose sources had detected the signal, did not see fit to share its interception with the other services who continued to anticipate an invasion, even though PRU reconnaissance showed that barge accumulations in the invasion ports were beginning to disperse. From this moment JIC reports to the Chiefs of Staff no longer contained the phrase 'invasion may be expected at any time' to 'situation unchanged'.

The level of support given to Fighter Command efforts by intelligence intercepts of encrypted Enigma traffic has been much discussed and is analysed elsewhere, but essentially it seems to be the case that Luftwaffe Enigma 'red' traffic (Luftwaffe communications) suffered from poor operator security procedures and was regularly broken by British cryptanalysts throughout the Battle of Britain, but the value of the resulting information was variable. Identification of the units sending and receiving signals gave good indications of the Luftwaffe order of battle and any movements of units. The existence of radio directional navigation beams was also uncovered by Enigma decrypts, as was the deployment of Freya radar stations in France, but high-level communication was mostly by fixed-line telephone and no detailed insight of strategy or tactics at any level was ever acquired through Enigma decrypts. It seems likely that Dowding was apprised of the content of Enigma decrypts, without being informed of the source, but there is some evidence that he was initially sceptical about its veracity, as were many military commanders who were not privy to Bletchley Park operations.

All squadrons and *geschwader* had Intelligence Officers attached to them to investigate claims of enemy losses. The criteria for verifying claims varied and was undoubtedly tightened up after the first few weeks; both sides consistently over-estimated their successes throughout and this resulted in a distorted view of enemy strength as the battle progressed, but the consequences of this were much more damaging to the Luftwaffe. Fighter Command strategy was actually influenced very little by its assessment of overall Luftwaffe strength. That was really irrelevant to their daily efforts. Their strategy was simply to focus on each attack as it came and respond appropriately. Be there many or few aircraft in an attack, the strategy was the same: respond with appropriate force. If few, then scramble the minimum number of fighters to meet the threat; if many, then put up all available aircraft. Careful management of resources was at the heart of their effort. The Luftwaffe, however, based much of its strategy, after Adlerangriff, on Schmid's estimation of Fighter Command strength and it is clear from subsequent analysis that this was wildly inaccurate, prompting injudicious deployment of resources and inappropriate choice of targets.

The large number of aircraft and crews forced down on British soil once the Battle commenced was an important source of intelligence, as was the highly proficient technical and scientific establishment that analysed the information gleaned. Captured Luftwaffe aircrews were interrogated by AII(k) branch at the Combined Services Detailed Interrogation Centre (CSDIC) at Cockfosters, while recovered aircraft were examined and analysed at AII(g) branch.[43] Hidden microphones in PoW areas together with captured documents allowed the RAF to build up a quite accurate picture of Luftwaffe order of battle, equipment, bases and operating procedures.

Throughout the summer, Fighter Command Intelligence worked assiduously to analyse Luftwaffe strategy as a means of countering it.

From the very first assaults in June, they reported daily summaries of their assessments. The following are summaries of their briefings.

27 June	Night attacks have never been an accepted part of German Air Force bomber tactics, because such attacks are not sufficiently accurate to permit bombing to destruction. The present phase (has been) to exploit nuisance value and to train pilots on navigation for large scale raids. The enemy fly in groups of three or four at heights of around 10-15,000ft. AIR16
1 July	There are indications that preparations for a land and sea invasion are at an advanced stage. AIR16
5 July	The Germans were practising large-scale disembarkation using up to forty vessels.
10 July	There has been a marked increase in the movement of transport aircraft up to the Antwerp area and sea transports are being prepared.
12 July	Sources indicate that the German High Command is hesitating and losing confidence in the prospect of a successful invasion in the immediate future.
17 July	Reports indicate that Luftwaffe bombing attacks will be limited to single aircraft operating when cloudy conditions offer a measure of concealment. Attacks on convoys are expected to be carried out in strength with fighter escort.
24 July	Heavy attacks are restricted to convoys.
29 July	The German Air Force is now thought to be sufficiently strong enough to begin a large-scale offensive, despite a shortage of bombs and fuel in advanced airfields.
13 August	It was estimated that 102 enemy aircraft had been destroyed during the previous two days. The attack of the 12th was estimated to have included up to 1,000 aircraft.
20 August	A seaborne invasion was still very much a possibility, but dependent upon the success of the German Air Force against Fighter Command.
24 August	The German Air Force appears to have changed its tactics, whereby the number of fighter escorts has been reduced in relation to bomber aircraft and now included more Bf110s. The bombers were flying in larger groupings and bombing from a greater height.

27 August   There was an increase in enemy fighter sweeps over the Channel coast in an attempt to draw British fighters to combat.

31 August   This day saw the biggest attack so far with increased fighter protection up to a 3:1 ratio for the bombers. Bf110s flew alongside the bombers with Bf109s at least 5,000ft above them as top cover.

7 September   German bombers were showing great resilience by refusing to break formation even under the heaviest attack by British fighters and anti-aircraft fire from the ground.

Once the fighting had started in earnest an important function of RAF Intelligence was to build up a picture of Luftwaffe tactics by the debriefing of RAF fighter pilots immediately after combat. The results of these debriefings were distilled into reports which were disseminated throughout the whole of Fighter Command so that their pilots could learn from each other and be more 'savvy' in their next engagement. 'Each engagement produced its own lessons,' said Squadron Leader H.S. Darley of 609 Squadron.[44] A notable exception to the rule that valuable pilot experience was translated into instructions for others, however, was the early realisation that attacks from above were much more effective than following Fighter Command Intelligence advice to execute a steep climbing attack against dive-bombers, forcing them to overshoot the target. Furthermore, Luftwaffe pilot tactics, honed in conflict from the Spanish Civil War, through Poland and then France, were quick to exploit the antiquated Fighter Command tactics of flying in close formation which, often fatally, gave them little room for manoeuvre in close combat. Many RAF pilots had discovered the folly of this practice in the Battle of France, but a good number of them did not survive to teach others. Coming up against agile Luftwaffe fighters forced Fighter Command pilots to choose between attack manoeuvres against slower-moving bombers drilled into them during their training and the realisation that they were totally inadequate in practice against predatory Bf109s. New tactics had to be learned 'on the hoof', but some long-serving squadron leaders, steeped in tradition and obedience, were very reluctant to change, despite mounting evidence urging them to do so. They were reluctant to abandon skills that may well have looked impressive in training but proved almost suicidal in combat. Indeed, Fighter Command Operational Training Units continued to instruct new pilots in the old ways and many of these had to undergo rapid retraining when they joined active squadrons. Dowding agreed that 'at the beginning of the war we paid too much attention to close formation. … Circumstances forced us to relax that.'[45] In this regard, Fighter Command was slow to 'put intelligence into the hands of those who can use it'.

RAF pilots who found themselves in convoy escort-protection roles soon learned that flying too far out to sea was extremely perilous, since baling out of a damaged aircraft meant serious risk of drowning before rescue. Ironically, in this regard Luftwaffe pilots were much better served in that even though German military were much more orientated towards land warfare, they had a very efficient *Seenotdienst* sea-rescue service using both fast motorboats and Heinkel Hs59 seaplanes. Park specifically instructed controllers in 11 Group Directive 4 to 'Avoid sending fighters out over the sea to chase reconnaissance aircraft or small formations of enemy fighters.'[46]

Debriefings were important also to keep track of enemy casualties. Intelligence officers were attached to all squadrons to interrogate pilots returning from combat and record their claims of enemy aircraft destroyed, probably destroyed or damaged. Later, when combats were mostly over the land, claims of destroyed aircraft could be verified by evidence of downed aircraft or captured pilots, but during the early convoy phase when engagements were mostly over the sea it had been difficult, and the lack of material evidence coupled with the inexperience and eagerness of pilots fresh to combat led to a high level of over-estimation of enemy losses. Intelligence officers were reluctant to query claims too closely for fear of denting pilot morale which was going to be of vital importance, but soon began to demand better proof, especially in the case of enemy aircraft which had clearly been shot down but had been subjected to a number of separate attacks by pilots all of whom claimed the 'victory'.

The interception and breaking of Enigma signals was tedious and often produced little usable intelligence, but the discovery of German aircraft navigation beams used to guide bombers onto their target at night owed a great deal to the 'listeners' and the codebreakers. From the beginning of June, Cheadle listening station had intercepted radio traffic indicating that the Germans were installing a number of radio beam transmitters on the Channel coast in their newly occupied territories. These transmitters were apparently part of the Knickebein system of aircraft navigation.[47] This was an early indication that the Luftwaffe were planning extensive night-time operations over England with both bomber and fighter units eventually being equipped with receivers. 'The early detection and partial frustration of Knickebein … was an early and major British victory in the Battle of Britain.'[48]

Professor R.V. Jones, in one of the low-grade intelligence reports in circulation, had come across the transcript of a snippet of conversation recorded in March between captured German airmen, oblivious of the fact that they were being 'bugged'. One flier spoke about Knickebein (Crooked leg) while the other about 'X-Gerät' (X-Apparatus). Both flyers seemed confused about the nature of either, to the point where they didn't quite seem to know the difference between them. Both Knickebein and 'X-Gerät', however, seemed to be systems used by bombers as navigational aids. Jones contacted the interrogation centre at Cockfosters and asked that the prisoners be fed apparently innocuous questions that might tease out a little more intelligence, but the ploy failed. Jones was intrigued and believed that he had stumbled upon something important. He matched this flimsy intelligence with another source: a scrap of paper retrieved from a downed He111 of KG26 which contained the following (in translation) 'Navigational Aid; Radio Beacons working on Beacon Plan A. Additionally from 0600 hrs Beacon Dühnen. Light Beacon after dark. Beacon Knickebein from 0600 hrs on 315°.[49] Jones inferred from this that Knickebein was a 'beamed beacon' that had been set to transmit in a north-westerly direction. He filed this information away hoping for further intelligence to link into it.

On 5 June an Enigma-encoded 'red' signal was intercepted and decrypted by the 12th. It was sent by the Chief Signals Officer of Fliegerkorps IV at 14.55 hrs. and read: KNICKEBEIN, KLEVE, IST AUF PUNKT 53 GRAD 24 MINUTEN NORD UND EIN GRAD WEST EIN GERICHTET (Knickebein, Cleves, confirmed at 53° 24' north and 1° west). Jones was given the transcript simply because nobody else could make head nor tail of it. The word Knickebein leapt out at him and the meaning of the message was clear when it was confirmed that a German aircraft had flown over that location on the 5th. The Germans had established a radio beam transmitter at the town of Cleves, and one of its reconnaissance aircraft with special equipment had detected the beam at the given location (just south of Retford).[50]

It was known that Fliegerkorps IV used He111s of KG4 and KG27 and examination of captured He111 shot down over the Firth of Forth revealed that their 'blind landing' radio receivers were much more sensitive than were required for guiding them back to base after an operation, suggesting they had a different more specialised use. The frequency setting of this receiver was noted and thought to be related to Knickebein beams. After a meeting to discuss the new information, Air Chief Marshal Dowding, who was not privy to knowledge of Enigma and therefore had no reason to believe the intelligence to be of a high-level, described the evidence as 'nebulous'. Even to Tizard there seemed to be 'unnecessary excitement' about it.[51] Nevertheless, priority was given to fitting out aircraft with the means of locating such beams and a weekly report was submitted to Prime Minister Churchill, who authorised extra staff to work on detecting them. On 18 June, documents from a crashed German aircraft in France indicated the location of transmitters at Bredstedt and Cleves, while a couple of days later a captured document showed transmitters at Cleves and Stollberg. At this stage there was nothing to indicate whether Knickebein and X-Gerät were different systems or 'one and the same thing.'[52]

At a meeting in 10 Downing Street on 21 June, chaired by Churchill, the question of Knickebein radio beacons was discussed. Henry Tizard expressed reservations about the existence of the beams and suggested it might be an elaborate German hoax. Others doubted the need for such navigational aids and Frederick Lindemann declared that shortwave beams would not propagate far enough to be useful due to the curvature of the earth bouncing them off into space. Professor Jones, who was considered the authority on Knickebein by this time, had been invited to the meeting at the last minute. He found the atmosphere 'tense' and was forced to defend the evidence which, despite his lowly status among such a high-powered gathering, he did robustly in an address lasting some twenty minutes.[53] His disclosure of the position of two transmitters operating at known frequencies impressed Churchill, who ordered that an aircraft be sent up that night to try to intercept any transmission. A twin-engine Anson piloted by Flight Lieutenant Harold Bufton was put up over East Anglia with Corporal Dennis Mackey scanning the airwaves for signals.[54] They flew across the anticipated line of the navigation beam with receivers set to the frequency set on the Lorenz device of a crashed Luftwaffe aircraft, and reported back the next day that 'a narrow beam, some 400–500 yards wide was detected passing through a position just south of Spalding. The frequency of the transmission was 31.5 megacycles per second.' A second similar beam was detected just to the north of the first and the beams were both pointing to Derby, where half the Rolls Royce Merlin engines for Hawker Hurricanes were built.[55]

On 27 June another intercepted Enigma signal was translated as: 'It is proposed to set up Knickebein and Wotan installations near Cherbourg and Brest.'[56] Wotan was a Norse god with only one eye (a single beam). Jones postulated that it might mean that a German bomber could fly along a radio beam and, measuring its progress by detecting a radar pulse, locate a target while flying 'blind'. Another radio intercept suggested that Luftwaffe fighters had intercepted British bombers by using a Freya-Gerät radar system. In mythology, Freya had been a mistress of Wotan and an associate of Heimdall, a watchman who could see 100 miles by day or night. While not conclusive, certain inferences were drawn from the names given to these systems.

Knickebein had been developed by Telefunken but employed, in operation, the Lorenz blind-landing system. It worked by 'piggy-backing' on the Lorenz blind-landing system to aid navigation and landing in poor visibility and required no extra specialised training for operatives. The Lorenz system used two adjacent radio beams, one emitting Morse 'dots' and the other Morse 'dashes' extending some thirty miles from an airfield. When the receiver was on track the two signals would merge into a continuous note and the navigator could find his way back to the source of the beam.[57] This system was also used by the RAF. Knickebein transmitters were quite big at 100ft high and 300ft wide. They ran on a circular rail track to allow alignment in a particular direction. The Lorenz system had been modified to transmit a beam powerful enough and narrow enough to guide an aircraft to any location in the British Isles as a simple navigation aid, though because the beam widened imperceptibly with range, it became less accurate the further the aircraft flew. In order to locate a bombing target, a second beam from another station was set to intersect the first over the target. This was not pin-point accurate but would easily put the bombers over a major city on a cloudy night. By the beginning of 1940, the Luftwaffe had three Knickebein transmitters at Cleves, Stollberg and Lörrach, but after the fall of France further stations were erected along the Channel coast.[58]

On 27 July, a document recovered from a German bomber indicated that aircraft receivers were to be upgraded to receive Knickebein navigation signals, but each *geschwader* had to request the upgrade as required. On the same day, a decrypted Enigma signal showed that KG 54 had made such a request. It was known that KG 54 was in Luftflotte 3 and operated primarily over the West of England, which was outside the range of existing Knickebein signals. The inference was that a new transmitting station was to be set up on the Cherbourg peninsula in early August, presaging a major increase in precision night-time bombing of areas such as Manchester and Liverpool. The exact location of the new station was pinpointed on 8 September by another Enigma decrypt indicating that an aircraft of Kg100, call sign 6N+LK, was to be fitted with an X-Gerät device working with a beam so concentrated that it was no more than 20 yards wide at a distance of 200 miles. This was proof that Knickebein and X-Gerät were different systems. X-Gerät was more complicated in that it had to locate two beams and navigate towards their intersection point. Unlike the Knickebein system this new one required more elaborate radio receivers and specialised training for their operators. X-Gerät did not come into extensive use until November.

During September, a special flight of Anson aircraft, No. 80 Wing, blandly named The Blind Approach Training and Development Unit (BATDU), flew missions from Garston in Hertfordshire to try and disrupt Knickebein. Special 'jamming' devices were designed which could emit a muddled radio noise on the required frequency and these were positioned in a number of police stations along the path of the beams. Lorenz transmitters, currently used by the RAF, were modified to mimic a Knickebein signal, but with little success. Meanwhile, new transmitters were detected along the French coast at Dieppe and Cherbourg. Lindemann suggested 'masking' devices to emit signals in phase with the navigation beams (nicknamed Aspirins) on the three or four wavelengths used by the Knickebein bombers which confused, although did not entirely deceive, their signals (nicknamed Headaches).[59] Tests were carried out to see if it was possible to 'bend' the beam; although this was technically possible, there was never enough time to develop the idea.[60]

In fact, Knickebein fell out of use for two reasons. First, it was superseded by the X-Gerät system (and later in 1941 by the Y-Gerät), and second, because the Luftwaffe aircrews were aware of the interference on their receivers which made them very nervous, thinking that night-fighter interceptors were waiting for them further down the line.[61] When the new X-Gerät system came into play there was an immediate improvement in target location.

On the night of 13 August, twenty-one He111s of Kg 100 hit the Nuffield Spitfire factory at Castle Bromwich with spectacular accuracy and continued in a similar vein during the following nights. A new signal with frequency 74 MHz was detected coming from Calais and Cherbourg and codenamed 'Ruffian'. Professor Jones and Lindemann assumed that the two were linked and indicated that an enhanced navigation system was coming into play. The bombers of Kg 100 were based at Vannes in Brittany and had not yet been connected to Luftflotte 3 headquarters in Paris by landline, so they were forced to use Enigma radio communications. By this time Bletchley Park were deciphering enough Enigma traffic to ascertain the beam frequencies and targets for some night raids, but it took several days to complete the decryption and such information was useless operationally although sufficient to build up a picture of how the X-Gerät worked. The traffic indicated that the system was accurate enough to pinpoint a target at a distance of 100 miles to within 100 yards. Kg 100, using X-Gerät, became the pathfinder unit sent ahead of raids to drop incendiaries over the target to mark it for the main bomber fleet.[62]

In conclusion, it can be said that intelligence was an important part of both Luftwaffe and Fighter Command strategies but was applied in different ways according to differing requirements and crucially, collected and applied with significantly different levels of professionalism. RAF Intelligence was respected and, more often than not, put Fighter Command aircraft in the right position and in appropriate numbers to fulfil its two criteria: to resist and to survive. Luftwaffe Intelligence, however, was seen as having only marginal significance unless supporting Göring's prevailing military and political ambitions, and when it was utilised its fundamental flaws proved to be, at best, a hindrance and, at worst, disastrous. The differing fortunes of the intelligence agencies is indicative of the way in which intelligence is used as a political tool in a totalitarian regime where free discussion and dissent are not encouraged. For Fighter Command it was the free flow of information and support between agencies that allowed intelligence to play such a vital role and ensure its eventual survival during the summer of 1940.

The two significant areas of intelligence fundamental to the efforts of Fighter Command in 1940 were radar and the Dowding System of command and control. It was radar that met the first requirement of intelligence which, according to Hinsley, is: 'information has to be acquired', and it was the Dowding System that met the other two: 'it has to be analysed and interpreted; and it has to be put into the hands of those who can use it'. Given the importance of both it is important to look at the way in which each was developed before the war and how each contributed to the war effort during the summer of 1940.

Chapter 5

Air Chief Marshal Sir Hugh Caswall Tremenheere Dowding

[Dowding had] unquestioned technical and command competence … and an exceedingly reserved manner [which] had drawn upon him the nickname 'stuffy'[1]

In the famous picture of Dowding walking alongside King George VI and Queen Elizabeth at Bentley Priory on 6 September 1939, we see a serious, middle-aged uniformed man looking distracted and a bit uncomfortable. With the declaration of war three days previously it is almost impossible for anyone to understand the responsibilities that were now bearing down on him. His personal experience of war itself (he had served in the Royal Flying Corps during the First World War), coupled with an acute awareness of the threat now facing not only the men in his command but the whole civilian populations of the British cities, was going to demand exceptional qualities of self-confidence, fortitude and sound judgement. He and the whole intelligence-based, and as yet unfinished, 'Dowding System' that he had spent so long developing was about to be tested in an existential struggle. With this in mind it is a reasonable interpretation of the picture to imagine that, while he was attentive to his monarch, he may well have been impatiently counting the minutes until he could get back to his desk and get on with the job in hand.

For three years, between 1930 and 1933, Sir Hugh Dowding had been responsible for the 'Supply and Research' arm of the RAF on the Air Council, its policy-making body, and had brought to the job a deep intelligence, pragmatism, sound common sense and a deep-seated intolerance of fools.[2] He had overseen the organisation, training and equipping of the service at a time when the international political landscape was changing in disturbing ways and coincidentally, or perhaps as a consequence, saw many advances in military technology. His tenure of that office had started out inauspiciously enough when he signed off the R-101 airship's certificate of airworthiness only days before it exploded, in a public relations debacle, on its inaugural passenger flight.[3] Dowding was much more circumspect thereafter about trusting technicians and signing off on anything before extensive trials.

As the technological revolution progressed through the thirties, Dowding adopted the unprecedented approach of liaising with aircraft manufacturers at much earlier stages of procurement by stipulating 'ideal' characteristics of future designs rather than focusing on the technical requirements. He particularly championed the monoplane design over another generation of biplanes. This put him at odds with the 'old guard' within the Air Ministry, such as Chief of the Air Staff Lord Trenchard, who were not ready for such rapid changes. His specification F.7/30, issued in September 1931, was the first step on the road to the RAF acquiring high-speed, low-winged monoplane fighters with fixed forward-firing machine guns. Adoption of this specification led to the development of the Hurricane and Spitfire.[4]

The transition, however, was not easy. He was challenged at every turn by many leading figures in the Air Ministry who argued that bi-plane fighters with movable machine guns were the most effective defence against what, at that time, was considered to be the main aerial threat: the heavy bomber. A new Chief of the Air Staff, Sir Edward Ellington, had no sympathy with Dowding's vision and nudged policy in favour of a two-man crewed aircraft with forward and movable guns which became the Boulton-Paul Defiant, designed specifically to attack slow-moving bomber streams from below, which it may well have done if bombers had not become more powerful and faster and, crucially, escorted by fast, manoeuvrable, destructive escorts.

The new generation of fast, self-defending bombers being developed, especially in Germany, convinced Dowding that the Defiant was too slow and cumbersome to defeat the bombers and that the RAF desperately needed agile, high-performance fighters with effective firepower. Cannon proved to be too heavy and destabilising for lightweight fighters and a step too far as the answer to armament, so multiple wing-mounted machine guns were adopted as the norm. As he pressed on with his plans for fighters, Dowding suffered a setback in his drive for a high-performance, heavily armed, multi-crewed heavy bomber, which was rejected on the grounds that it was too expensive and not quite what was required as a means of defending the islands at a time when disarmament talks taking place in Geneva were still felt to be productive. Large-scale production of any new type of aircraft, fighter or bomber, would entail massive investment in tools and training, which manufacturers were reluctant to make unless guaranteed substantial orders. The compromise design turned out to be the Fairey Battle, but the new Griffon engine which would have helped it achieve its potential as a high-performance aircraft failed to overcome design and production problems in time to be utilised.

With the rise of Nazis in Germany and a belligerent Japan in the Far East, the Air Ministry reviewed its Home Defence Air Force. Ellington seemed satisfied with a minimal increase in aircraft numbers, which Dowding and others flatly disagreed with in the face of the variety of threat and range of possible scenarios, but the failure of policy during this period was a collective responsibility and Dowding, as second-in-command at the Air Ministry, must shoulder some of the blame for not making a stronger case for more and better aircraft production.

The dominant figure in British politics in 1933 was the Chancellor of the Exchequer, Neville Chamberlain, whose budget for the armed forces, for reasons of economy, was weighted in favour of air defence and, on a broader political map, offered, to his mind, the best way of preventing Britain being drawn into another continental war. It was commonly held that the only real threat to Britain in the event of war, if it could avoid sending an army across the Channel, was from mass bombing of the British mainland. In 1934, the government promised that no country would be allowed to out-perform Britain in air power; a promise that was soon broken. Although plans were laid for a rapid increase in aircraft production and training, the Air Ministry proved unenthusiastic – even towards what in fact proved to be quite modest government schemes. The whole ethos of the RAF was based on entrenched elitist attitudes reminiscent of a 'gentleman's club', and the Air Ministry feared that government plans for expansion would lead to a dilution of the very principles and traditions of the service which were the legacy of the ironically named 'father of the RAF', Hugh Trenchard.[5]

Dowding's analysis of the potential threats in the event of war made defence a higher priority than attack. His enthusiasm for heavy bombers was lukewarm and he made no great effort to support a major expansion. Like most British leaders, he was anxious to avoid being drawn into another continental land war which would inevitably result in a large proportion of RAF resources being drawn into conflict far from home. If war came, the RAF was ill-equipped to launch any significant long-range bombing strategy and would be better served by concentrating on deterring such a move by an adversary. Key to Dowding's approach was his willingness to investigate innovative ideas in his, now reduced, role of research and development at the Air Ministry which, together with his previous position had placed him 'at the heart of development and expansion of Britain's fighter and bomber forces and also the country's air defences'.[6] His support for 'radio reflection' techniques that promised to deliver a system of early warning for aircraft attack was positive but restrained in its early stages. However, as a series of demonstrations proved very encouraging, he allocated substantial funds for its development. This would evolve into the crucial early warning radar system.

When, in 1935, Hitler officially confirmed what was widely known: that Germany was building a military air force, the British government felt the need to assuage public opinion by announcing a major investment in the RAF, but in practice, very little changed, and the pace of modernisation remained laggardly. However, substantial changes to RAF organisation resulted, whereby three commands were established: Fighter, Bomber and Coastal. Dowding, who was made Air Officer Commanding (AOC) Fighter Command at Bentley Priory, initially opposed the way in which this idea was implemented on the grounds that it would be too much for a centralised administrative controller to oversee operations down to station and squadron level. He felt that some command responsibilities should, instead, be delegated to Group level. Eventually, experience convinced the Air Ministry that Dowding was right and made the necessary adjustments.[7]

One of Dowding's priorities in 1936 was the development of an integrated air-defence system involving a network of command, control and communications. A key element of this was the introduction of a Filter Room which evaluated information before passing it on to controllers. Simultaneously, with characteristic determination, Dowding, now promoted to Air Chief Marshal, tackled the many problems associated with the introduction of new technology, not least the resistance to adoption of new ideas by long-service personnel. Instrumental in helping to break down prejudice, however, was the realisation that the German Luftwaffe was expanding at a rate with which British manufacturers were unable to compete.

The prospect of a massive and overwhelming bombing attack by the Luftwaffe if war broke out was the major preoccupation of the Air Ministry driving it, in October 1936, to create a new committee under Dowding's leadership, which was tasked with a comprehensive review of air policy in regard to this threat. Dowding's analysis was that, in the event of war, Britain could expect a concerted effort to destroy the basis of its air power as well as an attack upon its economy by a strangulation of its sea trade routes. He was supported by British Intelligence whose analysts predicted that the German economy was too overburdened with debt to sustain a long war and so would attempt a quick 'knock-out' blow, but the Air Ministry still persisted in its unchanged view that the best deterrent would be having the ability to launch a massive retaliatory bombing strike. Nothing went beyond discussion until after the Austrian Anschluss, when German ambitions were becoming clearer. The Ministry was galvanised into a serious expansion of aircraft production. Their belief that bombers would determine the outcome of war, however, was somewhat at odds with their policy because if the bombers always found their target, and the Germans had more and better bombers, Germany would inevitably win a bombing war. This logical contradiction, which did not seem to bother Whitehall, was not lost on Dowding, whose own strategy was to create a credible and sustainable defence against bombing attack. This did not rule out the need for a long-range bombing capability but that was of secondary importance and was, in the short term, never going to play a decisive role. Under increasing pressure, the government increased defence spending but only reluctantly.

Another problem for Dowding was the appointment of William Sholto Douglas as Chief of Air Staff, and Sir John Slessor as Director of Plans who, in direct contrast to Dowding, both favoured the Defiant over the Hurricane and Spitfire as the first line of defence against bombers. Their opinions, however, were based on the assumption that German bombers would attack without fighter escort given that the distance from German airfields to British cities was beyond their fighter range. As a consequence, hundreds of Defiants, which would prove quite useless against German fighters, were ordered in preference to the other fighters.[8] Dowding had no confidence in the Defiants as day-time fighters but he had been moved out of procurement and was unable to directly influence the decision. He did eventually manage to reduce the Defiant order to some extent and, when they were delivered to his command, he was able to deploy them where 'they would do the least harm'. Even so, Chief of the Air Staff, Sir Edward Ellington, still believed that every fighter built meant one less bomber, thus weakening the offensive capability. Dowding had to fight for every Hurricane or Spitfire that came off the production line.

In a lecture to the RAF Staff College in 1937, Dowding had given an insight into his philosophy and an appreciation of Fighter Command's wartime mission in the event of attack by a 'totalitarian state'. His primary objective, he said, would be to prevent a sudden knock-out blow by massive terror-bombing of London and to prevent the strangulation of sea lanes vital for the importation of food and raw materials. He tangentially alluded to the possibility that an enemy might choose to eliminate the British fighter force as a precursor to bombing.[9]

The distance between Dowding's vision of British air defences based on fighter production and that of his superiors at the Air Ministry, who still favoured bombers, was beginning to grow, which only increased the animosity towards him within the Air Ministry. Often letters he sent to senior officers for clarification of policy remained unanswered and requests for improvements to Fighter Command facilities were regularly met with obfuscation and delay. Clearly many in the Air Ministry were irritated by his implied criticism and expressed this annoyance with disdain. The strength of opposition to Dowding is illustrated by an internal Air Ministry memorandum describing Fighter Command as 'a one-man show', and Dowding as a man with 'inadequate mental ability and a very slow brain', who was a 'complete non-co-operator with authority'.[10] Dowding, for his part, was exasperated by the attitude of 'Whitehall Warriors' whom he saw as quite out of touch with the reality of Britain's increasingly inadequate defence capability. He complained to the Air Ministry that he was dealing with 'a number of vital matters which generations of Air Staff have neglected for the past fifteen years',[11] which did little to ameliorate his critics' opinion of him. Air Ministry frustration with Dowding was somewhat tempered, however, by the knowledge that he had been appointed to serve for three years in post and his time would be up at the end of June 1939, when they could put him out to grass.

While making his case for fighter production, Dowding was also turning his attention to fighter tactics. There were many gaps in his knowledge about the potential threat Britain would face in the event of war. German bomber capabilities were hard to fathom since such intelligence as was available was too often drowned out by the din of propaganda. The new fighters brought their own set of imponderables, such as determining the limits of human ability to effectively withstand the gravitational effects of high-speed manoeuvring without losing consciousness. Perhaps most important of all, more needed to be done to look again at pilot-training methods where close-formation flying was prized almost above all other skills. While the Luftwaffe had learned valuable lessons about fighter-to-fighter engagement in the Spanish Civil War which they were quick to apply in their own training schools, the Air Ministry had not taken much notice, believing that there was little prospect of their fighters being drawn into engagements of that nature. The problem, apart from RAF elitist attitudes and resistance to change, was the accepted assumption that enemy bombers would be flying without fighter protection which obviated the need to consider fighter-to-fighter tactics. Fighter against bomber was still the anticipated scenario. Dowding did, however, in a wide-ranging review, consider the matter of whether fighters were equipped with ammunition of the correct calibre and destructive power to destroy bombers. What, he asked, was the most effective distance at which a fighter should open fire to deliver the most telling blow? Should fighters be fitted with cockpit armour, and how would that affect the flying characteristics of the aircraft? What are the most effective methods of attacking the bomber stream? He demanded to know, 'If Chicago gangsters can have bullet-proof windows for their cars, why can't my pilots have bullet-proof windscreens?[12] As well as pondering these issues, he was obliged to apply himself to many other mundane questions, such as the supply and storage of fuel at aerodromes and, more importantly, the shortage of experienced pilots available to train the large numbers of recruits coming into the newly formed Auxiliary Air Force squadrons which, incidentally, were not universally accepted by long-serving RAF officers and administrators who doubted that such an influx could ever produce combat-ready airmen of the 'right sort'.

When considering the vital question of intruder detection, as well as championing the development of radar, Dowding realised the importance of good old-fashioned human observation, especially once enemy aircraft had crossed the coast thus putting them beyond the scope of radar, which could only track aircraft out to sea. He had, since 1936, advocated the expansion and modernisation of the Observer Corps, which was to employ some 30,000 people at its peak. Another separate command was set up to administer Barrage Balloons, which were not hugely influential in the Battle of Britain but did serve a purpose, if only to improve civilian morale.

He was also willing to consider all technical initiatives, if only to eliminate them as unworkable. He was sure that the Luftwaffe were looking at all sorts of ideas and it would be catastrophic to overlook any potentially important development that the enemy employed, and the RAF had missed. It was in this area that major advances were made in Britain's ability to withstand attack. Not only in the development of radar but also in the adoption of a crucial IFF (Identify Friend or Foe) system that allowed ground controllers to differentiate between friendly and enemy aircraft which were detected by the radar. Unfortunately, testing of both radar and IFF was hampered by the extreme reluctance of Bomber Command to cooperate in any training exercises. This is hard to understand given that Bomber Command would have benefited as much as Fighter Command from the experience. It has been mooted that this refusal to cooperate meaningfully was in part due to the lack of confidence Bomber Command had in its crews and their understandable reluctance to have this failing exposed. There were also quite simple practical policies put in place, such as the method of dispersing aircraft at an aerodrome to create a much less concentrated target for enemy bombers.

There was widespread acceptance in the Air Ministry that Britain would face an overwhelming German bombing attack in the event of war. This was the single most important factor influencing British foreign policy at the time and the threat of war was looming ever greater. It was not universal, however, and there were a few influential voices that prioritised defence over attack. Fortunately, the government listened to these dissenting voices and promoted production of fighters over bombers, although some caustically said that this was because they were cheaper and, in the context of propaganda, the extra aircraft numbers (two fighters produced for the same money as one bomber) showed that the government was acting decisively. The command structure of the RAF was closely examined in light of events and within the Air Ministry it was felt that Dowding, having few admirers and apparently not supporting the Ministry's bomber policy, was not the man to lead Fighter Command in time of war. He had already been passed over for the post of Chief of the Air Staff which went to Sir Cyril Newall, who was by no means an opponent of Dowding, but neither was he a strong political force in the Ministry. It was decided to terminate Dowding's appointment in June 1939, but that was thrown into doubt when events conspired in Dowding's favour. At the last minute, his successor, Sir Christopher Courtney, was rendered 'hors de combat' by an accident, and with no other candidate in the offing, the Air Ministry was reluctantly obliged to extend Dowding's tenure for another few months. After September however, his removal in time of war became almost a political impossibility. The knives may have been sheathed, but they did not lose their edge.

Once war had been declared, Dowding was quick to delegate responsibility, knowing that the scale of operations would require the application of personal initiative at all levels. This did not meet with the approval of headquarters staff who felt that it undermined their authority, but Park was in full agreement with Dowding and the policy of decentralisation was implemented throughout 11 Group. Sector commanders enjoyed almost total freedom over both strategic and tactical policy. The over-riding consideration under which they would operate, however, was that the primary role of RAF fighters was to shoot down the bombers, not to get into scraps with enemy fighters, and intercept the bombers where possible before they had reached their target, rather than when they were on their way back home. This put very tight constraints on controllers, who had to get fighters airborne and into position as quickly as possible. Relations between Dowding and his Sector commanders were not always amicable. While his rapport with Park in 11 Group was seamless, it was less satisfactory with Air Vice-Marshal Leigh-Mallory in 12 Group with whom he had a number of ill-tempered exchanges in early 1940. Park and Leigh-Mallory had a poor relationship which could have threatened to undermine Fighter Command efficiency, but Dowding chose not to intervene. This situation persisted throughout the Battle of Britain and resulted in the eventual removal of both Dowding and Park, but not before they had made their vital contribution to Britain's survival.

Dowding's extended tenure was due to terminate at the end of March 1940, but on the 30th Newall wrote a letter beginning 'My dear Dowding…', expressing his view that Dowding's command was 'of the very greatest importance', and requested that he stay in office until 14 July, since it would be 'undesirable' for any change to be made at such a critical moment. There was clearly no appetite for change under such circumstances in such a vital area of defence but it was understood that, regardless of the situation in July, Dowding 'must retire' on that date, despite the fact that the RAF would 'greatly regret the conclusion of [his] active duties'.[13]

Of course, at that time it was inconceivable that by July Britain would be facing a dramatic existential threat, but it would have shown the Air Ministry in a much better light if they had responded to Dowding's quite reasonable request to know the name of his successor so that a smooth transition could take place. Unfortunately, Newall remained silent on that issue, the most obvious conclusion to be drawn from which was that he had no idea who that might be. With no obvious candidate and British morale shaken by the defeat of France, he was forced, once again, to defer Dowding's removal on 5 July by going 'cap in hand' and asking him if he would stay on until the end of October. In a gloriously understated reply agreeing to Newall's request, Dowding discounted the 'question of discourtesy', but did point out that this fifth notice of retirement was typical of the 'lack of consideration' shown to him throughout the long, drawn-out sorry saga. It may have been of some comfort to Dowding that Churchill expressed his 'full confidence' in him and was 'taken aback' by the action of the Air Ministry against a leader whom, he thought, was 'one of the very best men [they] have got'.[14] Dowding was replaced as AOC Fighter

Command on 25 November by Sholto Douglas and days later his acolyte Park was replaced as AOC 11 Group by Leigh-Mallory.

In notes written by Wing Commander Douglas Bader dated 30 November 1969, he praised Dowding for his foresight in promoting the development of radar and for his part in the withholding of extra squadrons requested by the French in May. He did, however, criticise him for his 'failure' to assume full control of the air defences during the Battle of Britain, leaving Air Vice-Marshal Park to carry the responsibility, as AOC of 11 Group. Bader believed that Dowding had carried too much of the burden and should have shared the load with 12 Group (Air Vice-Marshal Leigh-Mallory), which had been desperate to get more involved, especially when London became the main Luftwaffe target.

WAAF plotters pictured at work in the underground Operations Room at HQ Fighter Command, Bentley Priory, in north-west London. A senior officer studies the unfolding events from the viewing deck above. (© MoD/Crown Copyright 2021)

A group of RAF radio operators at work, either monitoring Allied aircraft during a raid or listening in on enemy transmissions. (Danish National Museum)

Gravesend, Kent, 4 April 1940. Luftwaffe aerial image. (Alamy)

A Bildfeldwebel (Picture Sergeant) of the Luftwaffe teaching a student how to analyse an aerial photograph. (Alamy)

A recruit learns Morse at a radio unit in Germany. (Alamy)

Located at the mouth of the River Deben on the Suffolk coast, Bawdsey Manor was purchased by the Air Ministry in 1936 as the basis of a new radar research station. (Shutterstock)

Robert Alexander Watson Watt who established a small team at Orfordness on 13 May 1935 to construct the 'first prototype military radar'.

German inventor Johan Cristel (Christian) Hülsmeyer, who conducted the first successful demonstration of electric waves being reflected back to a receiver in 1904. (Alamy)

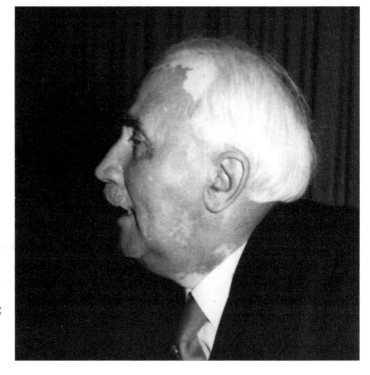

A portrait of Henry Thomas Tizard (1885-1959). (Historic Military Press)

The King of England
in RAF uniform,
accompanied by
Air Chief Marshal
Sir Hugh Dowding,
commander-in-chief of
Fighter Command at
the headquarters of the
Royal Air Force in 1940.

Hugh Richard Arthur
Grosvenor, the 2nd
Duke of Westminster,
a Nazi-sympathiser
and member of
the Rights Club,
a 'patriotic', anti-
Semitic organisation.
(Alamy)

Hermann Göring and Hans Jeschonnek during a meeting of the General Staff. Göring is wearing the Grand Cross of the Iron Cross. Jeschonnek wears the Knight's Cross. (Alamy)

Carinhall, Göring's residence at Veldenstein named after his first wife, Carin. (Alamy)

Above left: Three-rotor enigma machine, circa 1940. (Giorgio Rossi/Shutterstock)

Above right: The memorial to the Polish cryptologists Marian Rejewski, Jerzy Różycki, and Henryk Zygalski that can be seen in front of Poznan Castle. (Shutterstock)

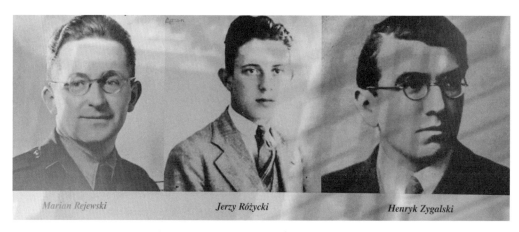

Polish cryptologists Marian Rejewski, Jerzy Rozycki and Henryk Zygalski who broke Enigma codes before the Second World War. (Alamy)

Chapter 6

British Radar

> From the very beginning the English had an extraordinary
> advantage which we could never overcome throughout the
> entire war: radar and fighter control.
>
> Adolf Galland; Geschwaderkommodore
of JG 26 in 1940[1]

The British Air Ministry struggled to come to terms with the technological advances in aircraft design and capabilities in the 1920s and, given Britain's geographical position – separated from mainland Europe, and its political landscape – torn between rearmament and appeasement, found itself in a quandary over how to create the right strategic balance between defence and attack. The predominant philosophy, in line with that of most European air forces, was strongly influenced by Douhet's theories which emphasised the role of bombers in any future war. Little had changed in that regard in the years since British Prime Minister Stanley Baldwin had told the House of Commons on 10 November 1932 that there is 'no power on earth that can protect him [the man in the street] from being bombed. Whatever people may tell him, the bomber will always get through.' Air defence against bomber attack was seen as almost impossible, leaving retaliation in kind as the only viable strategy.

This did not entirely eliminate the search for technological means of countering the threat however, albeit in poorly resourced and little recognised sub-committees that did themselves no great favours by pursuing unproductive research into acoustic mirrors to detect enemy aircraft, and 'death-rays' to destroy them. Military research lacked vigour during the first half of the twentieth century despite Britain enjoying its golden years of scientific research. It was the case that few in the vanguard of this scientific enquiry were attracted to the military. Apart from the fact that most scientists held themselves aloof from politics there was the important issue of publication of scientific papers, which were essential for a researcher to advance his or her career. Military research was, of necessity, secret and closed off any prospect of public recognition, however ground-breaking the achievements.

As early as 1925, the Air Defence Experimental Establishment (ADEE) at Woolwich (later moved to Biggin Hill) was asked to look at long- and short-range aircraft detection, but it attracted little attention and minimal funding.[2] This was followed by the setting up of the Signals Experimental Establishment (SEE) that conducted experiments using short-wave radio waves 'to locate ships from the coast … under any conditions of visibility or weather', building on the work done by the Royal Navy Signals School in 1928.[3] This work became increasingly important as the speed and range of bombers increased meaning that 'the importance of extending the period of warning' was crucial and there emerged an urgency to develop more effective air defence technologies.[4]

In 1934, Frederick Lindemann, who considered himself to be the pre-eminent authority on the subject, appeared before the Sub-Committee on the Re-orientation of the Air Defence System of Great Britain, demanding that they investigate new means of air defence including 'reflection of radio waves'.[5] The Air Ministry was forced to look for civilian help and brought in scientists as members of a new Committee for the Scientific Survey of Air Defence (CSSAD), which became better known as the Tizard Committee after one its founder members, Henry Tizard, Rector of Imperial College. Tizard was by no means an outstanding scientist, but he was a first-rate administrator. One of his first acts was to seek the opinions of Robert Alexander Watson Watt, a radio scientist working at the National Physical Laboratory in Slough (he changed his name to Watson-Watt after his knighthood in 1942). He was a hands-on, erratically brilliant experimenter with little time for administration, but little experience of the way in which scientific research was applied in practice. In 1935, H.E. Wimperis, Director of Scientific Research in the Air Ministry, asked Watson Watt to take a look at electromagnetic 'death rays', an idea currently under investigation by the Tizard Committee. Watson Watt's assistant, Arnold Wilkins, didn't take long to report that any such weapon would require an energy source 'far beyond current technology',[6] but he was anxious not to be too much of a disappointment and suggested instead that there might be more potential in an idea mooted by Wilkins: that of using radio waves to detect aircraft in flight, a technique that was already being used by ships to detect icebergs at night.

Watson Watt's report was discussed by the Tizard Committee, which invited him to submit a follow-up report. In this, Watson Watt included details of a Post Office report 233 of June 1932, in which engineers found that aircraft interfered with radio waves and reflected some of the signal back to source. This was no more than an annoyance for the engineers at the time, but the US Navy had also recognised this anomaly and filed a patent for a 'system for detecting objects by radio' in 1932. The German Navy stepped up its own research in 1933, but not until 1935 was any serious work done on radio detection in Britain. Watson Watt was approached by the Air Ministry and advised to take out a secret patent for RDF, which he did – but excluded Wilkins from the application. Watson Watt later also filed a patent for IFF even before it had been trialled.[7] Reading the Post Office report, Watson Watt and Wilkins had recognised that it illustrated a fundamental principle which could be applied to aircraft detection. His paper was so well received that Tizard presented a follow-up paper to the Air Ministry on 12 February 1935 entitled: 'Detection and Location of Aircraft by Radio Methods', along with a request for £10,000 for further research. Air Marshal Sir Hugh Dowding, at that time responsible for research and development, showed mild interest but demanded a demonstration before releasing funds. An experiment was duly organised at Weedon in Northamptonshire on 26 February 1935 and produced 'outstanding' results by locating a Heyford bomber by reflection of a 10Kw radio signal. Work began immediately for further research on Radio Direction Finding (RDF, sometimes just DF) under the guise of 'ionospheric investigations'. (It was only later in the war that RDF became universally known as radar.) Early experiments showed great promise, so Watson Watt was asked to gather a small team of researchers and, on 13 May 1935, he set up at Orfordness to construct the 'first prototype military radar'.

In April, £12,300 was approved for the establishment of a radar research facility at Orfordness, an isolated location on the Suffolk coast but within easy reach of London.[8] Here, a transmitter sent out a very broad radio pulse, the reflection of which was picked up by a receiver connected to a cathode ray display tube (CRT). The signal manifested itself on the display screen as a distortion on a line, the position of which varied in accordance with the distance to the reflecting object. Watson Watt realised immediately that this was an imperfect system which did not give a reliable indication of the distance, nor would it detect low-flying aircraft, but it did have the advantage of utilising existing equipment and the staff familiar with that equipment. Also, it worked with the sort of radio wavebands currently used for broadcasting and so experiments would not alert eavesdroppers that anything new was being tested.

On 15 June 1935, Watson Watt invited the members of the Tizard Committee to a demonstration of their equipment at Orfordness. Wilkins was astonished to learn that Watson Watt intended to show Tizard evidence of signal 'echoes' when none had so far been seen by the staff. Unfortunately, extreme weather in the form of low cloud and thunderstorms interfered with the signals and no echoes were observed. Wilkins viewed this as 'a useful excuse', but lamented that it 'was not to be the only occasion on which we were rushed into demonstrations for which we were not adequately prepared'.[9] Much to its credit, the Tizard Committee was not put off by this and authorised continuation of funding with agreement that shorter wavelength transmissions should be investigated and suggested that 'nothing had occurred to justify any relaxation of the urgency and importance of the general investigation.'[10] Tests performed subsequent to this in better weather conditions showed marked improvement, but a fair-weather system was of little practical use.

Straight away it was clear that in order to achieve an effective range the radio signals would have to be transmitted from a tall tower at least 200ft high. Even so, early tests proved successful only under certain clear atmospheric conditions. Such limitations could be mitigated by reducing the wavelength and a delegation was sent to Germany to observe ultra-short-wave radio work being done there in civil aviation while work progressed at home on modifying equipment according to the new requirements. The result was a huge advance in performance of the system within a few short weeks. So much so that by the end of July the equipment was capable of detecting aircraft up to seventy miles away and could differentiate between single aircraft and a group of aircraft. Crude calculations gave an approximate height of, and distance to, the target and a small modification to the receiving aerial gave a good indication of the direction to target. A revolving transmitter had been suggested as a means of determining direction but the idea was not followed up due to cost implications, although it is worth noting that the idea was later incorporated into CHL systems and adopted by the Germans for use with their Freya radar. By late 1935, the scientists at Orfordness were confident that they were working along the right lines but there was much to do to make it a practical and reliable working system.[11]

Watson Watt's attitude to research was that it was better to proceed with third-rate equipment rather than waste time waiting for better to come along, a philosophy that changed little even after funding was massively increased. This worked very well in the early days when the limitations of equipment were offset by the excellence of the research scientists. Emphasis was placed, where possible, on using equipment already available which restricted research to the 50m wavelength. This wavelength was currently used by commercial organisations; it had been hoped to hide radar signals in the background 'noise' to deflect the attention of enemy agencies, but the level of interference caused by this overlap and the tendency for signals to be reflected off atmospheric boundaries before reaching the ionosphere brought this line of attack to a halt. A solution to this problem was to build transmission towers much higher to give the signals more range beyond the horizon. A reduction of the wavelength of the signal improved the system, but every step in this direction required more and more transmission power.

While the detection of aircraft was slowly improved and a crude method was devised to relate the signal strength to the number of aircraft, it was still not possible to determine its altitude which was vital to know if a successful interception was to be made. A method was devised but, crucially, it required an accurate measurement of the target's direction from the receiver. This in turn was determined thanks to a 'light-bulb' moment when Watson Watt struck on a simple solution using a 'crossed dipole arrangement' connected to a 'goniometer'. [12]

By now the team at Orfordness had proved that they could provide long-range early warning of approaching aircraft and were well on the way to determining its exact position in the sky. Watson Watt was so confident of progress that in July 1935, he began specifying the location along the coast from Newcastle to Portsmouth of thirty radar stations required to give total radar coverage of the coastline at a cost of £200,000. [13] The Air Ministry approval for the plan was remarkable in that no prototype RDF station actually existed at the time. [14] The urgency with which radar was being developed and the readiness of the Treasury to stump-up the cash is testament to the government's growing unease about the fragile political situation in Europe. Watson Watt confided in his staff that personally, he expected war to break out before the end of 1938. [15] By now Orfordness was becoming a little cramped and research was relocated to Bawdsey Manor a few miles away.

On 9 September Watson Watt submitted a report to the Tizard Committee outlining progress. He duly reported that an aircraft had been detected up to ninety kilometres away at over 10,000ft. He outlined proposals for the chain of stations but he did not shy away from describing the several major problems awaiting solution, which included better distance and height estimation and the difficulty in detecting aircraft over land due to interference from uneven topographical features. It was clear from the support coming from the Air Ministry that the worsening political situation in Europe was considered sufficiently worrying, and the Douhetist theories of bombing devastation so widely accepted, that continuing to invest on a huge scale was deemed to be entirely justified politically. To maintain a veil of secrecy over the whole enterprise, all funds now being channelled to radar research were put under 'Miscellaneous Air Defence Works'.[16] The research was referred to by the acronym RDF in Treasury budgets and all other references to disguise the true significance of the work, but with constant exchange visits of scientists and the military between Britain and Germany it came as no surprise that during a visit to Bentley Priory later in October 1937, Göring's right-hand man Erhard Milch casually asked Dowding how he was getting on with 'experiments in the radio detection of aircraft'.[17]

Thus far all research had been carried out by civilian scientists, Watson Watt included, which had freed it from the dead hand of military inertia. The Air Ministry was fully on board, but Lindemann still agitated for more attention to his own pet projects, such as aerial mines, and Churchill continued to plague the government about its overall preparedness for war, but desisted in pursuing public debate of the more secret areas of military research. Lindemann, however, was most complimentary about Watson Watt's research and even pushed Churchill to apply political pressure to increase support for radar research. Watson Watt became embroiled in a bureaucratic spat over his status, remuneration and responsibilities that dragged on for some time.

There was some agitation for research into radar detectors that could be housed in aircraft but Watson Watt, while optimistic that such devices were possible, argued for retaining all his staff on perfecting the ground-based early-warning system which was still far from satisfactory. A major advance came when Watson Watt abandoned the idea of alternating transmission-receiving stations in favour of two separate masts at each station: one to transmit the signal and the other to receive it.

Meanwhile Lindemann's continued criticism of the Tizard Committee threatened to destroy it. Watson Watt was persuaded to meet Churchill secretly to apprise him of the state of radar research and took the opportunity to complain of bureaucratic obfuscation and delay within the Air Ministry. Churchill confronted Tizard who was able to retain the support of most of his committee, but it was made clear that an accommodation had to be made with Lindemann. Churchill threatened public exposure of the dispute if Lindemann was forced to resign. Pressure was applied to Watson Watt, with whom the Air Ministry was annoyed because of his disclosures to Churchill, to resolve his disputes and he was coerced into accepting new conditions of employment.

The dispute came to a head at a meeting of the Tizard Committee on 15 July 1936; Lindemann was furious at the way he had been treated and a heated argument resulted in dissolution of the Committee through the resignation of two of its members. Lord Swinton, the Secretary of State for Air, refused to accept the resignations and called an emergency 'back-room' meeting of the committee. Swinton had taken up his role in 1935 and had brought a refreshingly intelligent and hard-driving spirit to his command.[18] He had been able to work closely with Dowding, something others found impossible, and was an admirer of Tizard. With a keen appreciation of the importance of the work of Tizard's committee, Swinton was not ready to see it interfered with and took radical proposals for resolution of the dispute to Cabinet. He had enough sway there to persuade it to back the reconstitution the Tizard Committee without Lindemann. It was a humiliation for both Lindemann and Churchill. Lindemann's opposition to radar became more acute beyond this point, expressing to Professor Jones his grave reservations about its effectiveness against massed aircraft formations and its susceptibility to 'jamming'.[19]

Watson Watt, possibly chastened by his exposure to political machinations, retired to Bawdsey and concentrated on new trials beginning in September, to which he rashly invited Tizard and Dowding among others. The first trial was a disaster when aircraft came within visual range without appearing at all on the radar screen. Only Dowding was persuaded to stay and witness further trials, which were markedly more successful. However, progress was erratic and criticism of Watson Watt mounted for what Sholto Douglas called his propensity to 'run before he could walk', and what Tizard described as his 'lack of good judgement'.[20] New trials scheduled for January were cancelled due, according to Watson Watt, to a shortage of trained staff at Bawdsey resulting from the paltry salaries on offer, but according to others because of his inability to concentrate his efforts on the day-to-day operation of the research establishment, preferring to spend time at the Air Ministry discussing policy matters.

The morale among staff at Bawdsey, however, was excellent. The informal atmosphere which encouraged debate and cooperation bore fruit during the early months of 1937 when even Watson Watt's myriad of new ideas and constant change of focus (or maybe because of them) could not slow the pace of development. Tests, upon the results of which rested Air Ministry support to extend the number of radar stations, were scheduled for April. Much progress had been made since January, especially by the introduction of dipole antennae which focused the transmission beam out to sea avoiding landward interference, and the reduction in transmission wavelength down to thirteen metres. Tests were generally convincing, despite some having been designed to yield results by running them in conditions much more favourable than any ever likely to be encountered during conflict. Funding was at unprecedented levels.

By the end of 1937 it had become obvious that Watson Watt's management style was no longer appropriate for the scale of research and development required to perfect radar. There were simply too many people and too many lines of exploration for one man, let alone a man who shied away from day-to-day involvement. He bridled at the suggestion that he be given one of the deputy director roles, but eventually agreed to be appointed Director of Communications Development for which he was not particularly well suited at all, and which actually demanded more of the type of administrative skills he so clearly lacked.

Lindemann's objections to radar proved prescient when it became apparent that the whole radar chain could be put at risk by quite rudimentary 'jamming' techniques. An enemy could simply transmit at the same frequency as the radar stations and swamp the receivers with signals. There was a solution, but it was not cheap. Each station would require the means to transmit at four distinct frequencies so that if one was jammed it could switch to another.[21] This demanded a total of eight antennae: four transmitters on 350ft steel towers, and four receivers on lower wooden towers.

Two significant developments were introduced as part of the ongoing process of radar defence. Each radar station was provided with a Filter Room to allow preliminary analysis of data to avoid overloading the operatives at the main Filter Room at Bentley Priory. This further increased the technical skills required of operatives who would be required to assess the strength, altitude and track of the signal source. This was quite a complex process and operatives could only master the techniques through experience and intuition. The training period for each operator was about five months. At the same time, development of airborne radar continued apace alongside the research being carried out at Bawdsey. An impromptu exercise, unofficially organised by Watson Watt, when an Avro Anson aircraft set out to locate British ships in the North Sea proved to be a spectacular success. Important advances were made at Bawdsey throughout the year and by the end of 1937, all previous calamities had been forgotten and radar development was advancing apace – which was just as well because in 1938, the political landscape altered dramatically, starting with the Anschluss in March. Churchill continued to demand that Parliament accelerate its pace of rearmament.

All through the life of the Tizard Committee there had been serious discontent and discord between its members and influential people close to it. The need for utmost secrecy was vital during the development of the radar chain which was just one of many projects undergoing research under its auspices. The press was 'advised' not to report on them and duly complied. The government opposition leader, Clement Atlee, was privately informed of the true nature of the towers, which effectively silenced any parliamentary debate. Only Churchill, with cloaked threats to go public in his disputes with Tizard, posed any danger to the security of radar research, although it must be doubted if he would ever have prejudiced such an important defensive development.

The existence of radar now caused the Air Ministry to revisit its attitude to air policy which had previously been dominated by the idea that 'the bomber will always get through'. It had been assumed that since there was no practical defence against the bomber, the most effective deterrent was to have a long-range bomber force of one's own. Radar now allowed for the possibility of a defensive air strategy to operate alongside an offensive one and this translated into modifications in policy whereby fighter aircraft production was given higher priority. It is important to note that throughout the tumultuous months of 1938, despite construction of the radar stations all across the south coast, there was not a single mention of radar in the press or in Parliament.

Churchill continued his attack on government policy during 1938 with the help of Lindemann, who did not share Tizard's enthusiasm for radar believing that the Germans would easily find counter measures to 'blind' it. The only time that the veil of secrecy was imperilled was when Churchill used the threat of exposure to champion the cause of Lindemann and challenge the government's level of rearmament but, as a member, was unable to publicly denounce it.[22] Instead, in a letter to the new Air Minister Kingsley Wood dated 9 June, he criticised the 'slow-motion' pace of air defence research. Tizard saw the letter and threatened to resign if nothing was done to refute Churchill's 'outrageous memorandum'.[23] He compared the work of his committee with what he cited as Churchill's 'total lack of real scientific imagination and foresight'[24] during his time as First Lord of the Admiralty when Britain had entered the First World War with no defence against German submarines. It is doubtful if Churchill would ever have carried out his threat but continued with what Tizard referred to as 'pin pricking' criticisms.[25] There was clear anger and frustration within the Air Ministry over Churchill's unwarranted criticisms, which he was apparently using in a broader attack on the government's rearmament policy. Churchill was temporarily restrained but by October he was back on the offensive and threatened he would 'free [himself] from the silence', and 'with due regard to the necessity for secrecy … endeavour to get something done by parliamentary action', unless Lindemann was co-opted back onto the ADRC (Air Defence Research Committee).[26]

Tizard initially found Churchill's attitude intolerable and again threatened resignation and dissolution of his committee. Huge pressure was put on Tizard from within the Air Ministry, who understood the vital importance of his work, to reconsider in the interest of national security. He reluctantly agreed to stay in place. Back on the ADRC, Lindemann, while not dismissive of radar, resumed his championing of aerial mining and parachute bombing as the areas of air defence most likely to be available by the middle of 1939, especially in night defence where radar, without visual back-up, had proved to be of little use. Radar, however, was the only research project that was based on sound scientific principles and incorporated existing technology. Tizard thought the best way of convincing Churchill was to invite him along to a full test of the system which was scheduled for June 1939. Churchill was duly impressed and began to heap praise on Tizard for the work of his committee. By this time radar had been incorporated into a fully integrated daytime air defence system.

Meanwhile Watson Watt was forging ahead with work on a new Chain Home network designed to work on a much shorter wavelength and so be more precise. Quick and reliable communications systems were designed. Investigations were carried out to prevent deliberate 'jamming' of the radar signal while the previous work on airborne radar continued apace. By the end of 1937, progress was sufficient for the government to authorise the building of two more – but only two – radar stations.

Important design modifications were made. A reflector was applied to the antenna to prevent radar signals being transmitted over land since there was too much interference from aircraft which were clearly neither enemy nor interceptor, and the wavelength of thirteen metres was adopted to reduce interference from other radio sources. More new tests in April were successful at detecting aircraft at ranges of up to 100 miles but it was proving difficult to estimate the height of the aircraft and well-nigh impossible to determine the number of aircraft in any given plot on the radar screen. Based on the results of the April tests, the Air Ministry, galvanised by the deteriorating political situation in mainland Europe, released a further £1 million for the construction of the rest of the radar stations, most of which at this stage would not be operational until September 1939.

The Munich Crisis of September 1938 had given impetus to the completion of the whole chain of radar stations. Mobile radar control rooms were also created as a back-up to the system in the event of damage caused by enemy action. Early trials were inconclusive and varied widely in their measure of successfully detecting and assessing 'dummy' raids by Blenheims of No. 2 Bomber Group. Such trials did, however, pinpoint the need to differentiate between friendly and hostile 'plots' on the screen so that British bombers returning from operations would not be mistaken for enemy aircraft.

During the radar development process, a number of issues were identified as being major stumbling blocks to progress. During tests it was clear that radar screens were being contaminated by aircraft in the test area which were not part of the trial and there was insufficient priority given to keeping airspace clear for trials. Controllers were still finding it very difficult to separate friend from foe on their plotting tables. The answer was development of IFF transponders emitting a high-pitched signal for fourteen seconds every minute (pipsqueak) which could, in theory, be easily recognised by radar operators above the background 'noise' of radar contacts, but again this required a 'trained ear' to separate out the signal. The device was colloquially known as a 'cockerel'. Controllers would remind pilots who did not have their IFF sets switched on by asking 'Is your cockerel crowing?'[27] Dowding placed this at the top of his research agenda realising that no attack could be authorised on an aircraft until it had been identified as a 'bandit'. Watson Watt claimed that he had considered IFF right at the start of RDF research, but Wilkins insists that it was he who first mooted the idea long before there existed any equipment to test it and that it was he who had pioneered the practical work in 1937.[28]

Many aircraft, mostly fighters, had to wait to get IFF fitted, but in reality, it was returning bombers that were most at risk from misidentification. A clock with a second hand in the Operations Room was divided into four different coloured quarters, each of fifteen seconds, and each pipsqueak was set to transmit for fourteen seconds during a particular colour quadrant. The system allowed controllers not only to locate an aircraft but also to identify it. It was clear also that IFF would become extremely counter-productive if the enemy realised that it was being used, which would allow them to adopt it in their own aircraft to disguise their aircraft as 'friendly'. This would be easily done by examination of British bombers forced down over the Continent but remaining essentially intact. If the Germans recovered a device from a downed bomber, they would quickly learn how to duplicate its signal and render the whole system redundant. To counter this, crews were ordered to activate a destruct mechanism if they were going to bale out, and as a back-up, each IFF set was fitted with two electronic detonators that would do the job automatically if the aircraft crashed.[29] Naturally, crews were nervous about carrying explosive devices in the cabin so all IFF sets were put in a steel protective envelope. Despite this, many British bomber crews secretly refused to use it fearing that in combat zones it would reveal their position to the enemy; it is said that some crews deliberately disabled such devises during a mission.

The Luftwaffe had brought up IFF in 1938 at OKW but Kriegsmarine refused to meet them halfway on the issue of frequencies to be allocated. The Army then hijacked the debate and veered it towards radar, insisting that it should be developed as part of anti-aircraft systems, thereby ending any discussion of IFF. When Martini later tried to bring the subject up again, the Army demanded that the Luftwaffe should justify their demands for IFF. When he did so, it was only with great reluctance that resources were allocated for Gema to work on a Stickleback (Stichling) system on 125 MHz for use with their Freya apparatus and another for the Würzburgs. The Stickleback system proved to be a disappointment at which point Dr Brinker and Herr Preikschat started work on the FuG 25a Erstling (First Child), operating on higher power. This too gave a lot of trouble, but found its way into use by 1941 after which it 'matured into a reliable system.'[30] By 1940 all German aircraft were fitted with the Würtzburg FuSE 62 apparatus with a 160MHz transmitter and 555MHz receiver.

Chain Home, or CH for short, was the codename for the coastal radar early warning stations all around the British coast from the Orkneys to Cornwall and North Wales. They were initially known as RDF and given the official name Air Ministry Experimental Station (AMES) Type 1. A radio direction finder (RDF) is a device for finding the direction to a source of radio transmission. The act of measuring the direction is known as radio direction finding, or sometimes simply direction finding (DF). RDF systems can be used with any radio source but very long wavelengths (low frequencies) require very large antennas and are generally used only on ground-based systems. These wavelengths can travel very long distances. Early British radar was referred to as RDF.

At a CH radar station, the 'line of shoot' was the bearing on which the transmission was fixed. Aircraft approaching along this bearing would show a strong signal, but the signal would be progressively weaker the further off this bearing the aircraft was. The area swept by the radar beam (lobe) on a horizontal plane described an elongated oval and relied on overlap with other stations to acquire total coverage. There were gaps also between the 'lobes' as they spread upwards. Meaning that a 'plot' at high altitude could suddenly disappear from the screen only to reappear later. Judging whether this was the same 'plot' or a new one was one of the many essential skills required to interpret the data. Low flying aircraft, such as the specialist attackers of Erprobungsgruppe 210, could exploit the curvature of the earth to fly under the lobe and avoid detection until close to its target. Plots 'acquired' by the radar operators were converted to visual displays on the main plotting table through an electric calculator which completely filled a room, a crude forerunner of modern computers. This equipment was required because of the complicated calculations that radar stations had to perform before sending their intelligence through to the Filter Room. The position of each aircraft had to be described as a grid reference and the observed elevation had to be converted into an altitude using a chart. It is not hard to see what a logjam would ensue if multiple aircraft were detected. The calculator devised at Bawdsey could convert polar coordinates into a grid reference, height reading into an angle of elevation, and an angle of elevation into a range and altitude and was installed in twenty-one radar stations by July 1940.[31]

In October 1936, as part of radar research at Bawdsey, the War Office had started research into Coastal defence radar (CD) to improve the accuracy of their anti-aircraft guns. Using 1.5m transmissions, their aerials (transmit and receive) were rotated together and swept the sky like lighthouse beams. This achieved an accuracy in determining range and location of a target far better than Chain Home but was useless in estimating altitude. Watson Watt immediately saw that CD technology would be an important supplement to CH and ordered twenty-four modified sets operating at the shortest wavelength possible to reduce the size of the rotating aerials.[32] Tests showed that aircraft as low as 50ft could be detected up to fifteen miles away.

Radar Coverage in 1940. CH Station (long-range radar) coverage shaded dark grey and CHL Stations (low-level radar) light grey with station names italicised.

CD stations were commissioned and set up alongside existing CH stations and the technology was renamed Chain Home Low (CHL). While the new CHL stations would become hugely important with their much better estimate of the bearing of an intruder, they added enormously to the amount of information coming into the Filter Rooms and this prompted a move to raise the level of performance there by employing higher-grade staff with mathematical and scientific backgrounds who only finished their training around the time that France fell.[33] Because of their ability to detect low-flying aircraft and because, even then, warning time was squeezed, CHL stations were given orders to report directly to Sector Filter Rooms and bypass Bentley Priory.

Radar stations were normally composed of two sites. The first housed the transmitter towers and the second, a few hundred metres away, contained the receiver masts and receiver equipment block. Power was supplied by the National Grid with 75Kw back-up generators. The transmitters operated on 22.69, 27.00, 48.00 and 50.50 MHz. The transmitter aerials consisted of four steel towers 110m tall with about 50m between them. Three large platforms were stationed on the tower at different heights and a transmission cable was suspended from the top platform to the ground on either side of the platform. The resulting signal was directed forward along the perpendicular to the line of the towers. This direction was known as the 'line of shoot' and was generally aimed out over the water. The broadcast pattern covered an area of about 100 degrees in a roughly fan-shaped area, with smaller side-lobes. The closer to the line of shoot a contact was the stronger the signal.

The receiver consisted of four 70m-tall wooden towers arranged at the corners of a square. Each tower had three sets of receiver antennas at different heights. Using various combinations of antennas, the receivers could measure the bearing of a contact and also its vertical angle. The operator sat in front of a 12-inch cathode ray tube (CRT) which showed a horizontal bright line, or trace, and a fixed scale in tens of miles above it. This trace, in fact, looked like a waving line of short grass as the 'background noise' caused small vertical deflections in it which could easily be read off against the scale. However, the variation of shape and amplitude of such spikes gave an experienced operator some indication of the number of aircraft in an approaching formation. Radar operators worked in hour-long shifts in front of their screens while the 'recorder' maintained a log of plots as they were called. A 'plotter' then marked the contacts on a Perspex screen overlaying a gridded map and passed on these coordinates to Bentley Priory Filter Room.

It was a complex process to work out what a blip on the radar screen meant in terms of what and where the contact was. Upon receiving a contact, the operator had to search using the goniometer (an instrument that rotates the line of shoot) to find the maximum deflection on the screen. Then a correction factor had to be applied and this was determined by reference to tables which had been drawn up when the calibration of the equipment had been done during the commissioning of the station.

Calibration was a laborious process involving an aeroplane flying in very tight circles over eight different points spread across the line of shoot and at various heights, while remaining in sight through a theodolite mounted on the top platform of a transmitter tower. Afterwards the radar coordinates were compared with the true visual plots and correction tables duly created. Any change of frequency or aerial system required a new calibration run.

In use, a target's bearing and range had to be corrected by reference to the tables and then applied to a map to obtain a grid reference for it. This caused a delay of up to four minutes which was greatly reduced by the introduction of a 'calculator' (a single program analogue computer) designed in 1939 by G.A. Roberts at Bawdsey and built by Siemens in conjunction with the GPO Chief Engineer's Office. It tracked the angle of the goniometer by means of a hidden ring of switch contacts to provide its input, in both bearing and height, and automatically added the correction factors which were hard wired in from data obtained during calibration. The output was displayed visually on a panel of small bulbs as a four-figure grid reference, together with height and estimated number of aircraft. The radar operators referred to this display as 'the fruit machine' because the lights would repeatedly change as the operator rocked her goniometer knob. The calculator could also be mechanically linked to a teleprinter and so send the data automatically by dedicated telephone line to the remote Filter Room.

They would then apply a scale to determine the distance and bearing of the contact. This allowed the operator to describe the contact in terms of its polar coordinates (a two-dimensional coordinate system in which distance and angle are measured from a given point). These polar coordinates could then be converted into a point on a map overlain with a Cartesian grid (a grid with x and y coordinates). CH could not see aircraft flying much below 5,000ft, nor those much above 20,000ft. Indeed, at Ventnor no heights at all could be established as the ground sloped away too steeply on the south-east side, but this was rectified with the introduction of CHL radar.

The next step in this process was to report the target's grid reference and height by voice via dedicated landlines to the Filter Room at Bentley Priory, where staff determined which targets were friend or foe and eliminated any obvious anomalies. Repeated plots became the direction of travel (vector) with the height and estimated number of aircraft repeatedly confirmed. By cross referring reports from several different lines of shoot, further confirmation was provided. The edited data was assembled as markers on a large plotting table and this showed the situation as it had been something like four minutes previously: since then the bombers would have flown on about another fifteen miles by then.

With the separate raids thus identified, the information was passed to the Operations Room staff who could then make the tactical decisions regarding the deployment and vectoring of the defending aircraft, either those already in the air or presently on the ground, towards their ever moving targets. It was found that those best equipped to calculate the required courses were recuperating experienced pilots, as they were able to visualise better the everchanging relationships between defending and attacking aircraft. However, once the enemy aircraft had crossed the coast CH could no longer detect them and then the Observer Corps became the sole means of tracking the enemy.

By the beginning of 1940, Sector controllers were using CH data to position their fighters with an accuracy of about five miles. This was usually sufficient on a clear day but useless in poor weather conditions. Another flaw in CH coverage was that aircraft approaching at very low level came in undetected 'under the radar' giving very little warning. Efforts were stepped up to remedy this by the use of CHL.

In 1936 the War Office had established a small group at Bawdsey under Dr E.T. Paris and Dr A.B. Wood to work on radar for anti-aircraft guns and coastal defence (CD). The CD equipment worked on a frequency of 180–210 MHz. By July of 1939 the CD set could detect an aircraft flying at 500ft up to twenty-five miles away with very good accuracy and in August 1939, on Watson Watt's recommendation, the Air Ministry ordered twenty-four CD sets from Pye Radio with the intention of placing one at each CH site. These stations became known as CHL stations and the equipment as Radar Type 2. CHL transmitters did not require tall towers and could be made small enough to allow for rotation thereby compensating for the narrower beam. The new CHL systems were set up alongside CH stations.

In July 1940 Watson Watt reported on the state of CH radar. He found the system to be fairly robust and dependable, but that calibration of stations was well behind schedule and aerials were generally found to be below standard. Range-finding and direction-finding were usually good, but estimating height would require more aerials fitted to the towers which would further set-back the calibration process. Filtering of the intelligence was complex, but the necessary skills could only be acquired through experience, a problem exacerbated by a serious shortage of able and qualified personnel.

The new radar stations under construction had incorporated several major modifications to minimise the risk of jamming. This proved to be crucial during the Battle of Britain when even the most accurate Luftwaffe bombing failed to destroy them as the force of the blast was dissipated through the lattice framework of the towers. The extra towers also added resilience to the system's capacity to absorb damage. When stations were hit and put out of action it was damage to the control rooms and communications, not to the towers, that caused the breakdown.

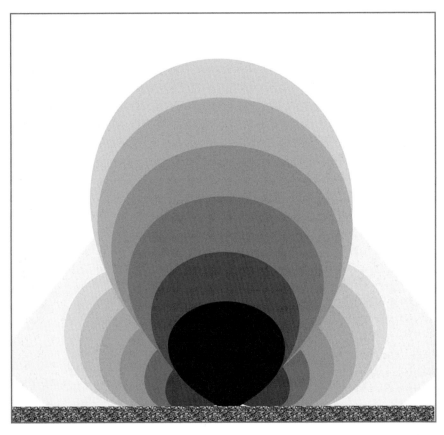

Diagrammatic representation of a radar sweep with the main lobe and secondary lobes to the side. The darker the colour the more sensitive the radar. The maximum range might be in the region of 100 miles.

Alongside the development of radar was the intimately connected question of efficient communication between aircraft and ground controllers so that pilots could obtain constant updates from the most recent radar tracking information. The two systems were intertwined to become what is now referred to as the Dowding System of fighter control, which played such a vital part in the Battle of Britain.

The diagram below is what an operator might have seen with showing contacts at twenty miles and thirty miles. By changing the direction of the radar beam and working between different aerials on the radar towers, the operators had to estimate the line of approach, number of aircraft and height before sending the information to Bentley Priory Filter Room. The complexity of this process and the urgent need for speed is testament to the great skill and expertise of the radar operators and analysts.

The author recognises *http://www.ventnorradar.co.uk/CH.htm* as a significant source of information for this section.

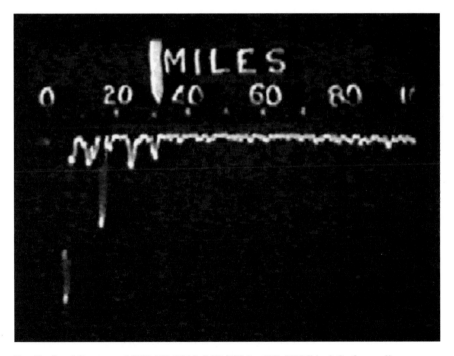

By Radar Museum, NEDAD.2013.047.058A, CC BY-SA 3.0, *https://commons. wikimedia.org/w/index.php?curid=32661852*

Chapter 7

The Dowding System

The war will be won by the science thoughtfully applied to operational requirements.

Sir Hugh Dowding, AOC Fighter Command.[1]

The Dowding System incorporated a number of components, all of which had required political will and substantial investment to create. The radar chain was the first line of defence but the translation of a 'blip' on a radar screen into the destruction of an enemy aircraft also required a vast integrated telephone communications network, a series of command and control centres, again with secure communications and a radio communications system capable of passing information to aircraft once they had been sent up. When a radar station in the chain detected a threat, the radar operatives had to make an assessment of what the information meant in terms of numbers, height and trajectory of the aircraft, and then transmit their analysis to a central hub where it could be cross-checked with information from neighbouring stations and reports coming in from the Observer Corps and the Y-Service. Officers at the central hub would then decide which elements of air defence should be deployed against the threat and orders were relayed down through Group and Sector command centres to aerodromes that would send aircraft up or signal to aircraft already on patrol and guide them to an interception.

One does not need to look too closely at the whole of the Dowding System before realising just how complex it was and what exceptional levels of skill were required every step of the way. The system was only as good as the people who operated it, and its success in standing up to the Luftwaffe onslaught under the most extreme pressure is testament to their dedication and expertise, much of it acquired 'on the job'. From Observer Corps 'spotters' out in the wind and rain, to radar operators peering endlessly into their glowing screens, to analysts who turned the intelligence into usable information, to controllers who looked at the big picture and applied resources in the most effective but sustainable manner and last, but by no means least, the pilots who got the orders to scramble and went, not knowing if they would ever return.

The Observer Corps had its origins in the First World War when a number of observation posts were set up as part of the War Office early warning system against Zeppelin raids over south-east England. It acquired its formal independent status in response to the advancement of aircraft technology, acquired its official title by 1925 and was transferred to the Air Ministry in 1929. In 1935 it was expanded and split up into sixteen different commands but could still make only a small contribution to air defence since 'the problem of early warning was still unresolved'.[2] Although a vital part of Britain's defences, it was manned entirely by volunteers who took part in exercises only when they could get time off work.[3] Wood and Dempster were sure that 'The success of the Observer Corps system [was] accounted for almost entirely by the enthusiasm of its volunteers.'[4] When Dowding became AOC Fighter Command, as part of his plan for an integrated air defence system, he saw that it was vital to move the Observer Corps onto a war footing. Observers were obliged to attend aircraft recognition classes and studied methods of estimating aircraft height, but for the most part were carried along by their impressive enthusiasm and relied on aircraft recognition booklets and a pair of binoculars.[5] Exercises conducted in August 1939 to test the way in which all components of air defence were coordinated showed promise. Observer Corps reports were matched to radar intelligence and Dowding reported satisfaction with the results but was concerned by the number of reports indicating serious errors by inexperienced members who failed to differentiate between friendly and enemy aircraft. He even went as far as to say that Observer Corps reports should be ignored unless supported by radar intelligence. Churchill was unimpressed and described the Observer Corps as operating as if from the 'Early Stone Age'.[6]

Radar stations were improving their ability to detect aircraft approaching from across the sea, but were significantly less successful at tracking them once they had crossed the coast. Topographical features of the landscape required elaborate calibration of the systems and there was neither time nor expertise to carry that out in the time available. Not only that, but the huge increase in the numbers of 'friendly' aircraft operating over land swamped the radar screens.

The only available recourse was visual observation in which, as previously stated, there was limited confidence especially in cloudy conditions.

The obvious limitations placed on observation posts meant that they could not be more than ten miles apart for complete coverage; this required not only a large number of men and women to staff them, but also an extensive network of telephone cabling linking the posts to their headquarters. Despite his misgivings, however, Dowding was a great admirer of these volunteers and, given the full range of services they provided, strongly supported a proposal that they all be paid for their time. Not only did the observers report sightings of aircraft, they also kept a log of where bombs were dropped (to locate unexploded devices), crash sites and enemy aircrews parachuting down out of damaged aircraft. They even occasionally lit flares, in direct contravention of 'black-out' restrictions, to guide stricken aircraft back to land at night. Even when visibility restricted direct observation of aircraft, if the operatives knew, from intelligence passed through from radar contacts, roughly where the enemy had crossed the coast, they could track them to some extent by sound. It should be said, in recognition of the enthusiastic and dedicated contribution made by Observer Corps volunteers, that once war was declared, they worked around the clock in all weathers: sun, snow and ice, without protection from the elements and without complaint.

Observer Corps local headquarters, of which there were thirty-two across the whole country, each had a table upon which 'plotters', connected to observation posts by telephone, placed and moved counters according to the reports coming in. This was similar to the system used by Operations Rooms at Fighter Command even down to the use of colour-coded clocks. For each recorded incursion an arrowed marker of the appropriate colour, corresponding to the colour indicated by the minute-hand on the clock, was introduced on the board. The arrow indicated the direction of flight, while the counter itself showed data corresponding to the estimated height and strength of the enemy. Each was numbered in line with a code already allocated from radar contacts. 'Tellers' would then record the tracks of enemy aircraft using pencil and gridded paper. These centres passed their intelligence directly to Fighter Command Group headquarters.

When the 'Phoney War' turned 'real' after the German invasion of France and the Low Countries, the Observer Corps felt a Shakespearian 'summoning of the blood and a stiffening of the sinew', as the prospect of an invasion loomed. Posts were protected with earth revetments and by the summer of 1940, Observer Corps posts were equipped with a rather ingenious and complicated looking, but aptly named, 'Observer Corps Post Instrument' (although colloquially known as the 'Heath Robinson'), a mechanical sighting device mounted on a circular plate depicting a map of the surrounding area.[7] By focusing the sights on an enemy formation and estimating its height, a needle would point on the map to the approximate point over which they were currently flying.

The Luftwaffe Adlerangriff offensive of August 1940, with its target portfolio now including many sites inland away from the coast, plunged forward posts of the Observer Corps into feverish activity. Some posts were almost overwhelmed with the numbers of aircraft crossing overhead at heights varying from tree-tops, in the case of Erprobungsgruppe Bf110s, to more than 20,000ft in the case of Bf109 fighter escorts. It is the case that Fighter Group Operations Rooms became frustrated at the number of Observer Corps tracks reported, which bore no resemblance to any reported by radar, and inaccurate height estimations – quite understandable given the difficulty in estimating them. Indeed, radar operators had similar difficulty with this last issue and on many occasions during the second part of the Battle of Britain, Fighter Command aircraft were deployed at altitudes which severely disadvantaged them against Bf109s or, in some cases, meant that they completely failed to make interception at all due to flying too high or too low.

Heinrich Hertz had first demonstrated the existence of radio waves in 1888 but he also showed that, just like light waves, they could be reflected, deflected and refracted. Research into the nature of radio waves of different wavelength opened up huge areas of long-distance communication using wavelengths of 200 metres or more. Shorter wavelengths were considered to be of less interest since it required greater power to produce them and they were believed to travel in straight lines and so would beam out into space rather than follow the earth's curvature. After the end of the First World War, for reasons of national security, the use of long-wave radio wavebands was restricted, but amateur enthusiasts were allowed free access to short-wave radio bands. It was soon apparent that short-waves could, in fact, be detected thousands of miles away by repeated reflection off the upper atmosphere but lost much of their clarity in the process.

However, research into the military application of radio transmission opened up a whole new field with seemingly boundless potential, namely the ability to locate the position of aircraft within a given area well beyond the range of human vision. As early as 1924, the first experiments in RDF had been devised to develop navigation aids for aircraft flying 'blind' in bad weather or at night. Two RDF stations picking up radio signals from the same aircraft could determine its location by simple triangulation. In the same year, Fighting Area Headquarters had been set up to control fighting aircraft in an air-fighting zone. The first area to benefit was the London Air Defence Area, which was divided into sectors each with its own fighter squadron(s) and Operations Room which was directly connected to a Fighter Area Headquarters Operations Room. The Operations Room was to provide 'an intelligence centre upon which are focused all sources of intelligence which may furnish information of value to the Defence Commander', and were designed to 'direct and coordinate the activities of all units of the defending force'.[8]

By 1935, advances in technology using RDF had resulted in trials being held at Biggin Hill and Hornchurch which detected aircraft 'with surprising accuracy'.[9] A more advanced system using cathode ray tubes was installed at Northolt a year later at the behest of Tizard, but curtailed owing to a shortage of qualified technicians, most of whom had been seconded to radar work. What did result from this, however, was the laying down of secure telephone and telegraph lines between Biggin Hill, Hornchurch and Northolt that was the start of a communications network connecting all Fighter Command stations. This was carried out by GPO engineers who continued to maintain the lines all through the bombing raids. Notwithstanding, Tizard was able to instigate a series of experiments centred on Biggin Hill and continuing for seven months designed to improve the range and efficiency of RDF sets fitted to aircraft. These experiments were fundamental to the development of techniques that would become crucial during the Battle of Britain.[10] Dowding, now Air Officer Commanding (AOC) Fighter Command was anxious to keep abreast of all technical developments and eagerly accepted Tizard's invitation to discuss applications. Predictably, reports were over-optimistic, based upon the results of experiments set up to provide the very best conditions for success. While this was essential to test embryonic technology it was no basis for one of the researchers, Dr B.G. Dickens, suggesting that 'daytime standing patrols could be eliminated, and most raids intercepted'.[11]

Up to this point there had been a 'crying need ... for Operations Rooms at all command stations with tables on which courses of all aircraft, hostile and friendly, could be tracked'.[12] The Operations Room would become the intelligence centres of all Fighter Command Group and Sector headquarters, and even stations in some cases, and would go on to play such a vital role in the Battle of Britain. Their initial function would be to collect information from radar stations about all aircraft approaching their area, identify each as friend or foe, and monitor their progress. In order that each Operations Room receive only such information as was relevant to them it first passed through a 'filter', at the central hub of Bentley Priory, which had its own 'master' Operations Room buried deep underground as defence against bombing. Each had a central large-scale map on a table surrounded by a ring of telephones with direct connections both up and down the command chain. The idea was to receive and assess information quickly and accurately and create a dynamic representation of the conflict by the use of markers on the map. They would be required to process large amounts of information in as short a time as possible in order to fulfil their basic function of guiding British fighters onto incoming enemy aircraft before they could reach their target.

These Operations Rooms were manned day and night once war broke out, and all conformed to a basic pattern. There was a central controller on a raised dais where he had full view of the whole map. The map itself was surrounded by plotters who received information from the Filter Room and moved markers on the table that corresponded to the position of aircraft, friend and foe, or groups of aircraft. These positions were adjusted at regular intervals according to what the plotters were being told from the Filter Room. The controller would make continuous assessments of the combat situation based on his reading of the table and it was he, having up-to-date information about the strength and readiness of squadrons in his Sector, who would call up aircraft from their stations or direct airborne aircraft onto interception trajectories. The effectiveness of the Operations Rooms was crucially dependent on radio telephone communications (r/t) both ground-to-air and air-to-air. Since 1932 all British fighter aircraft had been equipped with the new TR-9B system with a ground-to-air range of thirty-five miles, and five miles between aircraft in flight.[13]

The essential components of Fighter Command's strategy in the early phases of the Battle of Britain can be studied in the light of Professor Hinsley's quote 'Information has to be acquired; it has to be analysed and interpreted; and it has to be put into the hands of those who can use it.' Dowding's strategy, which became known as the Dowding System, relied on successful detection of raids at an early enough stage to allow fighter deployment and included:

- deploying a fixed number of squadrons in 10 and 11 Group areas, leaving about half of all squadrons in reserve in 12 and 13 Group areas
- a minimal number of aircraft deployed on standing patrol
- early detection of attack by radar stations

- rapid analysis of radar data
- rapid communication of analysed data up to a central control room at Bentley Priory
- rapid dissemination of information about enemy raids down to Sector control rooms
- rapid deployment of aircraft to intercept the raid
- number of aircraft deployed related to estimation of enemy strength
- continuous communication of situation reports to aircraft as they attempted interception

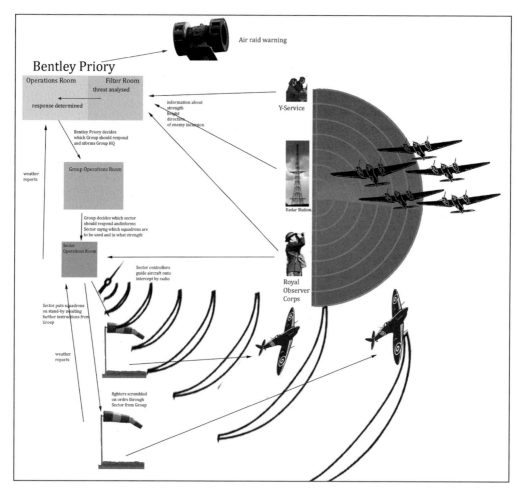

'(The) Operations Room should focus on broad direction, inter-group reinforcement and the dissemination of information'[14]

RAF Inland Area headquarters was established at Bentley Priory at Stanmore in Middlesex in 1925, but in 1936 it was handed over to Fighter Command where they established their own HQ. By 1939 its function had become so vital to British air defence that whole sections of it were bomb-proofed in a bunker some 40ft deep underground. This became the centre of a communications web that underpinned the Dowding System of fighter control. This system essentially was a chain of command that trickled down from Dowding himself to each individual pilot.

The first lines of defence were the radar stations and the Observer Corps which fed raw intelligence into the system, but as with all such information it had to be analysed to find exactly what it meant. Radar stations would report the detection of enemy aircraft (a contact) in a particular location and would initially assess what the 'blip' on their screens meant in terms of how far away the enemy was and how many aircraft were in the formation. This was a difficult and time-consuming operation involving complex calculations – and was by no means foolproof. The local station would then plot the information on their own maps and send it by telephone to the Filter Room at Bentley Priory. As the enemy incursion developed, they might be able to add further information such as how fast the enemy was approaching, what its trajectory was and maybe its altitude, although the emerging and inexact science of interpreting 'blips' meant that some of this information was more reliable than others. No doubt the analysts in the Filter Room at Bentley Priory grew accustomed to the varying quality of intelligence that came in from the different radar stations.

The Filter Room, arguably the most important link in the chain, had, as its first priority, to collate information from the various intelligence sources, resolve discrepancies, and create an overall view of what was happening. This involved determining whether the contact was friendly or hostile. Its staff included liaison officers from other commands such as the Observer Corps, Bomber and Coastal Command and the Admiralty, who could provide information about their own aircraft movements and so eliminate them from being categorised as hostile.[15] It is not hard to imagine the pressure on staff as enemy activity increased during August and September when the Luftwaffe started making 'dummy' raids, i.e. aircraft starting out as if to attack and then turning back when squadrons are scrambled to intercept. It was the fundamental responsibility of the Filter Room to assess the level of threat of each contact and pass on to the Operations Room only those which they believed required an immediate response. In this way the attention of controllers in the Operations Room was focused on the most important issues at all times. It is clear that decisions made in the Filter Room were of the utmost importance and, after a less than impressive performance early in 1940, it was recognised that the work was of highly specialised nature. The level was significantly raised by the assignment of staff, many of them women, with the appropriate level of scientific and mathematical skills.

The Filter Room, remember, was receiving intelligence from all coastal radar stations, which was burdensome but had the advantage of corroborating and reinforcing intelligence from adjoining stations plotting the same contact. Filter Room staff had to make rapid assessments of the threat level and pass that onto the Operations Room. Here the contact was represented on the General Situation Map (GSM), showing Britain and the eastern approaches on a 20ft table, by a wooden block displaying such information as was known about the height and strength of the enemy force. A known hostile plot would show a black **H** on a yellow background, while a friendly plot would be a red **F** on white (unidentified was a black **X** on yellow). Friendly plots would show the squadron number, altitude and strength. Given the size of the table, the blocks were moved according to constantly updated information by (mostly female) operatives using sticks (their similarity to gambling croupiers has often been alluded to). Depending on the overall situation, the staff there would decide whether an immediate response was required, or whether they would wait to see how the threat developed. Intelligence would continue to arrive updating their information about the contact; when the threat was identified as real, the Operations Room would pass information down to a Group Headquarters, or possibly two Group headquarters if the enemy raid was heading towards a target on the border between them as would be the case with Luftflotte 3 raids against Southampton, which might draw in RAF fighters from both Middle Wallop Sector in 10 Group and Tangmere Sector in 11 Group.

Only at the Bentley Priory Operations Room was it possible for controllers to have an overview of the country-wide situation. They would have an up-to-date knowledge of which squadrons were at which stations, how many serviceable aircraft they had, how many fighters were currently airborne, how long they had been in the air and which of them was best placed to meet each threat that developed. They would base all their decisions on their reading of the GSM which, by September, had become so congested with markers that a lot of the information was transferred to a 'tote board', so called because of its passing similarity to a bookmakers board at a racecourse, which showed which squadrons were based at each airfield along with the local weather conditions.[16] The board was manned and updated by members of the Women's Auxiliary Air Force (WAAF).

Group Operations Room controllers would have a centre similar to that at Bentley Priory but their maps would cover only their Group areas, allowing for a more detailed display. This was still thought to be at too high a level to control the movement of individual squadrons, but it did give Group controllers a clear view of what was happening in their zone. It was they who would now decide which of their Sectors was best placed to respond and it was to Sector Operations Rooms that all relevant information was relayed. Group Operations Rooms were the tactical control centres of the battle.[17] A crucial element of the 'Dowding System' was that intelligence was amalgamated and constantly updated only in the Bentley Priory Filter Room, and once information from there went through to Bentley Priory Control Room and down to Group and Sector Control Rooms, they were all looking at exactly the same picture.

Sector Operations Rooms had two units: one room whose sole function was to locate and identify friendly aircraft from their 'pipsqueak' transmissions, and the other which was set up in a similar fashion to Group except, of course, covering only the Sector on the map. These were housed in what were sometimes no more than flimsy brick-built huts with little or no protection against bomb damage. There were boards showing the states of readiness of all squadrons in the Sector in colour-coded format. Sector operatives would now put up a marker on their own table corresponding to the contact's estimated strength and height. Sector would call squadrons in their area to a state of readiness, but aircraft were only sent up on the orders of Group controllers. At this stage it was still impossible to know if the contact was enemy fighters or bombers, so there was no question of deciding whether a Hurricane or Spitfire squadron should be sent up; the idea, therefore, that bombers were attacked by Hurricanes and enemy fighters by Spitfires, as ordered by Park in his Directive of 11 September is problematical. It may well be the case that by this time there were usually a number of squadrons in the air at one time against massive raids which allowed controllers to implement Park's directive by deploying aircraft closing in on the combat zone to pursue different tactics.

Typically, a Sector controller might get a 'hostile' plot on his table and call an adjoining Sector controller by telephone to compare assessments of the threat level. Depending on the level of threat, he might call up a single aircraft, a section of three or four, a whole squadron, or all available aircraft. The call would go down to airfields to send up aircraft. Information about which squadrons had been called up and in what strength now went back the other way through Sector and Group to Bentley Priory so that their tables could be updated with 'friendly' markers. Back up the chain also went information about weather conditions, cloud cover etc. collected at each of the fighter stations in the Sector and also intelligence from local Observation Corps spotters. Once the squadrons had engaged in combat, the controllers had little or no contact with them and did not follow the progress of encounters.

'The efficiency and foresight of Group and Sector controllers were of prime importance to the conduct of the battle.'[18] A lot of these men were ex-pilots who had replaced the much less qualified operatives who had been employed in this role until Dowding saw that pilots flying into extreme danger needed controllers who had experienced battle and understood what they were asking them to do. These controllers performed admirably throughout, despite Luftwaffe Intelligence chief Schmid's assertion in his June report to OKL that they were little more than hopeless geriatrics.

It was crucial to constantly update information not only about the enemy, but also about RAF units in the air. Of utmost importance was information about how recent the information was and for that the markers on the table were colour coded. A clock in the room had each five-minute period marked by coloured triangles (three colours repeated four times) and so if a plot was updated while the minute hand pointed to a yellow triangle the plot was given a yellow arrow. The colour sequence was yellow, blue, red, so, for instance, if the minute hand had progressed to the next yellow triangle and the colour of the plot arrow had not changed in between, the information about that plot had not been updated for at least ten minutes.

Dowding summarised the role of Operations Rooms by saying that Bentley Priory had responsibility for identification of incursions and for informing Group controllers into whose area the incursion was taking place. Group would then decide which of the Sectors within their Group was best placed to respond and in what strength. Sector controllers would then decide which squadron in their area would be called up. It was Sector controllers who would then guide the interceptors onto their target through radio telephone communications. Interception points were predicted and constantly updated by applying the Grenfell method. It is estimated that the average time from first contact to information arriving at airfields was a little over four minutes.

Having an enemy 'plot' on the operations table was only useful if fighters 'scrambled' to intercept could be guided to a location where they would intersect the enemy's path at the precise moment the enemy arrived there also. It says something about the level of mathematical skills of British Intelligence that, for some time, the rather simple answer to this puzzle eluded them. They looked upon the problem with awe as if it required some sort of higher calculus using first and second order differential equations for a solution. The fact that two entities were in constant motion and flying in different directions, probably at different speeds completely floored them. A number of complicated calculating instruments were devised, at not inconsiderable expense, none of which seemed to offer a solution that would guide the fighters to their target. They arrived either too early or too late. Fortunately, Biggin Hill station commander, Wing Commander E.O. Grenfell, was a practical man with common sense to spare and he instinctively saw that the answer was simple geometry, not even requiring calculation. During one exercise he noted the position of 'friend' and 'foe' on the plotting table and mentally drew a line between the two. Using that as a base line, he projected the path of the 'foe' and noted the angle between that and the base line. He applied that same angle to the position of the 'friend' and extrapolated that until it crossed the path of the 'foe'. This now became the trajectory the 'friend' was ordered to follow, and the position where the two lines crossed was where the two aircraft would meet. Of course, that assumed that they were travelling at the same speed and that the 'foe' had not altered its course so it would be necessary to plot the positions a few minutes later and reapply the method. This might well give a slightly different intercept position, but that was not a problem. After each calculation, the 'friend' was redirected along the new path and although further plots and calculations might give slightly different 'solutions' for the intercept position as the two aircraft got closer, the difference between the 'solutions' became smaller and eventually merged into one.

On 4 August, the famous Biggin Hill Experiments began, 'which would develop the techniques which would be crucial during the Battle of Britain', but they were crude and a 'far cry from the realistic simulation desired'.[19] On the 7th more realistic tests were carried out and repeated over several months as the technique was refined. Tizard called it the 'Principle of Equal Angles'. Henceforth an Operations Room supervisor, when given a 'plot' to track, might ask for the 'Tizzy angle' when working out an interception.[3] The system was an extraordinary success.

The Grenfell Method

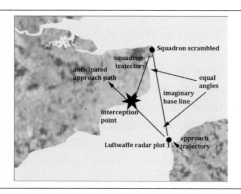

Luftwaffe aircraft detected off Cap Gris Nez and their flight path projected by extrapolation.

RAF fighters scrambled from Manston and given a bearing to follow based upon the Luftwaffe anticipated trajectory and the *Principle of Equal Angles*.

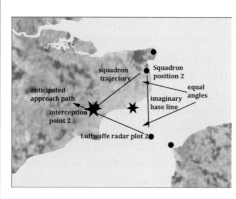

New plots show that the Luftwaffe aircraft have changed course so the Grenfell method is applied again to estimate a new interception point.

RAF squadrons are contacted and advised of the new interception point and are given a new bearing to follow that may be significantly different from their first bearing.

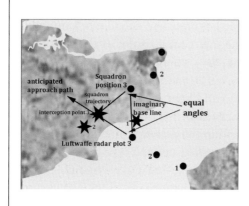

As the Luftwaffe and RAF aircraft get closer together, even if the Luftwaffe aircraft change course, the new estimated interception points are grouped closer together which means that the RAF fighters have to make only minor adjustments to their trajectory.

As the distance between the two sides decreases even further the Grenfell method becomes more and more accurate leading to a successful interception.

The Operations Room was to become the control hub into which all information flowed and out of which orders emanated. The tests being continuously flown to perfect the system were designed to allow ground controllers to guide fighter aircraft onto an interception path before the enemy bombers had crossed the coast, the reason being that once aircraft had done so, radar signals were severely interfered with by reflection from undulations in the landscape. It was also found that the siting of a station and the contours of the surrounding land affected the radar signal in such a way as to reduce its ability to predict an aircraft's height, so each station's equipment had to be calibrated to suit its environment which meant extra tests and delays. All components of the system – transmitters, receivers, generators, cables, aerials and telephones – had to be in place before calibration and if there were any changes the whole lot had to be recalibrated.[20] When enemy aircraft had cleared the coast the only reliable source of intelligence about them was derived from the Observer Corps but of course they were hampered by cloudy skies, haze and mist. It was clear, also, that the RDF signals were not differentiating between friendly and enemy aircraft with obvious consequences.

The key to a successful interception proved to be the speed and precision in translating radar plots into position markers on the plotting table. Once a raid was confirmed, a code word would be used to 'scramble' intercepting aircraft which would be given a course and height to follow – once airborne, and radio links from ground to air would send continuous information to the pilots to guide them to their target. The length of coastline along which a raid may be expected stretched from Lincolnshire to Devon, and the height at which it might proceed was anywhere from sea level up to more than 20,000ft. The odds against a chance encounter were very high and to miscalculate the interception by only a few miles and several thousand feet was an obvious problem, so accuracy was of the essence.

Now came the question of how to utilise the information coming through on the radar screens. How could these distortions of signal on a cathode ray tube somewhere on the coastline of southern England be used to knock down enemy bombers? A number of steps were required to translate the intelligence data into usable information. Tests were carried out at Bawdsey and the station at Dunkirk, near Canterbury, using an experimental mobile unit, but there were immediate problems. First of all, personnel had to be trained to interpret the radar signals in terms of what they might represent in the real world. The signals indicated the presence of aircraft at ranges of up to 100 miles, but it was proving difficult to estimate the height of the aircraft and almost impossible to determine the number of aircraft in a given 'plot'. The test tracking of commercial aircraft proved difficult, mostly because unlike military aircraft that were used in military trials, these airliners were not adhering to predetermined flightpaths and altitudes. This gave early indication that the enemy's natural aversion to cooperate with RAF defensive systems was going to necessitate a rapid improvement in operator skills. Improvements in equipment and recruitment of experienced staff slowly began to increase the reliability of interpretations, but radar tracking was far from being an exact science.

Once the operator had made a judgement about the radar source, that information was passed via telephone link to Bentley Priory Filter Room where it was compared with information from other nearby stations and firmed up into an assessment of the threat. Information was then compared with that coming from other radar stations, the Observer Corps and the Y-Service listeners and, in practice, usually proved to be fairly consistent. It became increasingly apparent, however, that low-flying aircraft could come in 'under the radar' and escape detection. This was exploited by specialist Luftwaffe gruppen who flew across the English Channel at wave-top height making them 'invisible' to radar until almost over the coast. Other aspects of the programme such as DF, direction-finding and r/t communications proved resilient and became important components of the system. Despite the vital requirement of DF sets, however, a shortage of cathode ray tubes slowed their introduction.[21]

Radio telephones fitted to the fighters were equipped with a quartz crystal which was 'tuned' to receive signals on a specific frequency and usually two, but never more than three, squadrons operated on the same frequency. This meant that the airwaves were not cluttered with too much traffic, but it also meant that aircraft flying into the airspace of adjoining Sectors lost contact with their ground controllers. However useful the radios were, it was soon found that they lacked range and Dowding ordered urgent research into the much more powerful Very High Frequency (VHF) radios. Code words were introduced to speed communications between ground controllers and pilots. Some examples were 'angels' meaning height (angels one-five means 15,000ft.), 'orbit' was circle and search, 'bandit' was enemy aircraft, 'tally ho' was the signal to attack, and 'pancake' was return and land.

By April 1938, unease about the priorities being adopted in radar research prompted a paper, 'Suggested Tactical Analysis of Large-Scale Air Defence operations in relation to RDF'. The paper looked at which level of the command chain was best suited to operate the Filter Room and

Operations Room, and what procedures were required to allow rapid transfer of information from there through Fighter Command channels down to the level of pilots. As well as questioning the design of radar receivers it asked at what point responsibility for each step along the chain should pass from operator to Filter Room to Operations Room and then how orders would pass down through Group, Sector, station, squadron and pilot. Crucially, it queried at what point the whole system might become overburdened with information and effectively cease to work.

A major exercise was carried out in August 1938 under the direct guidance of Dowding to see what progress had been made. The five active radar stations transmitted information through to the Filter Room at Bentley Priory and from there it went down to 11 Group headquarters and the Sector stations in the Group. The Observer Corps were employed to track aircraft after they crossed the coast. Bomber Command provided the 'enemy' aircraft. In many respects the exercise was a major success, but it also served its purpose in identifying weaknesses. Too often the screens were swamped by signals and radar operators were unable to differentiate between them, and even when the signals could identify individual raids it was proving difficult to determine the numbers of aircraft and their altitude. Once again it was clear that low-flying aircraft evaded detection. The Filter Room staff were equally swamped with information and struggled to translate it into clear plots on their tables. The increased level of activity was now throwing up anomalies between information coming from radar stations and reports from the Observer Corps. Park thought that the situation map on the main table was getting too complicated and cluttered up with duplicated and sometimes spurious 'plots' and persuaded Dowding, after much resistance on Dowding's part, to introduce a second table to which 'plots' were passed when queries and anomalies on the first table had been resolved. All in all, the tests showed that, as presently constituted, the system was practically useless on an operational level due to the time lag between initial detection of a raid and useful information being transmitted to aircraft. Dowding, however, was not disheartened and continued to give the work his full support with the proviso that ever more realistic conditions must pertain in future exercises to get everyone used to the pressures that would be experienced in time of war. A whole new level of senior management was created in the Air Ministry to oversee the radar programme under the directorship of Watson Watt.

After the German annexation of Czechoslovakia, the British government made strenuous efforts to prepare the home defences for war. Only five radar stations were operational at this time. Dowding urged the completion of the others and a deadline of 1 April 1939 was stipulated by the Air Ministry. Under this constraint Watson Watt reported that the stations would only be working with a single wavelength and would not be fully calibrated in respect of direction and height assessment. Although technical research had progressed well, the production of transmitters was behind schedule, giving the prospect of a radar chain which offered the very minimum of cover against air attack.

Emergency measures were approved in an effort to complete the building and equipping of stations but simple manpower shortages, owing to the secret nature of the work and weather, impeded construction of the towers during the winter in some of the most exposed coastal sites. Potential technical recruits were discouraged by the poor remuneration on offer and lack of career advancement prospects. Existing technicians were also having to work on airborne radar which was thought to have important long-term applications and so further reduced the number of qualified staff to work on CH radar.

Despite the impediments and due in no short measure to the 24-hour operation put in place, eleven stations in the intermediate chain were operational by the 1 April deadline, but the project leader A.P. Rowe admitted to Tizard that 'I shall never quite understand how it has been done.'[22] To deal with the shortage of trained radar operators, Watson Watt claims to have pioneered the idea of women being trained as radar operators. The five main grounds for favouring women to men were that women:

- had a higher powers of sustained concentration and lower liability to boredom
- had higher average finesse in relatively delicate manipulations such as the fine tuning of dials on the receivers
- had a higher scale of general conscientiousness
- had lower tendency to disclose secrets
- had longer periods of availability for service in a fixed location[23]

Women were recruited and were found to have 'performed excellently' in tests, although Dowding's second-in-command, Park, doubted that more than a few would have 'sufficient technical skills' to reach the required standard.[24] The move also raised concerns about placing women in locations that were likely to be the target of enemy bombers. The first four women operators joined Poling station in October 1939.

The whole radar chain in the spring of 1939 looked barely half-finished and of little use operationally. The tracking stations were able to detect approaching aircraft but were still unable to provide information about height and location. With only a single transmitting tower, they did not have the capacity to switch wavelengths if a jamming signal 'blinded' them. There was no protection for the operators against bomb attack and they had no anti-aircraft gun placements. Fighter Command Sectors lacked the specified three RDF stations. Identification of friendly aircraft and detection of low-flying aircraft were still major problems. Communications by telephone and teleprinter throughout the command were incomplete. The next most pressing issue was the detection of low-flying aircraft which received a boost from naval radar coastal defence (CD) research using much shorter wavelengths and especially developed to detect ships at sea-level rather than aircraft high in the sky. Tests with this short wavelength equipment proved very successful and it was immediately incorporated into the air defences, now called CHL Stations which were set up close to the CH stations.

By this time, the number of fighter squadrons had been increased to fifty, radar stations were being built and constantly upgraded, sector control rooms were under construction and the complex telephone communications system linking the whole from radar station to Filter Room to control room and back down to sector and airfield was being installed by Post Office engineers. Dowding ordered more frequent tests and exercises then full 24-hour operation of the completed stations as a means of improving operational efficiency and ironing out the flaws in the system. He convened several major conferences during which senior officers of Fighter Command sat with Tizard, Watson Watt and Air Ministry officials. One of the recommendations emerging from these conferences was that Observer Corps sightings of aircraft should not be responded to unless there is a corresponding radar plot conforming it as an enemy formation.

A major exercise was carried out in August 1939 in which hundreds of Bomber Command aircraft, given complete freedom of approach, acted as enemy formations. The new Operations Room at 11 Group was properly tested for the first time. The exercise was only a qualified success, with aircraft numbers still difficult to determine and their height almost impossible to estimate. Ground controllers were, understandably given their lack of experience, hesitant in calling up fighters until they were sure, but all in all, Dowding, unlike some of the Bawdsey staff, was confident that great improvements had been made since the big 1938 exercises. In the face of scientific evidence that the system had not been greatly improved and still left much to be desired, Dowding chose to be optimistic and continued to give 100 per cent support to the programme.[25] Throughout the whole development of radar in Britain it is clear that Dowding's encouragement and unfailing support was a major factor in it being ready, or at least as ready as it could be, by the summer of 1940. There must have been times when optimism faltered, but Dowding knew that if radar could be made to work, even if less than perfectly, it could well be the vital difference that narrowed the gap between Luftwaffe power and British resistance.

There was no disguising the fact that when war broke out on 3 September 1939 the British radar chain was still essentially unfit for purpose. No stations had been fitted out to the final specifications. Most had not yet been properly calibrated to account for its unique location, which made it almost impossible for all but the most experienced plotters to make sense of the data. Possibly most important of all was the failure of the system to detect enemy aircraft flying at very low altitude. The Operations Rooms lacked confidence to make swift judgements and there was general hesitation and delay at all stages of information transfer due to inexperience and uncertainty. The stations themselves lacked adequate spare parts, or indeed even a means of identifying the many parts of the equipment needed when ordering replacements except by lengthy description of the item. Completion of the radar chain and improving the operational performance of the staff was high on Dowding's agenda. With inadequate numbers of aircraft and trained air crews, Fighter Command was already well below the required strength to meet the demands of air defence, and was desperate for any glimmer of hope that the emerging technology would give it an operational advantage.

In November 1939, the first CHL stations came on-line to combat the threat posed by low-flying aircraft. The last link in the chain was ground-to-air and air-to-air communications which was greatly improved by the use of VHF radios. The TR 1133 system that used these new sets, however, was not compatible with the existing system making piecemeal implementation impractical; and so their introduction was delayed until there were sufficient sets available so that whole sectors could be changed over at one time which delayed their use until August 1940, but even so, it was the end of September before an appreciable number of aircraft were fitted out.

On a political level, the ADRC and the Tizard Committees had been dissolved on 21 June after Churchill had overruled Tizard on the issue of Knickebein at a Cabinet meeting some days previously, seriously undermining

Tizard's position and leaving him no option but resignation. Tizard, who maintained a close relationship with Dowding, was much too valuable to let go, however, and was quickly appointed as a scientific advisor to the Chief of the Air Staff. His first job was to investigate the many problems with the radar chain and make recommendations for improvements.

The control and command operations in the Filter Rooms and control rooms were streamlined in accordance with Instruction No. 1 issued in September. Its most significant recommendation was that each aircraft track was assigned a letter and a number which identified it on the plotting table. While the actual radar detection equipment had improved over the months, the way in which information was handled through the Filter Room and control rooms had been given rather less attention. The filtering process required a certain amount of assessment of probabilities and a weighing of the accuracy of information coming in from various sources, which demanded a higher level of operator skills as the amount of information increased. Immediate attention was given to replacing many of the Filter Room staff with more qualified personnel, but recruitment and training bottlenecks prevented rapid improvement.

In March 1940 the new underground Filter and Operations Rooms at Stanmore were completed. These were essentially bomb-proof, but similar facilities at Sector level were very much open to bomb damage and some were put out of action during the Battle of Britain. Radar stations were also, for the most part, open to attack. While money was now available with little restraint, the actual work could not be completed quickly due to manpower and material shortages. Where possible the CH stations, by now thirty in number, were upgraded with new transmitters and new techniques for interpreting radar plots on their screens. Operators were required to ascertain, from the information on their screens, the location of the contact and its height. In order for the Filter Room to make use of this information, the location had to be converted into a map reference, and angles of elevation combined with distance had to be converted into an altitude. This was obviously a process which consumed precious minutes, so an electric calculator was designed by Post Office engineers which speeded up the calculations considerably.

Meanwhile the radar chain had its own problems which Watson Watt, not a man to mince his words, was ever-ready to enumerate in July:

- Aerials were not up to specification
- Calibration of radar sets was incomplete

- Height estimation of the target was difficult
- Estimating numbers of aircraft still only possible by the most experienced operators
- Continuity of tracking a 'plot' through the system was difficult when large numbers of plots were detected
- Displaying the information on the control room plotting table was still confused
- Availability of suitable staff was very limited

Perhaps the one aspect which continued to have the most deleterious effect on operational efficiency during the Battle of Britain was the height problem. This could have been alleviated by the installation of extra antennae at different height on the towers but this entailed recalibration of the all the station's equipment and there was never, at any stage of the Battle of Britain, enough resources allocated to this task.

At the heart of the whole command and control system was Dowding, who micro-managed the whole thing. He had insisted that all information from all the radar stations be channelled through Fighter Command headquarters Filter Room and Operations Room at Stanmore and only after it had been analysed and assessed by a senior officer could the appropriate orders be funnelled down to the fighter stations. Park had praised Dowding for his 'capacity for delegation'[26] by insisting that tactical control should lie with Group or even Sector Operations Rooms rather than with Bentley Priory. Strategic control, however, rested with Bentley Priory which had direct command of the radar chain, the Observer Corps, barrage balloons, searchlights, anti-aircraft guns, rotation of squadrons and air raid warnings. Dowding remained the sole authority in deciding which Sectors should be called on to meet each particular enemy raid, since only Bentley Priory could see the whole picture and control was most efficient when exercised from a single authority. In January 1940, Dowding resisted Air Ministry pressure to force the establishment of Filter Rooms at Group headquarters by, in effect, demanding a vote of confidence in his decision. The Air Ministry feared that Bentley Priory would be swamped and overwhelmed with the sheer volume of intelligence once hostilities broke out leading to 'a time lag ... between the receipt of RDF information and the despatch of the fighters'. Dowding agreed to 'consider the matter'.[27]

An efficient link between ground controllers and pilots was fundamental to the system. Dowding had enormous faith in the abilities of his pilots and tailored his 'system' to give them as much responsibility as was practicable. Controllers had the daunting task of working out which enemy contacts were 'feints' and which would result in an actual raid, in what strength the enemy was approaching and at what altitude. Putting fighters up to intercept too soon or too late or at the wrong height was a constant problem. Aircraft remained under the direction of ground controllers until the enemy was sighted. Once contact was made, responsibility shifted to flight commanders who took complete control of their actions without interference.

The essential feature of the Dowding System was its communications network; the rapid transfer of intelligence into action and the crucial communication 'hubs' underpinning the whole system were the Operations Rooms. These had been located at Group and Sector aerodromes in close proximity to the runways and aerodrome administration buildings which, in hindsight, was questionable since there was no practical reason why they could not have been located a little further away thus avoiding unnecessary risk from bombing. The two factors that may have influenced the decisions were security (all buildings within the secure aerodrome perimeter) and communications (using pre-existing networks), both of which had economic implications. In fact it was the second that proved to be the most serious failing on the increasing number of occasions in late August and early September when bombing of aerodrome administration buildings destroyed power and communications which not only isolated the aerodrome, albeit temporarily, but also, critically, knocked out the Operations Rooms, breaking the link between intelligence and action, putting extra strain on the undamaged stations and inevitably sending up fighters to tackle the burgeoning threat with diminished resources.

Biggin Hill aerodrome was the most seriously damaged, having come under repeated attack from 18 to 30 August. There were many fatalities when administration and accommodation blocks were destroyed. After the raid on the 30th the station was 'silent and the scene was one of complete devastation'.[28] The total loss of communications meant that the Biggin Hill Operations Room, which had been the control centre for Sector C, ceased to exist. Its function was then passed on to Hornchurch which had to carry the extra burden and which itself was the focus of much Luftwaffe attention. At Biggin Hill, the Operations Room staff were moved into an old Victorian house, Towerfields, two miles away, from where they started to integrate back into the system. It was an indication of what other Operations Rooms might have been required to do had the pounding of the aerodromes continued. The system may well have survived further punishment, but there can be no doubt that it would have suffered a major drop in efficiency. One of the popular areas of speculation for historians has been how the Battle of Britain might have had a different outcome if Göring had not altered his strategy by turning away from attacks on aerodromes in favour of the mass 'terror' bombing of London on 7 September, or indeed if he had listened more to Martini and taken less notice of Schmid at the outset.

Chapter 8

Testing the Dowding System to Destruction

I became conscious of the anxiety of the Commander, who now stood still behind his subordinate's chair. Hitherto I had watched in silence. I now asked, 'What other reserves have we?' 'There are none,' said Air Vice-Marshal Park.[1]

Prime Minister Winston Churchill
at 2.35 on 15 September 1940.

The radar chain was far from ready when war broke out and was working at only partial efficiency, but the time was coming when it would be required to perform under real battle conditions. Desperate efforts were made to address all the prevailing issues in anticipation of an immediate attack in September 1939. After Munich Dowding might have been forgiven, in perhaps one of his more pessimistic moods, for giving radar technology a less than ringing endorsement by saying that whatever its shortcomings, '… anything was better than nothing', but his insistence on 'construction, upgrading, expansion, experimentation, training, operational testing and operations' had driven real progress.[2]

Real progress? Possibly, but events were to show how just much more was needed. The Dowding System had its first trial just a few days into the war in what became known as the Battle of Barking Creek. Unfortunately, it did nothing to instil confidence and was more of a timely reminder of serious issues that needed urgent attention. Squadron Leader E.M. Donaldson of 151 Squadron said, 'It had a devastating effect on [the] North Weald Wing.' These North Weald squadrons had been called to action just three days after Prime Minister Chamberlain told the British people that they were at war. Given that air raid sirens had wailed almost as soon as Chamberlain switched off his microphone, the events that unfolded on 6 September should not have been too much of a surprise. Having been on high alert for a couple of days, at just after six in the morning a searchlight battery reported to North Weald Sector HQ that they had spotted unidentified aircraft flying at high altitude over West Mersea. North Weald controller, Captain D.F. Lucking, informed the Observer Corps and ordered twelve Hurricanes to go up and investigate (six from 56 and six from 151). At 06.40, not only did 56 Squadron put up all twelve available Hurricanes instead of the six requested, but a further two reserve aircraft were also airborne a few minutes later. Unbeknown to the other pilots of 56 Squadron, these two followed some half-a-mile astern. This put twenty RAF fighters in the air

Radar and the Observer Corps picked these aircraft up and reported them as twenty unidentified aircraft near Southend. Fearing the worst, Lucking sent up the rest of 151 Squadron's Hurricanes plus eighteen Spitfires of 74 and 65 Squadrons from Hornchurch at 06.45. There were now forty-four RAF aircraft speeding east across the south Suffolk sky. Squadron Leader Donaldson, leading 151 Squadron's Hurricanes, spotted the Hornchurch Spitfires and initially believed them to be hostile aircraft but warned his pilots not to shoot until they had been positively identified as enemy aircraft. The leader of 74 Squadron's Spitfires, Flight Lieutenant Adolf Gysbert Malan, however, turned toward the Hurricanes and gave the 'Tally Ho!' order to attack the two trailing aircraft of 151 Squadron, L1985 flown by PO Montagu Hutton-Harrop and L1980 flown by PO F.C. Rose. Malan claims to have called off the attack immediately, but the three Spitfires of 'A' Flight, flown by leader FO Vincent Byrne, PO Freeborn and Sergeant Flinders, pressed home their attack. Donaldson saw the three aircraft coming, recognised them as 'friendly', and ordered his pilots to hold fire and not retaliate. Instead, they hastily dispersed to avoid the attack, but the tail-enders, Hutton-Harrop and Rose, failed to see the attackers and were hit as the Hurricanes opened fire on them. Hutton-Harrop was killed instantly, shot through the head by Freeborn, and his aircraft glided down to crash at Manor Farm, Hintlesham, just west of Ipswich. Frank Rose's Hurricane had its radiator punctured by Byrne and just managed to make a safe crash-landing at Whersted. Meanwhile, anti-aircraft batteries, manned by young inexperienced soldiers at Sheerness who could not read the Morse code signals being flashed to them from the aircraft, had opened up on 65 Squadron hitting and damaging one aircraft.

In the immediate aftermath Lucking was arrested, as were Byrne and Freeborn as soon as they landed, and a court martial was convened on the spot. The trial was acrimonious with Freeborn and Malan each accusing the other of lying. Freeborn claimed that he had received no order from

Malan to break off the attack and, for his part, Malan argued that Freeborn was impetuous and irresponsible. Anxious to avoid risking an embarrassing exposé, the authorities exonerated both Freeborn and Byrne, but Lucking was quietly relieved of his command with immediate effect. There seems to be no logical reason why this later became known as the Battle of Barking Creek. All anyone can say is that it was such a debacle that it had to be given a name that people associated with music-hall farce (as in barking up the wrong creek). Needless to say, the affair was covered up and such reports as were put out in the press to explain events referred to an enemy incursion that was repelled and praised the 'splendid work' of air raid wardens, assuring readers and listeners that 'Confidence in our system of air defence is very firm.'

During the battle of France in May and June 1940, Fighter Command was obliged to operate well outside the 'Dowding System' with no radar assistance and precious little control. The results were predictably catastrophic with devastating losses of men and machines. As British forces in France went into full retreat and the French Army Air Force was crushed, Dowding resisted pressure from Churchill to send more squadrons to operate from French airfields. He was able, instead, to persuade the Prime Minister to allow aircraft to cover the British retreat and evacuation from Dunkirk

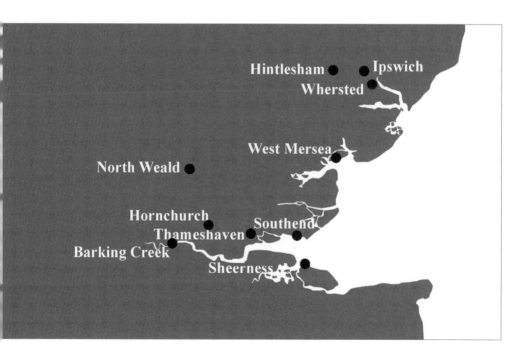

flying from English airfields. The destruction of the French Air Force and the decimation of British squadrons stationed in France was a clear indication of what happened in a modern war to an air force with inadequate early warning systems. The relative ease with which the British squadrons had been routed in France, as a consequence of repeated abandonment of airfields which fell to the advancing panzers and the lack of a coordinated air-defence system, might have instilled into the Germans a belief that Fighter Command was ill-prepared for war and would struggle to oppose a concentrated aerial assault. As confirmation of Britain's unpreparedness to face attack, the Germans had captured a British mobile radar set abandoned at Dunkirk of very basic design and of little practical use. If this was the level of British technological achievement in aircraft detection, far behind even their own rudimentary level, it failed to impress them.

When the Battle of Britain began with the raids on Channel convoys, radar was not the only means of anticipating Luftwaffe movements. Interception of low-grade Luftwaffe radio communications (Sigint) was a vital clue to Luftwaffe intentions and often, by dint of the volume and content of traffic intercepted, gave important indications of the imminence of an attack, the types of aircraft employed and the numbers involved. This information would be received in the Operations Rooms and used to augment and interpret intelligence coming in from radar stations. Sigint, according to 11 Group controller Wing Commander Thomas Lang, proved 'indispensable in providing Park with a clear tactical appreciation of developing German attacks'.[3]

The first attacks came from Luftwaffe bases only minutes from the convoys, the radar screens were able to detect them almost from the moment the aircraft were airborne, but because they were constantly climbing and their height constantly changing it was difficult for the radar operators to estimate at what height the defenders should meet them. In any event, it was only the small number of fighters kept on coastal patrols that had any chance of reaching an adequate combat altitude before the Bf109s struck. Other fighters hastily scrambled in response to radar contacts took the best part of twenty minutes to reach a height that did not put them at a murderous disadvantage against Bf109s attacking from above.

Radar operators were, for the first time, working in real situations which, of course, proved to be quite different in many respects to the training exercises they were used to. It is little wonder that, in these early stages, the estimation of aircraft numbers and height was often mis-reported. One raid was reported as containing just a few more than nine aircraft and turned out to have about eighty which, according to Park, left the defenders 'shot up rather badly' and, in a fine example of understatement, made 'economical fighting very difficult'.[4] Fortunately, the relatively low level of Luftwaffe activity during the Convoy Phase was a boon for British radar operators, giving them a great deal of practice in improving their skills before the much more intense attacks of Adlerangriff. It could be said that the Luftwaffe might have had more success in August if they had waited until they were ready and attacked in force instead of giving the radar operators so much invaluable practice during July.

At first, raids were being detected and met with an inappropriate response. Air Vice-Marshal Park, now in control of 11 Group, complained that he was unable to deploy his fighters in the most effective way because of inaccurate estimations of enemy numbers and feared that the whole RDF system might fall into disrepute if such errors continued. Investigations showed that the mistakes were usually the result of inexperience and lack of training. This situation had developed because, in order to speed up the flow of staff to the ever-expanding number of radar stations their period of training had been reduced; this was reversed with more resources being put in to the training programme.

However, it was not only the interpretation of tracks that was at fault, but Filter Rooms and Operations Rooms were having their own problems in displaying information on their plotting tables. Enemy raids would often comprise a number of formations flying at different heights. For instance, twin-engine Zerstörer Bf110s might fly alongside and ahead of the bombers at 12–15,000ft as close protection, but accompanying Bf109s flying 'top-cover' might be as high as 25–30,000ft. Radar operators were correctly identifying units within a raid as being at different heights but staff in the Filter Rooms were lumping them together as a single plot, which is how they went through to the Operations Rooms. On the plotting table they were all treated as a single formation which gave a false impression to the controllers and sometimes resulted in them instructing defending aircraft to proceed at the wrong altitude. Some pilots temporarily lost confidence in controllers' instructions which, from time to time, sent them into combat too low for comfort and they often added a few thousand feet to their flight path on their own initiative. While estimation of numbers improved with experience, the estimation of height remained problematical throughout the battle, awaiting improvements in the equipment as much as anything else.

Throughout the Battle of Britain, the radar chain was able to detect every major raid, although some smaller incursions were missed. Some of these smaller incursions, however, especially those made by the fast, low-level fighter-bombers of Erprobungsgruppe 210 were far from trivial and this gruppe was often able to strike at major targets before they could be detected and intercepted. Unfortunately for the Luftwaffe, they had too few specialist low-level gruppen to make more use of this tactic. Erprobungsgruppe 210 had been specially tasked with destroying radar stations, but the low weight of the bombs their Bf110s were able to carry meant little permanent damage was ever done and almost all stations continued to operate with full 24-hour efficiency throughout August and September, by which time there were at total of seventy-six stations in operation from Scotland, down the east and south coasts round to Swansea.

In July 1940, General Martini's 3rd Abteilung mobile listening stations (recently moved up to the Pas de Calais) had discovered that the 12-metre band of radio frequency was alive with signals apparently emanating from places on the English coast that coincided with the locations of the tall spindly masts he had long suspected of being part of an elaborate radar chain. The ones at Dover, for instance, were also clearly visible from the French mainland, but the problem for the Luftwaffe, which was never properly addressed in 1940, was that there existed a deep division of opinion about what their function actually was. Martini eagerly advanced his theories, but it was an uphill struggle to convince Schmid and Göring, who seemed to believe that they were radio transmitters for ground to air communications. Kesselring supported Martini's views and between them they eventually managed to persuade Jeschonnek and Göring to give the towers priority on the target list for the Adlerangriff offensive in August, but the attention of the Reichsmarshall was fleeting and he soon lost interest in them.

When Adlerangriff started in August, the radar chain was inundated with information and threatened to break down as had been predicted by Luftwaffe intelligence chief, Schmid. The fundamental flaw in the system, according to a report of 5 August, was that it was trying to fulfil two distinct and separate functions: namely, the early detection of threats and the formulation of a response to them which required different types of information and equipment.[5] CHL radar stations could focus on tracking a single target to facilitate interception, but only at the cost of neglecting to make wider sweeps to detect new incursions. Concentrating on the one meant sacrificing attention to the other. The two functions worked better if they were entirely separate, but that sort of reorganisation was impossible at such short notice; the solution lay in personnel not equipment. Staff learned to be more flexible and not become too 'blinkered' in their approach. They were able to step back from the detail and take a broader perspective of a raid by reporting the 'characteristics of the activity as a whole.'[6] Information was filtered at source before it swamped the Operations Room tables. Just enough of the essential raw intelligence was passed along the line to allow controllers to maintain a sufficient grasp of the overall situation, but all non-essential detail was withheld. Even so there were still occasions when a particular station was told to stop sending reports through to Bentley Priory Filter Room to prevent it going beyond saturation point. Again, the solution was to assess the threat posed by each raid, prioritise and concentrate on those reports that presaged the greatest danger. Dowding ordered that, 'The telling of information in these circumstances must be selective.' A later analysis of the problem by a team set up by Dowding concluded that the problem had been in understaffing of the Filter Rooms.[7]

On 12 August, sixteen Bf110s of Erprobungsgruppe 210 crossed the English Channel at wave-height, under the radar screen. As they reached the coast at Eastbourne in the early morning, they split into four groups and made surprise attacks on the four CH radar stations at Pevensey, Rye, Dunkirk and Dover. Radar trackers detected them but the aircraft had turned and were flying parallel to the coast, which confused the radar trackers and caused them to register the contact as 'undefined', meaning that no interception was made. Pevensey was hit by eight one-ton bombs and suffered major damage, including severance of its main power lines. Rye and Dover were hit next and then Dunkirk received eight bomb strikes. The transmitters at all four stations remained essentially operational despite the accurate hits, but it took some hours before all four stations were working at full capacity again. Meanwhile Sperrle had sent a large force of Ju88s to strike at Portsmouth docks. Fifteen of them with dive-bomber capability broke away and attacked Ventnor radar station, destroying most of the buildings and 'blinding' the station. A mobile transmitter hastily brought in continued to send signals which, although of no use operationally, persuaded Martini's listeners that the station was continuing to operate normally.

Despite Göring's insistence that attacks on radar stations were not profitable and should be discontinued, Ventnor was again attacked on the 16th by Sperrle's Ju87 Stuka dive-bombers of Luftflotte 3. A large raid on Gosport and Lee-on-Solent saw five Stukas peel off and strike at Ventnor again. This time the damage was more serious, with fires breaking out and destroying all the buildings and weakening the towers. The station was put out of action and not brought back into service for a full seven days and even then, a mobile radar station was brought in to resume coverage. On the

18th, thirty bombers struck at Poling CH station dropping ninety bombs and causing extensive damage to buildings and one of the towers. Again, a mobile unit was brought in to maintain radar coverage and while they were much less efficient, able only to act as early warning, they were, to echo Dowding's phrase, 'better than nothing'. On 25 August, Park reported that the damaged stations were now working with 'lash-up equipment', supplying much less comprehensive cover and less accurate assessments of raids.[8] The reduction in reliability of the information coming through to the Filter Rooms made it difficult to differentiate between actual raids and the diversionary attacks which were becoming a more common component of Luftwaffe strategy. Park admitted that the time when he most feared that his 11 Group would falter was when the radar chain was disrupted.

There was little effort put in by the Luftwaffe to 'jam' the radar signals and when they did make an attempt, it was without conviction, and countermeasures such as switching frequencies proved to be more than enough to nullify it. Afterwards, Göring diverted his attention away from the radar masts, apparently adjudging attacks on them to be wasteful of resources and unworthy of continued attention given their resilience to damage. He ordered his Adlerangriff commanders to ignore them in favour of attacks on actual airfields. It is interesting to note how one Stuka pilot describes his mission on 16 August, which clearly illustrates the Luftwaffe's confusion over the role played by the radar stations and their lack of in-depth understanding of how Fighter Command controlled its aircraft in combat. His gruppe was to 'knock out Ventnor radar station on the Isle of Wight which was serving as a British fighter control HQ'. [9]

All throughout the Battle of Britain, British radar plotters were plagued by difficulty in estimating the height of approaching enemy formations. this meant that on many occasions fighters found themselves vectored into positions which put them at a disadvantage, either because Luftwaffe fighters were above them or because bombers could slip through well below them, especially if there was intermittent cloud cover. Official records describe at least thirty-three occasions between the 8 and 18 August when Luftwaffe aircraft had clear and decisive height and numbers advantage over Fighter Command interceptors.

Fighter Command survived Adlerangriff and the ensuing attacks on their airfields, but only just. When the Luftwaffe revised its targeting strategy on 7 September to concentrate on London, the radar stations faced a new problem. Because the target areas were much broader, i.e. London docks as opposed to airfields, bombing could be carried out from a greater altitude which meant that the enemy formations were operating at heights which the CH stations struggled to cover effectively, and at which the Observer Corps struggled to follow – especially in poor visibility. Raids were now much more likely to remain undetected until close to target. Park countered this threat by increasing the number of standing patrols, but this was exhausting for pilots. His other solution was to form specialist units, 421 Flight and 422 Flight, to go out on forward patrol along the anticipated avenues of attack. Individual sorties by reconnaissance Spitfires from Biggin Hill and Hornchurch had been used previously to patrol along anticipated attack lines well forward and at great height, but their r/t equipment was unreliable under such conditions and although they had some success in spotting raids early, their intelligence was rendered useless because it could not be used. The two new Flights were established in late September with new MkII Spitfires using the more reliable VHF TR 1143 sets which allowed the aircraft to report back directly to 11 Group Operations Room.[10] When the first flights operated in early October the results were less than promising, however. Single Spitfires often came into contact with Bf109s flying ahead of their bomber streams and four of them were shot down in the first ten days. This was somewhat ameliorated by sending out pairs of aircraft.[11]

Eventually, the Luftwaffe abandoned their strategy of heavy daytime bombing and adopted a new one of employing fighter-bombers which, with their small bomb load, posed a much-reduced bombing threat, but these often came in at more than 25,000ft and at great speed. They were more of a nuisance than a strategic threat, but nevertheless had to be dealt with. Wood and Dempster claimed that Luftwaffe fighter-bombers approaching at high altitude 'flew too high for detection by the radar chain'.[12] However, in *The Birth of British Radar,* Wilkins counters this suggestion by stating that RDF showed 'no such failings', and that there was 'no fundamental technical reason why performance should be poor at great heights'. He goes on to say that the explanation was that 'the Filter Room at Fighter Command would not accept plots beyond a certain range and, as a result, the RDF operators took no notice of echoes at long range'.[13] By now the threat of invasion had disappeared, at least for 1940, and daytime bombing was reduced to a nuisance level. The night-time Blitz of London was beginning and essentially the Battle of Britain was over. Radar and the Dowding System had played its part; an essential part, in preventing the annihilation of Fighter Command. The story of its creation, growth through many difficulties and implementation with constant danger of breakdown was, in many ways, a triumph of scientific achievement, dogged endeavour and the determination of one man, Air Marshal Sir Hugh Dowding, to champion the cause in the face of sometimes unpromising results and against, at times, considerable internal Air Ministry opposition.

The opposition, however, had not faded away under the glare of Fighter Command achievements in the summer of 1940. The Air Ministry contained many who had agitated for Dowding's dismissal since as early as 1939. Events, sometimes precipitous as in the accident suffered by Air Chief Marshal Sir Christopher Lloyd Courtney which prevented him from replacing Dowding as AOC Fighter Command in February that year, somehow always stifled attempts by the Air Ministry to put a new man in place. The Chief of the Air Staff himself, Air Vice-Marshal Sir Cyril Newall, had embarrassed Dowding on 17 October when he 'ambushed' him at a Bentley Priory conference by allowing Douglas Bader, a mere squadron leader, to openly criticise Park, and by association Dowding himself; but the most galling attack of all had come on 25 September when the Air Ministry tried to force Dowding to make important changes to his system of air defence by introducing Filter Rooms at Group level.

The attack on Dowding was led by Air Marshal Philip Joubert de la Ferté, who had been a fierce critic of his since having been snubbed over the issue of a separate command for radar in 1939 and subsequently continued to criticise Dowding's handling of the whole air defence system. Dowding wrote to Churchill, his most vocal political ally, and received his immediate support. Joubert told Churchill that the Air Ministry was 'alarmed' by the way that the system was apparently 'slowing up', and feared that it would be swamped by any new Luftwaffe offensive in 1941.[14] The issue no longer directly concerned Dowding after 25 November when he was removed from office.

During the winter of 1940/41 Britain was subjected to the night-time blitz offensive when London and other cities suffered incessant bombing, but with a lull in daytime fighting and the lifting of pressure on Fighter Command it allowed some analysis of what became known as the Battle of Britain, and in particular a look back at the part radar had played. Watson Watt was in no doubt that radar had been a key element in survival and Park declared that, at its best, radar had been 'quite invaluable'. Dowding agreed and described it as 'a vital factor in the air defence of Great Britain'.[15]

Chapter 9

The Tizard Committee

> These men were scientists, Britain's best and ... they carried
> with them ... the country's top scientific secrets and [they]
> were on their way to America to give them away.[1]

The friendship between the chemist Henry Tizard and the physicist Frederick Lindemann began in 1908 when they were both students at the University of Berlin, but ran aground in the mid-1930s when they found themselves at loggerheads over British air defence strategy. Lindemann had been born in Germany in 1886 to a German father and American mother. In many ways he appeared European, speaking German and French fluently, and English with a pronounced German accent. Tizard was a year older and exuded British middle-class credentials with a public-school education and a First-Class degree from Magdalen College, Oxford.

Germany was a powerhouse of scientific research, which attracted both men to study there, although Tizard with his reserved, conservative manner shied away from becoming close to the more extrovert and somewhat reactionary Lindemann. Apart from anything else, Tizard's family were not all that well off and Lindemann's confidence was underpinned by a wealthy background. Their relationship seems to have been based on a mutual love and respect for science.

When Britain was galvanised into rearmament after the rise of Nazism, both men were doing scientific research at Oxford. Lindemann had become a confidant of Winston Churchill and they made a 'formidable team,'[2] sharing a fear of German militarism and a contempt for British appeasement, while Tizard was championed by the Director of Scientific Research in the Air Ministry, H.E. Wimperis, and his assistant A.P. Rowe, who were keen to bring Tizard into the Air Ministry fold to oversee aeronautical research which, they felt, was getting nowhere. They persuaded the Secretary of State for Air, Lord Londonderry, to sanction a new 'Committee for the

Scientific Study of Air defence' (CSSAD) with Tizard as its chairman (it would become known as The Tizard Committee), which predictably met with hostility from some quarters.[3] At the insistence of Dowding, it remained under the auspices of the Air Ministry and actually had a significant degree of independence which had the unfortunate, unintended consequence of denying it adequate administrative facilities. Although devoid of executive power, the committee was still able to exercise a measure of influence, not least because of the close ties which had been formed with serving officers. They understood the vital importance of its work, which was to assess the value of all new ideas – especially in air defence. It was the committee's policy of immersing itself in the details of its work before making recommendations which had earned it the trust of senior members of the armed services.

The first meeting of CSSAD was in January 1935, at which committee member Robert Watson Watt presented a number of ideas. For the Air Ministry, the burning issue was detection of enemy aircraft, especially those approaching at low-level. Tizard enumerated all the failings of the current system including the reliance on visual detection of enemy aircraft and the extreme paucity of experimental research into the problem. However, his first report, which was rather scathing in its first internal draft, included a paper by Watson Watt on 'Detection of Aircraft by Radio Methods' which offered some optimistic forecasts when edited for presentation to his political masters.[4] Watson Watt's paper proved to be a turning point in the development of radar detection which went on to play such an important part in the Battle of Britain. The paper led to experiments and eventually funding for research into what became radar. Meanwhile, Lindemann had built up a head of steam over the bomber threat and insisted that not nearly enough was being done to deal with it. He shamelessly used his political connections to inveigle his way onto another committee, headed by Lord Swinton: 'The ADRC' that had executive powers way beyond anything the CSSAD had. Tizard was invited to sit on the ADRC, but it was clear where the power rested. The situation got worse for Tizard after Stanley Baldwin's accession to the Prime Ministership when Churchill was invited onto the ADRC and was sufficiently emboldened to demand, and get, a place for Lindemann on the CSSAD.

In November 1934, almost as an afterthought, Lindemann had ended a submission on the 'Reorientation of the Air Defence System of Great Britain' by referring to 'other means of detecting aircraft' by the reflection of wireless waves, in what was the first documented evidence of government interest in the phenomenon of 'radar'.[5] The study had been requested by the Air Ministry which had examined a total of fifty-three ideas for improving Britain's air defences and found merit in none of them.[6] Up until that point, they had given scant attention to scientific developments in air defence but as a result of the study, a memorandum was sent to members of the Air Council, including Sir Hugh Dowding, outlining the possibility of some form of air defensive equipment utilising radiation to destroy aircraft and recommending the formation of a special committee to strengthen the present methods of defence against hostile aircraft.

Lindemann ruffled the CSSAD feathers with his bluff, no-nonsense, 'I'm right and you're wrong' attitude. Among the things that Lindemann thought he was 'right' about was that radar took up too much of Tizard's time when there were much more promising ideas, such as aerial mines, to pursue. By 1936, Tizard and Lindemann were on a collision course. Lindemann dominated CSSAD meetings with an overbearing attitude and let his political friends know that he resented the fact that too little funding was given to his pet projects while radar ate up much of the budget. Tizard was sensitive to unpleasantness and felt aggrieved that his erstwhile friend should try to undermine him in this way.[7] As German troops were reoccupying the Rhineland, substantial funding was going to radar projects at Bawdsey Manor and Churchill complained to Swinton that Lindemann was being side-lined. Exchanges between Tizard and Lindemann became vitriolic, resulting in two members of the CSSAD resigning.

Swinton was not prepared to leave a rump CSSAD with Lindemann holding the whip, especially since he had been encouraged by the results of recent tests and believed that Tizard's work on radar was vital for the country; there could be no question of progress being held up. His solution was to dissolve the committee and start again with a new membership which excluded Lindemann. Lindemann's involvement with the Air Ministry was paused, much to his chagrin, but he continued to advise Churchill and it was this relationship that would catapult him back into the limelight as Churchill's star rose. Tizard asked Professor Jones to tell Lindemann that he 'should be glad if we could stop this ridiculous quarrel at least for the period of the war and concentrate on fighting the Germans', but Jones reported back to Tizard that his overtures had been met with 'a mild snort'.[8]

In the same year, the Tizard Committee considered a proposal to build a weapon which might create a powerful beam of infra-red electromagnetic radiation capable of heating surfaces at a distance (e.g. an enemy aircraft) and causing the target to explode. A quick calculation confirmed that the power required was way beyond anything remotely available at the time, but the discussion then ranged widely and drew attention to a recent observation made by Post Office engineers. Apparently, radio reception was interfered with whenever an aircraft flew near their radio receivers. This had been known for many years ever since the early days of radio and had been tried out as a means of Atlantic liners detecting icebergs, but only now was it investigated for military use.

A test was carried out using the 49-metre waveband which proved successful in detecting an aircraft flying at 10,000ft. As a result, further research was quickly authorised into radio detection of aircraft. At the same time, research was ongoing into the possibility of detecting infra-red radiation emitted by aircraft engines. While this was shown to be possible, it was also discovered that it would be relatively easy for an aircraft to avoid detection by screening its engines

The committee was advised that there was little point in developing radar as a means of detecting enemy aircraft if no thought was given to ways in which such information could be made use of by British defences. Fighter Command was eager to cooperate given the pessimistic attitude within the service, which accepted that there was little or no current defence against enemy bombers which would 'always get through' to target. Bomber Command, however, was hostile to any suggestion from Tizard that the phenomenon of radio reflection had any relevance to their operations.

At about this time Jones had been appointed as a Scientific Officer at the Air Ministry and occasionally attended meetings of the Tizard Committee. He had studied Physics at Wadham College, Oxford, where he had been tutored by Lindemann, and was now working on infra-red detectors. Historian Max Hastings said of him: 'Dr Reginald Jones [was an] outspoken, combative … assistant director of Air Ministry Scientific research [in 1939]. [He] shines forth as an authentic star in the wartime secret firmament.'[9]

His research had discovered ways of creating 'thermal pictures' of scenes, work which was the foundation of modern 'night-vision' technology. Work was also carried out on infra-red detection of aircraft at close quarters which involved putting the detectors into other aircraft. Problems of heat screening were overcome to some extent and the work showed promise, but it only worked in close proximity to the target. However, the main focus of Jones' research was on radar which, although promising, was shown also to have severe limitations which were described by Lindemann in a memo dated 8 March 1938, in which he wrote:

Though undoubtedly excellent for detecting single aircraft or squadrons thereof, flying together, it seems likely that great difficulties may be encountered when large numbers of aeroplanes are simultaneously in the air. The difficulty may be materially increased if the enemy chooses to blind the operator with [such items as thin wires] each returning an echo just like an aeroplane.[10]

Despite the problems and continuing research into infra-red, radar was considered to be by far the best prospect for detecting enemy aircraft in flight, even though researchers held out little hope of a breakthrough. Professor Jones had by now become critical of the way the work was progressing and, having made himself unpopular with influential members of the Tizard Committee, was shuffled out of the Air Ministry to the radar research station at Bawdsey Manor. Jones was 'very annoyed', especially with Tizard and Robert Watson Watt, to have been inveigled into secret government research which had denied him opportunities to create a published body of his work to enhance his own career and achieve academic appointment.[11] Despite this animosity, Jones was eventually persuaded to have a reconciliation meeting with Watson Watt, who arranged for him to join the Admiralty Research Laboratory at Teddington, a move which Jones interpreted as sending him 'as far as possible from any place where I could cause trouble', and 'a rotten reward for three years of desperate work, from which I could not even recover the kudos of papers in scientific journals.'[12] Lindemann, Tizard and Watson Watt were definitely dropped from Jones' Christmas card list.

Before leaving for his new post however, Jones was side-lined into peripheral work and, as part of that, proposed a method whereby bombers could receive signals from a number of locations and by analysing the signals could pinpoint its position in relation to its intended target. Bomber Command continued to ignore advice and arrogantly claimed that its bombers were quite capable of locating targets at night using conventional methods, which was patently untrue. Jones' idea was simultaneously investigated by Luftwaffe researchers and was later exploited with good results in 1940 by using the X and Y-Gerät navigation beams.

The Tizard Committee, although essentially independent, was unable to remain aloof from politics and found itself ranged alongside Lindemann's much larger ADRC, which threatened to dominate the political research agenda. It fell to Dowding who, with Tizard, had been seconded onto the ADRC to intervene and reassure Tizard that he was not being side-lined or undermined. The ADRC had, to some extent, been created as a sop to Churchill and Lindemann, and there were obvious fears that it was wasting resources by duplicating much of the work of the CSSAD. Criticism reached such a level that the Prime Minister was forced to assure Parliament that there were no fiscal barriers preventing investigation into 'the bomber menace'.

However, with a virtual security blackout on the details of research done by both committees, Parliament became increasingly uneasy as reports on the burgeoning growth of German military strength proliferated. Critics embarrassed the government, which was unwilling to divulge details of its work, and continued friction created an atmosphere of distrust and suspicion that too little was being done. It was not clear, even to the scientists, which avenues of investigation would prove fruitful and policy decisions often failed to integrate into a coordinated strategy. Lindemann, Tizard's main critic, opposed any idea of 'radio detection' and championed a strategy of saturation barrages to fill the sky with miniature exploding shells and 'aerial mines' as enemy aircraft passed through. Lindemann's close association with Churchill, a fierce critic of government defence policy, was considered by ADRC to be a security risk which was addressed and overcome by Churchill's appointment to the committee in the hope that criticism could then be contained 'in house'. As a result, public debate on the issue of air defence became less prominent in Parliament and the press.

The CSSAD was advised that there was little point in developing radar as a means of detecting enemy aircraft if no thought was given to ways in which such information could be made use of by British defences. Fighter Command was eager to cooperate, given the pessimistic attitude within the service which accepted that there was little or no current defence against enemy bombers which would 'always get through' to target. Bomber Command, however, was hostile to any suggestion from Tizard as to how their navigation techniques, or indeed any of their operations, could be improved by radar.

When the threat of war loomed closer with the signing of the Molotov-Ribbentrop Pact on 23 August 1939, the Tizard Committee was confronted with the realisation of just how little they knew about German military research in those areas such as radar, which the committee itself had spent so much time exploring. It turned again to Jones realising that, for all his disconcerting readiness to hold authority to account and point out its flaws, his knowledge and experience was of vital importance when so much time had to be made up so quickly. He was recalled and sent to work with

Air Intelligence, initially at Harrogate, but subsequently at Bletchley Park, or 'Station X' as it was called, where all MI6 secret files were kept.

His first assignment there was to investigate the threat of a German 'secret weapon', evidence for which he searched in vain before realising that the whole 'scare' had been created by virtue of a mistranslation of one of Hitler's speeches. Soon afterwards, he was given a parcel said to emanate from a German spy and delivered through the British Embassy in Oslo (see Appendix A; The Oslo Report). It landed on his desk because, apparently, nobody else had much idea what to do with it given its dubious provenance. Among other things, the parcel contained a glass tube much like an electronic valve, which was said to be a close-proximity fuse for use in anti-aircraft shells. It also contained a surprisingly compendious quantity of information about German scientific and military research which Jones duly passed on to Air Intelligence. Perhaps because of his reputation for being a bit of a 'loose cannon', and having something of a pariah status, Jones was ignored. The report was dismissed by Air Intelligence as a hoax and was duly rejected despite the fuse being technically far in advance of anything the British had. Jones had little choice but to carry on beavering away in his backwater as the rest of Air Intelligence tried to ignore him.

He pressed ahead with his own research into why so little scientific and technical intelligence about German developments was available, but this report did little to repair his reputation and was also 'filed away' without comment. His report is worth looking at more closely since it says much about the work of military intelligence. What, he began by asking, are the aims of scientific intelligence? 'To obtain early warning of the adoption of new weapons by ... enemies', was his answer.[13] Then he considered how such a weapon might be created and concluded that it began with scientific research of an academic or commercial nature, followed by someone looking at its military implications. Then small-scale trials would be conducted before large-scale trials led to adoption. Jones scoured German scientific journals for papers about promising new ideas that then seemed to have no follow-up papers. This was a clue that the subject might have been adopted by the military for further research and, in consequence, subjected to a security clampdown. It pointed to possible lines of inquiry, but naturally made it difficult to find out anything more about them. Acquiring further information about any possible developments required the application of one or more of the following intelligence-gathering techniques: a) an accidental indiscretion, b) blackmail, c) interception of communications, d) capture of a device, e) espionage. Jones favoured interception of communications as the most practical and effective method, but was dismayed to find that there was no current British effort to systematically monitor German signals. He suggested that such an organisation should be set up immediately to listen in to German radio traffic and discover everything possible about new weapons or development of old ones. Assuming that the Germans had similar plans, Jones further suggested that Britain should transmit its own signals to mislead the enemy about British developments, mislead them about the success of their own weapons and, realising that secret communications would be encrypted, to set up a body adept at decryption.[14]

These ideas found favour with all except the Director of Research at the Admiralty who, alone of the intelligence chiefs, refused to support the formation of such a body and his intransigence forced its abandonment.[15] The argument that the Admiralty put forward was that existing scientific staff, rather than new intelligence officers, were best equipped to assess German developments, but in reality, the Admiralty simply had no intention of sharing any of its intelligence with other services. The weakness of their argument was that existing scientific staff could be burdened with memories of their own past failures which predisposed them to resist re-examination of ideas which they had rejected. It was a case of ingrained conservatism and unwillingness to expose themselves to scrutiny and possible embarrassment. The Luftwaffe proved to be equally prone to this kind of wilful blindness when they initially failed to believe that British radar was as far advanced as it was and consequently failed to grasp the fundamental principles upon which Fighter Command operated when controlling its aircraft.

Efforts were made to have Jones removed from intelligence work completely but he pleaded that 'sooner or later something useful would come from [his work]'.[16] He was allowed to stay, but essentially left to work alone. He did not sulk, however, and spent the next few months building up a body of contacts in intelligence. Many subjects of current research crossed his desk, but he was transfixed by a snippet of conversation recorded between captured German airmen, oblivious of the fact that they were being 'bugged'. This was indeed 'something useful', it was the first indication British Intelligence had revealing the existence of the German Knickebein and X-Gerät radio navigation beams.

As part of the ongoing reassessment of Britain's preparedness for war, attention had been drawn to the production of war materiel, in particular the ways in which it might be expanded in the short term and how such production might be sustained in the face of enemy bombardment of the aircraft and armament factories which, it was anticipated, would be almost impossible to prevent. The prospect of military aid from the United States was a distinct possibility, but Britain was still heavily indebted to the US as a result of the First World War. The idea of negotiating a deal with the US was mooted in which materiel and technologies might be traded. In particular, the US Navy had developed a much superior bomb-aiming device which the RAF was anxious to acquire. The question became: what might Britain be able to trade in exchange? In May 1938, The British Admiralty, which had little interest the bomb-aiming technology and lacked enthusiasm for dialogue, given its inherent sense of superiority from the days of Empire, had reluctantly agreed to an informal exchange of information on a quid pro quo basis, but it was quick to raise objections, claiming that 'the gain is entirely to the advantage of the United States'.[17]

It was clear that Britain and the US had many reasons to cooperate, especially given their mutual interests in the Far East, but there were significant political obstacles, not least the powerful 'isolationist' lobby in the US, generally supported by public opinion, which feared becoming embroiled in another major continental war thousands of miles from home. Notwithstanding the US 'neutral' political stance, the military of both countries, especially the navies, began informal discussions about what technologies could be exchanged. Naturally, neither side was keen to give up too much information initially and, as discussions progressed, a sense developed within the British contingent that British technological advances were far superior to anything they were getting in return. The one piece of technology that the British coveted, the American Mark XV Norden bombsight, remained strictly off the table, even though Britain tempted the US with details of their hydraulically powered gun turrets in return.[18] Despite this, and offers to include details of Britain's radar research, the bombsights remained strictly out of bounds, not least because the US doubted that British research was much ahead of their own and believed that there was little that Britain could offer in exchange for the Norden device.

As an interesting aside to these negotiations, as far back as 1937, the Abwehr officer Nicklaus Ritter had travelled to New York and met with a German-born informant, Hermann W. Lang. Lang was a US resident but had not yet been naturalised as an American citizen. He worked in a Manhattan factory producing the Norden bombsight and had access to some blueprints of the device. He agreed to copy whatever documents he could get hold of and duly handed them over to Ritter, who smuggled them out of the country wrapped inside a furled umbrella. More copies of supplementary material were made over time and spirited out of the country inside newspapers until the Luftwaffe had acquired enough information to reconstruct the whole device. The Germans, however, did not actually begin manufacturing the bombsight, but chose to incorporate its main features into a modified version of their own Lothfe apparatus, already in mass production and fitted to their bomber fleets.[19]

Negotiations reached a critical stage after German troops were detected massing on the Polish border in August 1939, which prompted the intervention of British Prime Minister Chamberlain who sent an 'urgent personal request' directly to US President Roosevelt, to 'make use of the magnificent apparatus [Norden Mk XV].' Roosevelt rejected the approach saying that his hands were tied by US neutrality and his military would never sanction release of the bombsight.[20] At the same time, Philip Kerr, the Marquis of Lothian, was appointed Ambassador to Washington and his arrival in the US was to have far reaching and positive consequences for British-US relations. Churchill, who had now been brought in from the political wilderness as First Lord of the Admiralty, took it upon himself to open up direct personal channels of communication with Roosevelt, despite the risk of 'mixed messages' reaching Washington through different diplomatic channels.[21] Churchill, apparently as an unsolicited gesture of goodwill, actually offered to the US details of the British ASDIC (an early form of sonar used to detect submarines) secrets with no reciprocal demands. The British Naval Chiefs, however, refused to comply and demanded the Norden bombsight in return.

Tizard intervened at this stage with a different approach. He could see that political obstacles were threatening to derail vital British-US cooperation and turned to his ally, Nobel Prize-winner Professor Archibald Vivian Hill, whom he asked to open informal talks with US scientists, believing they would be more amenable to reaching an agreement with significant mutual advantages. Hill was posted to Washington ostensibly as an Air Attaché in May 1940, when he set about contacting US scientists from a list that British scientists had compiled for him. Informally, he also made contact with Felix Frankfurter, a close ally of President Roosevelt who thought the President was 'receptive to the idea' of an 'open and frank technical exchange. And promised to 'do everything … to help secure the President's approval.'[22]

Hill reported to Tizard that, in his opinion, the official discussions of trading secrets had little chance of success but he was much more optimistic about his own contacts, which placed national interest above the mistrust and jealousies of military and political negotiators. He told Tizard that in his opinion Britain should make a full and complete disclosure of military secrets to the US and they would reciprocate in kind. Lothian was essentially supportive of Hill's views, but felt that there should be some kind of guarantee of reciprocity first. A second consideration which Lothian pointed out was that Britain would benefit hugely from the US production capacity of war materiel if a fighting war broke out, and a generous approach at this time might ensure further cooperation later. Tizard was very much in favour of an open exchange, but the Admiralty feared that US leaks would ensure that 'anything told to the American Navy went straight to Germany'.[23] For its part, the Army believed that the US had little to trade that was of interest to them.

The German invasion of France and the Low Countries on 10 May 1940 brought Churchill to power in Britain which, in turn, increased the influence of Lindemann who had continued his critical opposition to Tizard, especially after his removal from the CSSAD. On 19 May 1940, Churchill undermined Tizard's position by bringing in Lord Beaverbrook as head of the new Ministry of Aircraft Production and turning to Lindemann as his trusted source of scientific intelligence. Lindemann immediately made his presence felt when he urged Professor Jones to look into the newly discovered Knickebein signals apparently used to aid navigation in German bombers. Dowding had reservations about Knickebein and referred to the evidence for its existence as 'nebulous', Tizard agreed and decried the 'unnecessary excitement' generated by it.[24] When Churchill gave Lindemann instructions to give Jones' work the highest priority, Tizard realised that he was superfluous to requirements and resigned on 26 June.

On 15 May, during a very busy first week in office, Churchill had made his first appeal to Roosevelt for '40 or 50 of your oldest destroyers' to assist with convoy duties. Roosevelt was sympathetic but unable to openly agree because of the US policy of neutrality. He did, however, agree to the sale of twenty new motor torpedo boats.[25] Tizard urged Hill to return to Britain and put the case for cooperation directly to Churchill. Tizard noted that Churchill was not in favour of the interchange of information 'unless we can get some very definite advantages in return.'[26] Which is a little different from his position in September when he had wanted to give up ASDIC secrets with no request for reciprocity. Tizard could see that any agreement at government level was going to be hard to come by. Hill arrived in Britain on 13 June and quickly let it be known that in his opinion, the US had made substantial advances in radar but lacked any coordinated means of rapidly developing it. He described a fetish of secrecy on both sides of the Atlantic.

On 28 June Churchill cabled Lothian to 'impress on [the] President and others that if this country were successfully invaded and largely occupied … some Quisling Government would be formed to make peace on the basis of our becoming a German Protectorate.'[27] Churchill's subsequent attack on the French fleet at Mers-el-Kebir was meant to indicate to Roosevelt the level of commitment the British had to opposing the Germans, but in the face of strong isolationist feelings within the US population, Roosevelt still was unable to openly make any commitment of support.

When Hill returned from the US in June, he had found the mood in Britain somewhat altered. Jones had produced clear evidence that the Germans were using radio detection as well as an advanced Knickebein system of guidance for their bombers and the fear was that German technology was well in advance of what had been assumed. This prompted many within the Air Ministry, including the Secretary of State for Air Archibald Sinclair, to believe that Britain now had little to lose by opening up to the US with all their military secrets, since the Germans themselves seemed so advanced. Even Churchill agreed to widen the terms of negotiation by sending a special technical mission to the US with instructions to deliver 'specific secrets and items of exchange'. Lothian assured everyone that such an approach to Washington would be met with equal candour. He was authorised to contact Roosevelt directly on 8 July to suggest that there would be a 'secret British Mission bringing full details of all new technical developments, especially in the radio field'. When Lothian mentioned 'short waves' later in the telegram, he was referring to research which had been carried out in Britain on the cavity magnetron, invented by John T. Randall and Henry A.H. Boot at the University of Birmingham, of which the US had no knowledge but which would prove to be the single most important item in the exchange.[28] The device was a revolutionary development in radar research, having the capacity to operate at much higher power and frequencies, thus allowing much shorter wavelengths and making it suitable for small antennas which could be mounted in aircraft.

During their early research into radar detection, British scientists realised that in order for it to work effectively the radio beam would have to be very narrow and of high frequency. This meant, in effect, shortening the wavelength of the beam. This shorter kind of wave, if it was going to be of practical use, would need to be generated by a very compact and powerful energy source. A combination of careful research and inspired guesswork resulted in a cavity magnetron, a device which looked something like the cylinder of a 6-shot revolver, but which produced the required 10cm waves with sufficient power to be useful.[29] It is difficult to overestimate the importance and revolutionary consequences of this discovery which, simply put, made radar possible. By early June 1940 a fully functioning prototype had been built but, having invented it, the problem was that Britain did not have the means of producing such devices on a scale that would allow them to exploit it to full advantage quickly enough with the Luftwaffe now poised in northern France ready and waiting to attack.

Roosevelt responded to Lothian's appeal by sending a personal representative, William J. Donovan, to London with instructions to assess the prospect of British survival if the Germans decided to launch an offensive.[30] All doors were opened to Donovan when he arrived and what he heard and saw encouraged him to report back to Roosevelt that Britain, he thought, had a more than even chance of holding off the Germans. The US military thought otherwise and were wary of making any move towards actively supporting Britain or exchanging military secrets. US scientists, however, were generally of the opposite opinion and were eager to make unofficial contact with the British with a view to lobbying Roosevelt to go ahead with the exchanges. On 22 July, Lothian received word from the White House that Roosevelt would be glad to receive the British mission at the earliest opportunity for a full and free interchange of technical information. Despite the wording there remained doubt about the US military's willingness to give up its Norden bombsight technology, but the signs were encouraging, and plans were made for an early meeting.

In Britain, meanwhile, there had been more resignations from the CSSAD. Feverish consultations with a number of eminent people, including Lindemann, failed to come up with anyone willing to lead the mission to Washington. Watson Watt was suggested but was deemed 'insufficiently diplomatic'.[32] Churchill brought in his 'fixer', Lord Beaverbrook, to find the right man and Beaverbrook was quick to see that Tizard, eminently qualified and available now that his committee had been dissolved, was the perfect choice. Tizard was less than enthusiastic at first, fearing that he was being shunted into a cul-de-sac and would be simply a figurehead with no negotiating position, especially when the armed services disdainfully responded to requests for representatives to join in the mission by sending officers of junior rank. Churchill intervened by insisting on more senior officers and went further, instructing all armed services to prepare lists of technology that could be offered to the US with no holds barred. Tizard was encouraged by this show of support and agreed to lead the mission.[33]

As details of Tizard's mission were being drawn up it became clear that it was going to be difficult to convince the US that Britain had all that much to offer. Britain thought their radar technology was the key, but while radar was of interest to the US, it was of much less importance given their relative geographical isolation and immunity from attack. The US had, instead, compiled a list of information and equipment they were willing to trade against a similar list of British developments they were interested in. The list which they sent to Britain on 2 August was extensive, not to say exhaustive, but only in the areas of British research. It had little to say about what the US would give in return. Churchill, notwithstanding his eagerness for US involvement in the war, was not impressed by their reticence to discuss the Norden bombsight. Powerful voices in the British military and the War Cabinet led by Lord Halifax, however, persuaded him, on 6 August, to acquiesce and agree to authorise a British Technical Mission to the United States which would have full authority to disclose all secret information in the possession of His Majesty's Government.

The personnel for Tizard's mission comprised, for the Army: Brigadier F.C. Wallace; for the Navy: Captain H.W. Faulkner; for the RAF: Group Captain F.L. Pearce; a Cambridge scientist, John Cockcroft; a radar specialist, Edward Bowen; and Arthur Woodward-Nutt of the Air Ministry to act as secretary.[34] Tizard was clear, in the minutes of the first meeting of mission members, that while full cooperation would be given in areas where considerable mutual expertise was apparent, there were still areas in the early stages of development, such as jet engines, where information would be disclosed only when it was clear that the US was responding in kind.

All documents and equipment that would need to be presented to the US were collected and stored in a large black deed box about the size of a suitcase. The most important item in the collection was the cavity magnetron, but Tizard was clear that it would be held in reserve as a last bargaining chip in the negotiations. On 13 August, the deal for destroyers was effectively signed off by Churchill and Roosevelt and on the 28th, a thousand British crewmen were boarded onto the liner *Duchess of Richmond* at Liverpool, along with the members of Tizard's mission, to set sail across the Atlantic. Tizard and Pearce flew to Newfoundland separate from the other members of the mission. The US acquired access to British military bases in Canada and the Caribbean in return for the destroyers.

When negotiations got under way in Washington a serious problem emerged in the guise of patent rights. Many of the technologies used by the

US military were produced and used under licence from private industries there. It was made clear that where technology, whether involving the whole or part of a device, was subject to a patent, the British would have to negotiate separately with the manufacturers and come to a financial agreement with them directly. The next hurdle was soon evident when the US naval chief Admiral Anderson categorically stated that the bombsight was 'off the table'.[35] While this irked Tizard, he was not disheartened because by now it was clear to him that the most important aspect of his mission was to utilise the manufacturing capacity of US industry to deliver the military materiel that Britain so desperately needed but was unable, under its current wartime restrictions, to produce. Tizard had a private meeting with Roosevelt at the White House when the President assured him of his best intentions but explained that an open policy of support for Britain could cost him the election in November. Roosevelt explained that the greatest fear the US had was that they might hand over the Norden bombsight technology only to have it fall into German hands if it was recovered from a downed RAF bomber. Tizard asked that at least he be given the dimensions of the device so that modifications to British bombers would allow rapid deployment if it became available.

Once discussions were underway it became clear that US radar technology was ahead of the British in a number of important areas. They had developed a sophisticated system for separating outgoing radio pulses from their echoes and built it into their SCR-268 radar system.[36] The British had built separate towers at their radar stations, one for transmission and one for reception, but the US system required a single 'duplexer' which alternated between transmission and reception to give a clear 'echo' signal unaffected by the powerful transmission signals, thus giving a much clearer picture of an intruder. Having been granted leave to examine this system in detail, the British contingent were much more confident that cooperation was going to be at a gratifyingly high level. In return the British gave details of their IFF system which, based on radar, was used to identify friendly aircraft from the enemy on radar screens.

The British were now ready to open their box of tricks for US perusal. This box, containing documents and devices such as the cavity magnetron, had remained in England, but was now taken on board the Canadian ship *Duchess of Richmond* at Liverpool by a radar scientist Edward Bowen. For eight days Tizard nervously monitored the ship's progress through U-boat patrolled Atlantic waters. The *Duchess* was fast, but nevertheless, travelling unaccompanied, it had to constantly make small changes to its course to avoid contact with U-boats as it made its way to Halifax, Nova Scotia. It eventually arrived safely on 6 September.

The first full meeting of British and US delegations took place three days later when Tizard made sure that, to avoid any discussion of patent rights, none of his team was authorised to enter into any detailed discussions with any non-military members of the US team. While the British were ready and willing to discuss radar technologies, the US had a much broader agenda inquiring about a range of technologies, much of it concerning information gleaned from captured German equipment. The first week saw a significant amount of information exchanged and both sides seemed satisfied with progress, but the cavity magnetron remained firmly under wraps. The US, however, had a sense that the British were holding something back, as indeed they themselves were in the form of the Norden bombsight. Bowen eventually pulled the rabbit out of the hat during the second week and the US side, although having some idea of what was coming, were astounded by the technical sophistication of the cavity magnetron.

This changed the whole complexion of discussions as both sides now opened up with full disclosure. The US wanted to immediately go ahead with industrial production. The cavity magnetron was set to become one of the most important technological developments of the 1940s with a number of important applications not just militarily, but also domestically in, for example, microwave ovens. Unfortunately, the British had not applied for a patent on the device and on 24 October 1940 the US company RCA did so, thus depriving Britain of the massive financial benefits of having invented it.

Tizard returned to Britain on 2 October, satisfied that his mission had been a success even though the US did not deliver up its secret Norden bombsight until 1942, when it was installed in British bombers for the first time. In the US companies such as Bell Telephone Laboratories and RCA immediately set up industrial production facilities at a time when the nation was going to the polls. When Roosevelt was re-elected, the brakes were off. The US factories started a massive programme of war production, much of which was bought by Britain and much more besides would find itself on the continent of Europe on 6 June 1944. The cost for Britain, however, was immense. The whole of its dollar and gold reserves were spent before the end of 1940, but a full wallet would have been of no use to Britain if it had not succeeded in convincing the US, over the course of a few summer months in the summer of 1940, that it was capable of resistance and possible eventual victory.

While it was of small significance in 1940, the Tizard committee had coordinated research into nuclear fission. Many refugee scientists from occupied Europe worked with British researchers and made the crucial calculations that showed how it could be achieved using Uranium-235, opening up the potential for the production of a bomb of enormous power. Tizard had agreed to full disclosure of this information in his discussions in Washington in 1940. The US, while not unaware of the science, had done little up to that point in the way of nuclear research. It would not be until the Japanese bombing of Pearl Harbor that the US would step up to full war production and it was at that time that work began in earnest with the 'Manhattan Project' to produce the Atomic Bomb.

Chapter 10

Enigma

> Intelligence gathering is not a science. There are no certainties
> even when some of the enemy's correspondence is being read.[1]

Battle of Britain narratives have often claimed that Bletchley Park was routinely breaking 'red' Luftwaffe Enigma codes in 1940. There is some truth in that, but without qualification it has tended to give a misleading impression. Some Luftwaffe signals were certainly intercepted and decrypted but there was a time lag between one and the other because of the complexity of the decryption process. For instance, there was never any possibility of Enigma decrypts being completed in time to be of any use in predicting attacks. Furthermore, all important, high-level, Luftwaffe communications tended to go through fixed land lines, leaving Enigma machines to be used primarily for low-grade signalling such as weather reports, transport and movement orders. Last but not least, because of the secrecy surrounding the work at Bletchley Park, when operational decision-makers were given 'Boniface' material they tended to treat it with some scepticism, being unaware of its provenance and because many of them had a low opinion of the intelligence-gathering services at the best of times. Perhaps the most that can be said of Bletchley Park's work on Enigma is that 'In the first two years of war … it lit a candle of hope about what the codebreakers … might accomplish in the future.'[2]

Where military installations were static, all communication was by fixed telephone lines which, although not invulnerable to 'tapping', were generally quite secure. For mobile units, which were becoming more prevalent within the armed services, however, there were no fixed lines and all communications were by radio, whose signals were much more easily intercepted. It was necessary, therefore, to translate messages into code (encryption) that hid their meaning from all except those for whom the message was intended and who had the means of deciphering them (decryption).

A great deal of effort has always been invested in building and trying to break into such communication networks. The German military adopted and developed a commercial encryption machine which they called 'Enigma'. Throughout the 1930s other countries, most notably Poland, made strenuous efforts to 'break' the Enigma codes. It is worth repeating here Professor Hinsley's remarks at the start of this book and noting how these general principles apply to Enigma: 'Information has to be acquired; it has to be analysed and interpreted; and it has to be put into the hands of those who can use it.' Intercepting the traffic and breaking the code was only the first step. Next came the problem of interpreting the information and fitting it into an overall picture of enemy operations and intentions. Then last, but not least, was the problem of using the information in ways that did not alert the enemy to the fact that their communications were being intercepted and their codes broken.

The First World War saw a huge increase in the volume of secret military radio communications. This was a relatively new phenomenon and there was a serious shortage of trained operatives to handle both encryption and decryption. The different levels of competence at this time is illustrated by the 'Zimmermann telegram affair'.[3] The German government, in the person of a top civil servant Arthur Zimmermann in January 1917, sent a telegram to Heinrich von Eckardt, the German Ambassador in Mexico, instructing him to persuade the Mexican government to form an alliance against the United States to divert their attention from the war in Europe. The message began: 'We intend to begin on the first of February unrestricted submarine warfare....' Since all transatlantic telephone lines had been severed, they had to send this message, in code, through the US diplomatic wireless cable service in Copenhagen. This service used a relay station at Porthcurno in Cornwall which was routinely listened into by British Naval Intelligence. Being in possession of a German diplomatic code book captured in Mesopotamia in 1915, the British quickly decrypted the message but hesitated to make its contents public for fear of exposing their surveillance of German diplomatic communications. The text of the decrypted message was surreptitiously leaked to the US in March, at which point Zimmerman, somewhat bizarrely, publicly acknowledged that the telegram was genuine. The consequences for the German war effort were not good.

It was not only the military, but also diplomatic agencies and commercial organisations who were anxious to maintain secrecy about their activities. Interest in, and the use of, encrypted communications grew during the 1920s with Germany, in particular, taking huge strides in protecting secrecy.

Just before the end of the First World war in 1918, Arthur Scherbius, a German electrical designer from Frankfurt, had patented an ingenious and complicated cipher machine which he called 'Enigma'. He was immediately contacted by German Naval Intelligence for a demonstration. They were impressed, but at that stage of the war they could not afford to buy the large number of machines required to transform the whole naval communications network. Scherbius then tried to sell it to the German government for encryption of diplomatic communications, but they too lacked the means to take advantage of it. Scherbius was a businessman and naturally anxious to benefit financially from his invention so he bought the patent of another machine, this time Dutch, and incorporating the best features of both machines into an improved Enigma, he formed a company, Chiffriermachinen Akteingesellschaft, to manufacture and market it focusing initially on the Polish and Swiss governments.

When the war ended the German armed forces were reduced to a small fraction of their former size and Scherbius hoped that the Navy might reconsider now that it had a much smaller establishment. His persistence paid off when, in 1924, the German military had reasserted itself, albeit clandestinely, and agreed to buy a small number of Enigmas for Army and Navy intelligence services. Trials proved successful and the Enigma was adopted in 1928 for use throughout the services.[4] Unfortunately, Scherbius was not able to enjoy the fruits of his labours for very long. He was killed in 1929 in an accident involving a horse and carriage.[5]

Polish Intelligence had, for obvious reasons, been maintaining close scrutiny of German resurgence since the early 1920s and had routinely intercepted and decoded their secret military communications. Many European countries were developing more sophisticated encryption methods for military and diplomatic communications and they were all aware of Scherbius's Enigma machine which they admired for its sophistication and complexity, but none were interested in adopting it believing, with patriotic fervour, that their own systems were perfectly adequate. In 1931, while the Germans were in the process of testing and evaluating the Enigma machine, Hans-Thilo Schmidt, a German cipher clerk looking to make some money, offered to sell a book of German military 'keys' to French Intelligence. These 'keys' described the configuration of machine settings used to encrypt messages and were of immense importance in understanding how to break the encryption. The French, like the Poles, were motivated to keep a very close eye on German military developments and accepted Schmidt's offer of trade. Unfortunately, they discovered that the information Schmid provided was only useful in the encryption of messages and they could see no use for it in the decryption process. The head of the French cryptanalytical bureau, Captain Gustave Bertrand, wondered if maybe the Poles, whom he knew to have been working on German codes for many years, might find it useful. Three Polish mathematicians, Marian Rejewski, Jerzy Różycki and Henryk Zygalski, had spent years studying how to break German codes. They had been familiar with Enigma machines since one January day in 1929 when a commercial type had been impounded by Polish Customs and handed over to their intelligence service.[6] Bertrand passed the intelligence over to them on the understanding that any developments would be shared. When the Poles saw what they were getting, it was a revelation and proved to be a complete breakthrough in their work, allowing them to make huge progress. For a few years the two agencies were then able to work together, the Poles providing the mathematical and technical skills to break the codes and the French analysing the decrypted texts. At the time the British remained aloof, believing that trying to break the 'unbreakable' Enigma code was a waste of time.

Over the next few years, the Poles were able to routinely break the German codes and follow the development of their encoding procedures using a 'bomby', which consisted of six replica Enigma machines in combination. The whole process of decrypting Enigma communications at Bletchley Park during the Second World War owed an enormous debt to the Polish analysts who made many fundamental breakthroughs throughout the 1930s and laid the foundations for one of the most important operations contributing to the defeat of Nazi Germany.

On 15 December 1938, however, the Germans vastly increased the complexity of their communications by introducing two extra wheels, any three of which may be used at any one time. This development launched the process of decryption into an entirely new sphere of difficulty, forcing the Poles to look for means beyond their own resources. In March 1939, the British and French governments had given a security guarantee to Poland which inexorably tied the three countries into a military alliance and this binding of mutual support encouraged the Poles to approach French and British Intelligence in a bid to pool their efforts. A meeting was held at Pryn, near Warsaw, which the British still thought was a waste of time and showed little interest, but when the Poles demonstrated how their bomby worked the whole mood changed. The British and French delegations were convinced of the importance of the work. The Poles gave each of them a replica of the most up-to-date Enigma in use by the Germans.

The British replica was taken to the secret GC and CS at Bletchley Park. After the fall of Poland, Rejewski, Różycki and Zygalski and a dozen other cryptanalysts fled to Bucharest and requested asylum through the British Embassy. The British prevaricated, weighing up the advantages against the security risks of having Poles working at Bletchley Park. Frustrated by delays, the Poles then turned to France and ended up in Paris where they went to work at 'Station Bruno' in the Château de Vignobles at Gretz-Armainvillieres, just north of Paris. From there they made their first important breakthrough in January 1940, but when the signals were analysed, because of the time it took to decrypt them, they were found to be out-of-date and of low-grade material. Zygalski had devised a method of decryption using perforated sheets which, when placed one upon the other began to indicate patterns in a text. Using these sheets, a British mathematician, Peter Twinn, was the first Briton to decrypt an Enigma message. British Intelligence, in January 1940, made an urgent plea to the French to have Różycki, Zygalski and Rejewski sent to England to work with Twinn but the French would not allow them to leave.[7] However, the important fact was that the codes had been broken but further promising progress was halted when France also fell to the German war machine.

The Polish codebreakers were evacuated first to Paris where they succeeded in decrypting detailed messages warning of an attack on the capital by the Luftwaffe but then had to flee, with the staff of French Intelligence, to the south of France, the Poles setting up in the Château des Fouzes between Montpellier and Avignon.[8] The British were not happy about the Poles remaining in France, fearing that exposure would completely undermine their whole Bletchley Park operation, but they had little choice but accept the risk. Had any one of the Poles been captured, even if they did not give up their Enigma knowledge, it would have been quite impossible for the Allies to know if henceforth the Enigma intelligence was still genuine or if it had been compromised and manipulated to deceive.

Intercepts of German Enigma messages which had been collected by British Army personnel working in an old naval fort complex at Chatham, in the Thames Estuary, were routinely sent to Bletchley Park by motorcycle couriers during the first months of war, but with no means of decryption they were merely filed away. The staff at Chatham, mostly female, had a tedious and difficult job to do. Unaware of what, if any, use was being made of their laboriously collected transcripts, they struggled with two essential difficulties in their work. First, there was the problem with actually hearing the signals through their headsets. Such signals might be faint or interrupted according to atmospheric conditions and required 'a sensibility and delicacy of hearing that can only be gained by long experience';[9] and second, understanding which messages were more important than others so as not to waste time intercepting and transcribing communications of little interest. Straining to hear the fainter transmissions was exacting and exhausting work. The problem was to identify the very weak signals which would fade out with the slightest drift in frequency.[10] Operators listened-in on particular frequencies, but the most important frequencies could only be determined over time. The location, or at least the direction from which the signal was coming, was also of significance in determining its importance. The importance of each intercept had to be quickly assessed, but this required a great deal of experience. Sebag-Montefiore noted that, 'The margin between breaking Enigma and failing to do so [is] already so slender because Enigma traffic is so light that the task of breaking the code is exceptionally difficult.'[11]

By looking at a typical message sent from one military unit to another in the same network, the complexity of the work and skills required of the listeners is clear to see. It might include:

- Call sign (identifying the sending unit and intended receiving unit) changed daily for every unit
- Time (of transmission)
- Number of characters in text
- Whether the message was complete or part of a larger message
- A 'discriminant' indicating the type of traffic (level of command, type of military unit etc.) and which 'key' to use
- An 'indicator setting', which was a procedural setting
- The enciphered text in blocks of five letters

The cypher clerk intercepting the transmission would record each letter and then might augment the whole by including information pertaining to the intercept such as:

- Radio frequency of transmission
- Date and time of intercept[12]

When each transcript was analysed by the Bletchley Park cipher clerks their task was almost overwhelmingly complex requiring, above all, knowledge of the individual machine settings used out of a staggeringly high number of possible combinations. Each operational unit of the German armed forces had its own Enigma setting within its communications network which operated on an assigned frequency.

The 'call sign' of a message, which were changed daily, would inform the recipient about the identity of the unit sending it and which, if any, other units would be receiving the message also. Intercepted messages allowed British Intelligence to start, with painstaking deliberation, to build up an understanding of the German armed forces structure and the different types of traffic used in their radio networks. Slowly patterns emerged. It was soon discovered that the call signs were repeated month on month, which proved to be an exploitable weakness in the system.

Understanding the way in which communications were handled in the German armed forces was crucial to deciphering messages. The same Enigma machine might be used for different levels of communication and the operator needed to know which traffic was specifically for his unit. This was made clear by the 'discriminant' which told the operator which 'key' to use. If he did not have that key then the traffic was not for his unit. Security was in the key, which differed according to the type of traffic. At first, the encoded part of intercepted messages was totally unintelligible, but analysis revealed that any ranking officer mentioned in the message would be given his full rank and unit and the sender of the message would also give his full rank at the end. This offered important clues as to how the encoding machine had been set up. Daily discriminants were then analysed and found to fall into a number of different categories which analysts marked with different colours: red, blue, brown, orange and green. The green transmissions were usually of medium frequency which were difficult to pick up at Chatham due to their short range. The French, however, were able to identify these 'green' messages as all coming from German Army units.

All encryption processes involved the use of a key which was, essentially, the means by which encryption was implemented. The Enigma employed a hugely complex means of encryption which encouraged its users to believe in its total operational security. Ability to decipher an encrypted message depended on knowing the key that had been instrumental in the original encryption process. Keys were issued to stations for a month at a time with each key valid for twenty-four hours, changing at midnight. No information about the key was included in any of the messages.

At this time the German Enigmas used three wheels which could be inserted in any order. These wheels determined how the internal mechanism of the Enigma would function in the process of encoding a message. As well as a change of order, the wheels could be set initially in a number of rotational positions which would leave a particular letter showing at the top. Before coding a message it was necessary to record the position of each wheel and the letter each was displaying at the top. A third component of the key is a 'cross-plugging board' (steckerboard) in which letters of the alphabet are 'steckered', or connected to other letters by inserting electrical connectors (plugs) into the appropriate sockets. All three settings must be known in order to decode the message later, which is done by reversing the electrical current through another Enigma machine with the same key settings. Each section of the German armed services (network) used its own specific key which was changed at regular intervals. There were many networks, each with its own assigned radio frequency so that any message transmitted could, in theory, be picked up by any other station in the network. In order to avoid congestion, a control station would ensure that only one message was being transmitted on that network at any one time. There were also protocols for transmitting signals between different networks so that all became part of a whole.[13]

By the end of 1939 a number of things were clear to British analysts. Breakthroughs in analysis of intercepted messages was making cipher clerks increasingly confident that eventually the whole Enigma traffic would be readable, but the work of recording intercepted messages had to be absolutely accurate for the information to be useful to the analysts. Difficulties in interception of signals (sometimes faint or interrupted) and occasional lapses in concentration by listeners did not make this any easier. Finally, the volume of traffic being intercepted during a time of 'phoney war' indicated a requirement of a much larger staff to cope with the expected increase in the volume of traffic if the war 'hotted up'. It was clear that Chatham could not possibly accommodate the extra personnel, so new listening posts were established which included one specifically dealing with Luftwaffe signals. Luftwaffe traffic was designated 'red', but this also included Army-air communications which were so important to the German 'Blitzkrieg' strategy. Indeed, Guderian's Panzer Division used the 'red' key during their advance in May 1940.[14]

The Enigma had space for three wheels, each with a series of studs on one side, each of which was arbitrarily connected internally by a wire to a pin on the other side of the wheel which then made a connection with a stud on the next wheel. A typewriter keyboard was connected in such a way that every time a letter was depressed one of the wheels would move forward by one stud. When this wheel had moved a full revolution, it would click the next wheel forward by one stud.

Encryption was enacted by an electric current which ran through the studs and wires as a key was depressed and this illuminated a letter at the other end of the circuit. In this way a letter of text was converted into a letter of encryption. The next letter depressed would create a different circuit, one or more wheels having been turned, and so each encrypted letter was created by a different series of electrical connections. The receiving machine could be set up to reverse the encryption process, but it required knowledge of the original setting of the sender machine.

When trying to break the encryption of any message it was necessary to know the original position of each of the three wheels prior to transmission. Using a combination of cloned Enigma machines, the Polish cryptographers could take an intercepted encrypted message and try out all the possible combinations of wheel settings until it produced a message in plain German text and that would indicate which wheel setting had been used to encrypt the message and give them the key. The key was changed daily so this process had to be followed every day.

The steckerboards used by the German armed forces expanded the number of possible settings of the machine to a staggering extent (over 200 trillion). Polish cryptanalysts who had come to Britain in September showed how their idea of a synchronised array of Enigma machines, named a 'bomby' (so called, said one Bletchley Park wag, because its mechanism 'ticked' as it worked) could be used to break the codes. This bomby could analyse the enormous number of possible steckerboard combinations in less than a thousandth of a second. Two bombes were installed at Bletchley Park, exclusively used for breaking the many networks in the 'red' traffic.

Before work could begin on decrypting the message texts, they had to come to Bletchley Park from Chatham by motorcycle despatch rider, whose contribution to the whole Enigma narrative 'has never been properly recognised', since teleprinter facilities were 'utterly inadequate to handle so much volume'. The use of teleprinters was restricted to transmission of those messages that were expected to be of particular interest (referred to as 'Welchman Specials'). Chatham was given descriptions of the kind of message that might fall into this category, such as messages emanating from the same location at the same time each day (believed to be daily orders).[15] 'Red' traffic was handled at Bletchley Park in 'Hut 6', initially under the leadership of John Jeffreys, but run by Gordon Welchman after May 1940. Hut 6 had only thirty staff in January but saw a huge increase in staff working a 24-hour shift rota during the early months of 1940. A complex process of analysis usually resulted in the discovery of the day's 'red' key during the early hours of the following morning, which then allowed transcription of the original text. The problem now was how to make sense of the decrypted text, which might simply be a series of numbers or code words. British Army and Air Force Intelligence were quick to respond by setting up units at Bletchley Park in 'Hut 3', while in London, MI8 was set up to study German radio networks. Hut 3 performed 'the immense task of analysing ... and squeezing from it [Hut 6 decrypts] the last drops of intelligence'.[16] The staff of Hut 3 were all fluent speakers of German, unlike those of Hut 6 where there was no such requirement.

Just before the Germans attacked France on 10 May, the preamble of all German communications traffic changed by the addition of a three-letter group. At a stroke this 'blinded' British Intelligence, but two important failures of German procedure allowed Bletchley Park to very quickly start breaking the new codes. Cryptographers were able to make use of a particularly lazy practice of Enigma operatives, which allowed them to make huge assumptions about the contents of a new key which more often than not were correct and allowed them to break the key quickly. One codebreaker, John Herivel, assumed that Enigma operators might be inclined to shorten the tedious process of setting up their machines before each message by simply ignoring best practice and, when inserting the prescribed wheels for the day, would place them in the most convenient way and leave them in that position rather than spinning them to randomise the position. Consequently, when the operator sent the three letters by Morse to the person at the other end, enabling them to set their machine to the same start position, he actually sent, in clear (un-coded) text, the key for that day.[17] Using this 'Herivel tip', the 'red' key was broken only ten days later.[18] The other breakthrough was uncovering the practice of Enigma operators using obvious message settings, which made the task of working out the day's wheel order considerably less onerous.

Such laxity of procedure was the Achilles heel of the German Enigma. The Germans had immense confidence in the security of Enigma traffic, believing that the complexity of its design would defy any attempt to undermine it and they saw no reason to make any serious effort to test that theory by trying to break their codes themselves. One of the consequences of this complacency was that they did not routinely monitor operator practices and did not demand sufficiently strict operating procedures. As a result, operators developed the sort of lazy habits described above.

The Luftwaffe, in particular, was notoriously prone to short-cuts in procedure. One of their main preoccupations, and one which populated much of their communications, was weather forecasts for which they used uncomplicated code to save time. Although the code changed every day it was soon observed that the code was always the same as the connections in the steckerboard, so if one was broken then they both were. As early as 20 May, the Bletchley Park teams had broken the new coding and were able to read 'red' traffic again. It should be noted that while 'red' codes were being routinely broken, 'blue' naval communications were still very resistant to decryption because of much tighter control of operating procedures. As a consequence of British efforts to break Enigma codes it was realised that encrypted British military communication procedures had to be strictly enforced and so were routinely monitored throughout the war to ensure that all rules were meticulously observed.

None of the decrypted Enigma 'red' signals had given any indication that an invasion was being considered by the Germans, but in August the code-name Seelöwe started to appear, indicating that a large operation was being planned. This was conveyed to Prime Minister Churchill who initially discounted it, but when informed of the source accepted it; he insisted, however, that any British communications should refer to Seelöwe as 'Operation Smith', so that any security lapse would not compromise the Enigma work. Unfortunately, there was an existing low-grade operation of the same name (Smith) run by a colonel in Gloucestershire which resulted in much information about 'Seelöwe' going to this colonel who, seeing that it came from Bletchley Park but not having the faintest idea what it was about, locked it in a safe and told nobody about it, hoping that someone would come along at some point and enlighten him.[19]

Not all Enigma decrypts were so useful. An example illustrates how easy it was to misunderstand messages that had been incorrectly transcribed, even by a single letter. An Enigma intercept was decrypted as 'FLAK GAS', which set up a scare of poison gas fired in anti-aircraft shells until it was realised that a letter was missing from the text; it should have been 'FLAK GAST' which referred to an anti-aircraft equipment depot (Geräte Ausbau Stelle).[20]

Enigma intercepts could tell quite a lot even if they were not deciphered. In May 1940, after the German invasion of France, Enigma had been of little use to Allied troops in combat because of Bletchley Park's inability to deal, in detail, with the sudden, massively increased, volume of transcripts coming in over the first two weeks of the attack, but the overall picture emerging from the intelligence (location of source) was one of lightning German advance, complete rout of the French forces and a rapidly disintegrating defensive position of the British Expeditionary Force (BEF). Early indications were that the BEF would be cut off if it tried to hold its position along the Dyle in Belgium and might be forced to fall back to the coast. This may explain why preparations for the Dunkirk evacuation were started as early as 20 May, and it may also indicate that British Intelligence, and hence the British War Cabinet, were made aware of the impending catastrophe earlier than Lord Gort, the BEF commander in the field.[21]

It was a common problem with early Enigma intercepts that their value was often questioned by operational commanders who preferred to concentrate on their own field intelligence. In most cases 'Boniface' intelligence was disguised as having been derived through traditional clandestine means. The RAF Director of Signals, Air Commodore Nutting, on one occasion, believing that the intelligence had come from agents 'in the field', professed admiration for the 'brave chaps' who had so courageously provided it.[22] On 26 May, an Enigma intercept gave British Intelligence a clear eight hours notice of the time and place of a meeting between the Chiefs of Staff of four Fliegerkorps. Who knows what might have been the consequences for the German advance of a strike on this target by Bomber Command? In the event, the intelligence was not acted upon.

There were, however, other instances of Enigma decrypts being used in a positive way. As an example, British paranoia over the threat of invasion at the height of the Dunkirk evacuation was somewhat assuaged when, on 1 June, decrypted Enigma traffic clearly showed that the German forces in the Pas de Calais were preparing to move south across the Seine and encircle Paris. The French campaign had shown the modern armed forces to have an 'unexpected ability to carry out large-scale overseas operations', and were masters of 'secret preparations and rapid execution of plans', but the Enigma intelligence suggested that Britain, for the moment, was not the focus of their attention and was clearly instrumental in Churchill's ill-fated decision to send a second Expeditionary Force to France on 7 June.

Enigma traffic was reduced significantly after the fall of France as units became more fixed in place and landlines used extensively rather than radio for communications; it increased again at the beginning of July when it allowed British Intelligence to start building up a picture of the Luftwaffe order of battle in the newly occupied territories. It was noted that dive-bomber gruppen were being moved up close to the Channel coast, which made attacks on coastal convoys, when they came, less than a total surprise.

Piecing together fragmented intelligence, however, was not easy and it was not until 5 August that a comprehensive understanding of Luftwaffe deployment in northern France was arrived at. In any event, such information was of limited use in trying to determine the strength of Luftwaffe units as the Battle of Britain progressed. Enigma decrypts were equally unable to shed any light on Luftwaffe strategic shifts which were discussed and disseminated through landlines. Occasional signals were picked up in early July referencing an operation called 'Adler', but there was no indication of what it referred to.

A very serious flaw in the exploitation of Enigma decrypts was in the way British Air Intelligence dealt with the information. Only transcripts pertaining to the Luftwaffe order of battle were given high priority by intelligence analysts, and anything that looked like operational or tactical intelligence was considered to be of lesser value and side-tracked into departments that dealt with the question of long-term Luftwaffe strategy. In this way, much intelligence that could have been of immediate value was many weeks in evaluation before coming before RAF controllers. However, there were occasions during the Battle when intelligence gained from Enigma signals was of significant tactical use. Intercepted signals ordering the transfer of bomber units from Luftflotte 5 in Norway to Luftflotte 2 in France after August gave a clear indication that no more bombing raids were to be expected across the North Sea on targets in the north of England, so Dowding could afford to relocate his exhausted squadrons to 13 Group stations where they could be sure of a bit of rest, and fresh squadrons located there could be safely transferred south. Also, interception and decryption of signals confirming the disbandment, after 17 September, of a specialist staff which had been tasked with organising Operation Seelöwe was a clear indication that any invasion was highly unlikely before 1941.

The breaking of the 'red' key after 22 May allowed decrypts to be available within hours, but that was not the end of the matter. Decrypted messages were sent from Hut 6 to Hut 3, where analysts would translate the messages from German and interpret the contents. Typically, a text message would consist of five-letter groups, which may or may not make sense when concatenated. The text may be corrupted by the inclusion of incorrectly heard Morse code signals or an interruption in transmission when intuition or group brainstorming was required to ascertain the meaning by filling the gaps. When the correct text was arrived at, it was rarely a simple sentence. Often the meaning was only apparent to analysts familiar with German military establishment and practices.

Messages might be just a series of numbers or seemingly meaningless words. It required a certain amount of intuition, an example of which was when an analyst guessed that an apparently meaningless series of numbers were simply map references which related to movement of units from one place to another. While messages very rarely gave straightforward information of immediate use, they did contribute enormously to RAF understanding of the location of various Luftwaffe units over time, which allowed them to make assumptions about possible changes in strategy. Increased levels of communications from particular locations also indicated a potential increase in activity for units stationed there.

Every text which was successfully processed through Hut 3 was sent to intelligence officers at SIS headquarters in London, from where it was disseminated to operational commands. Army and Air Force related intelligence derived from Enigma sources in summaries and subsequently distributed under the codeword 'Boniface'. In 1940, special arrangements were made within the British Intelligence services for handling 'Boniface' (later changed to 'Ultra' in 1942) intelligence. Great care was taken to control the distribution of 'Boniface' intelligence to Allied commanders and units in the field. Liaison officers, part of MI6, were appointed for each field command to manage and control distribution. To begin with, even top commanders were not advised about the source of 'Boniface' intelligence and were inclined to regard it with some scepticism. Dowding himself was not made directly aware of it, but undoubtedly benefited from information which came to him through intelligence liaison officers, although such intelligence was generally broad and of questionable use tactically. Intelligence officers in the field who handled 'Boniface' material were kept well away from situations that risked their capture, and anyone who had worked at Bletchley Park never saw combat. Often 'Boniface'-based intelligence was wrapped up as Y-service radio traffic intercepts. There remained the tricky problem of using 'Boniface' in ways which would not alert the Germans to the fact that the Allies were reading their communications, and it was this that raised possibly the most difficult moral issues of when and when not to use it.

The use of 'red' Enigma decrypts in 1940 was undoubtedly of significant benefit to British Air Intelligence but its importance, in the short term, should not be overestimated. Its greatest value was in the slow methodical accumulation of seemingly mundane information which gradually acquired strategic relevance over time. Information was recorded on indexed cards and filed so that if certain words were noticed to be used with excessive regularity, other messages including that word could be quickly located to try to build a pattern of understanding of the context and meaning of messages which were otherwise apparently meaningless. While individual decoded messages might be trivial, in combination with others they might shed a light on a significant development but, in many cases, the importance of a message might not be apparent for some time due to a shortage of trained intelligence officers capable of making the connections.

Chapter 11

Polish Codebreakers

[his achievements] elevate [Rejewski] to the pantheon of the greatest cryptanalysts of all time.[1]

The contribution made by Polish codebreakers to the Bletchley Park's efforts to break the Enigma codes was enormous. 'Without it,' said Peter Calvacoressi who worked in Hut 3, 'the British would not have been able to read Enigma traffic in these early months [of 1940] and without the breaks made [before May]', could not have achieved the breakthroughs later.[2] When the codebreakers at Bletchley Park set out to break the Enigma codes they 'had the invaluable benefits of the Poles' experience and ingenuity',[3] and were, to quote Isaac Newton when he paid tribute to those upon whose work he had built, 'Standing on the shoulders of giants.'

Poland had been monitoring German and Russian radio messages from at least 1918 onwards. The Second Polish Republic had been established at the end of the First World War and sat uneasily between revolutionary Soviet Russia and a crushed, unstable Germany. They were, naturally, anxious to keep track of any signs of German rearmament and joint German-Russian military cooperation. The Germans had experimented with an Enigma machine for encoding secret messages as early as 1919 and it had become standard equipment for the Kriegsmarine in 1926. On 15 July 1928, when the first German machine-enciphered messages had been broadcast by German military radio stations the Poles intercepted them and tried, in vain, to decipher them. The Polish Cipher Bureau (Biuro Szyfrów) was run by Franciszek Pokorny, and a civilian Bureau associate, Antoni Palluth, a director of the AVA Radio Company in Warsaw which produced cryptologic equipment designed by the Cipher Bureau. Small and under-resourced, the Bureau acknowledged that a new phase of German resurgence was taking place and was forced to recruit more staff. In January 1929 Major Gwido Langer became chief of the Radio-Intelligence Office, and subsequently of the Cipher Bureau. The Bureau's deputy chief, and the chief of its German section (BS-4), was Captain Maksymilian Ciężki.

They approached Zdzisław Krygowski, professor of mathematics at Poznań University, with a view to setting up a cryptology course for selected student. Many of his students had been educated in German speaking schools so were equally fluent in both German and Polish. Krygowski recommended around twenty promising students to the Bureau recruiter Ciężki. All twenty attended secret cryptology classes run by Pokorny and Palluth at a nearby military establishment while simultaneously pursuing their university studies. One of these students was Marian Rejewski. Rejewski had been born on 16 August 1905 in Bromberg to Józef and Matylda (née Thoms) and was studying mathematics at Poznań University's Mathematics Institute.

Rejewski graduated with a Master of Philosophy degree in mathematics in 1929 before going to study in Göttingen, Germany. On his return from Germany, Professor Krygowski offered him a post as an assistant mathematics tutor, but he also carried on working for the Cipher Bureau at Poznań where the Polish General Staff had now merged the Radio-Intelligence Office (Referat Radiowywiadu) and the Polish-Cryptography Office (Referat Szyfrów Własnych) into a single unit in Warsaw. The new Bureau was charged with both cryptography, the generation of ciphers, codes and cryptology – the study of breaking them. It was here that Rejewski was reunited with two of his erstwhile fellow students Jerzy Różycki and Henryk Michał Zygalski. Zygalski had been born in 1908 in Poznan, the son of Michał Zygalski and Stanisława Kielisz Zygalski. He studied higher algebra and mathematical analysis and gained his Master's Degree in 1931, after which he went on to work full time at the Ministry of War building in Marshal Pilsudski Square in central Warsaw and later to Biuro Szyfrów-4, the cipher office dealing with German messages in Kabackie Woods outside Warsaw.[4] Różycki had been born in what is now the Ukraine, the fourth and youngest child of Zygmunt Różycki, a pharmacist and graduate of St Petersburg University, and Wanda (née Benita). He attended a Polish school in Kiev before moving with his family to Poland in 1918. In 1926 he completed secondary school at Wyszków on eastern Poland's Bug River. Despite being a wayward extrovert from a dissolute family background, he had graduated from Poznań University's Mathematics Institute with a master's degree in 1932.[5]

Rejewski was chosen to work alone on examining a copy of a German Enigma machine that had been acquired in January 1929. The Warsaw

Customs Office had received a package from Germany whose documentation described it as 'radio equipment'. Their suspicions were aroused when an agitated official of the German firm who had sent the package strenuously demanded that it be returned to Germany immediately as it had been dispatched in error. The customs officials notified the Polish Cipher Bureau, ever willing to learn more about German radio, who sent two experts, Ludomir Danilewicz and Antoni Palluth, to examine the package, which they found to contain a commercial Enigma cypher machine. They had been alerted on Saturday, which gave them almost two days to minutely examine the machine before carefully repackaging it and returning it to the German firm on Monday. They had learned enough to build a replica Enigma but all attempts to use it for decrypting German military codes came to nothing, which indicated that there were fundamental differences in the internal wiring between the commercial and military machines.

The major breakthrough for the Poles now took place not in Poland, but in Belgium. In June 1931, Hans Thilo Schmidt, a civil servant at the German Defence Ministry Cipher Bureau in Berlin, had walked into the French Embassy there and boldly inquired how one went about selling German state secrets to the French government. It is not hard to see how the French might have been sceptical, but they were sufficiently intrigued to eventually agree to a meeting between Schmidt and a charismatic and flamboyant French agent, Rodolphe Lemoine (Stallman) in the Grand Hotel in Verviers a few months later.

Despite having a steady job Schmidt, like many Germans was suffering as he tried to bring up a young family in a time of acute economic depression under rampant inflation, but he compounded his misery by being repeatedly unfaithful to his wife, Charlotte. He was something of a fantasist who saw a chance to improve his circumstances by treachery.[6] In his office, Schmidt had access to ciphers which were made up for use by the German armed forces and it was these that he was prepared to betray to the French.

Lemoine probed Schmidt's motives and quickly discovered that, far from any political motives, he was driven by pure greed which simplified things significantly for Lemoine. He promised to look at the ciphers and put a price on them at their next meeting. This was duly convened a week later at the same hotel, but this time Lemoine had brought along Gustave Bertrand, the head of Section D (decryptement) of the French Intelligence Service (Service de Renseignement). Schmidt, however, who had now been given the codename Asché, was being coy and had not brought any cipher codes to the meeting.[7] Instead he offered manuals to explain how to use the German Enigma machine. Bertrand failed to appreciate the difference between what Schmidt had promised and what he had delivered, but was convinced that the manuals were authentic and, with Lemoine, offered to trade and set about inveigling Schmidt into a web of intrigue from which he could never escape. The French anticipated that Schmidt would deliver priceless intelligence, but after an initial fairly large payment they would be able to manipulate him at minimal cost. Their optimism was short-lived when cipher experts in Paris examined photos of the manuals that Bertrand had taken, and explained that the documents in no way enabled decryption of codes, merely how to operate the Enigma machine. Unwilling to believe that he had been taken in, Bertrand took his photos to the British head of Secret Intelligence in Paris, Wilfred Dunderdale, but Dunderdale, after consulting British cryptanalysts, agreed that he had, indeed, been deceived.

Nothing daunted, Bertrand then thought of an old acquaintance: Gwido Langer at the Polish Cipher Bureau, whom he knew had spent time working on the German Enigma codes. The two met in December and Langer quickly saw that the documents, although far from enabling deciphering of Enigma messages, would be of great value in building on previous Polish research to achieve a better understanding of the internal workings of the military Enigma. Bertrand was urged to go back to his source and try to acquire current Enigma machine settings. This he did and Schmidt, this time, came up with the goods which were spirited away to Warsaw under diplomatic security. The German codes were changed every three months, but Schmidt was able to furnish the next two series in May and September 1932. While Bertrand obediently passed these over to the Poles, he received not a single notification that they were making any sort of progress.

Rejewski, Różycki and Zygalski had moved to the Polish Cipher Office in 1932, where Rejewski was selected to work on the captured commercial Enigma. First Rejewski tackled the problem of discovering the wiring of the rotors which he did by applying Group Theory, a mathematical theory of permutations, as opposed to using traditional methods such as searching for linguistic pattern or letter-frequencies in the coded messages. Before receiving the French intelligence material, Rejewski had made a careful study of Enigma messages, particularly of the first six letters of messages (called the 'indicator') intercepted on a single day. Each message was encrypted using different starting positions (settings) of the Enigma rotors. A setting consisted of three letters arbitrarily chosen by the operative. All Enigmas in a particular network were given a 'ground setting' for the day which was repeated. This repetition was intended to act as a sort of error-check but was, in fact, an Achilles heel. Rejewski knew that the first and fourth letters were the same, the second and fifth were the same, and the third and sixth were the same. These relationships could be exploited to break into the cipher.

Enigma operators also had a tendency to choose predictable letter combinations as indicators, such as a girlfriend's initials or a pattern of keys that they saw on the Enigma keyboard. These later became known to Bletchley Park cryptanalysts as 'Cillis'. Using the data thus gained from the study of cycles and the use of predictable indicators, Rejewski was able to deduce six permutations corresponding to the encipherment at six consecutive positions of the Enigma machine. These permutations could be described by six equations with various unknowns, representing the wiring within the entry drum, rotors, reflector, and plugboard. At this point, Rejewski ran into difficulties due to the large number of unknowns in the set of equations that he had developed. He had set about trying to construct a replica machine starting with the internal wiring of the first wheel which was beyond him until he was given settings which had been supplied by Schmidt, after which he succeeded in reducing the number of unknowns and solved the wirings of the rotors and reflector. This enabled the Poles to build a prototype machine at which point Różycki and Zygalski were brought in to start decoding German messages.

Meanwhile, Bertrand was having trouble with Schmidt who had begun pursuing a lavish lifestyle which Bertrand felt sure was bound to attract attention. Schmidt had even bought a small soap-making factory. In desperation, Bertrand drew up a bogus contract which identified Schmidt as earning royalties from a new method of making soap in an effort to disguise the source of his new-found wealth. Furthermore, Bertrand, having heard nothing positive from the Poles, was starting to doubt the value of Schmidt's product and he upbraided him at the Hotel d'Angleterre in Liège, but Schmidt assured him that it was genuine and up-to-date and now started including, in his briefings, intelligence about German High Command conferences to which his brother, a serving general, was privy. With growing Nazi dominance of all German life, there was also the risk that increased security measures could expose Schmidt's perfidy. This almost came about when German intercepts of the diplomatic signals between the French Embassy in Berlin and French Intelligence in Paris revealed that a source was passing secret intelligence about German ambitions in Austria and Czechoslovakia. That the Berlin Embassy should have trusted the security of diplomatic communications in such a place at such a time is amazing. Schmid panicked as a full-scale investigation into the leak was launched by Canaris, head of the Abwehr secret service. A new procedure had been established for clandestine meetings, 'Uncle Kurt has died', being the emergency signal to warn of danger and Schmidt duly called it up.[8] He was encouraged now to leave the Cipher Bureau and his work with Enigma came to an end. Schmidt had a lucky escape in March 1938 when Lemoine was arrested by the Gestapo in Cologne and, although released, was never again fully trusted by French Intelligence who feared he might have been turned. Fortunately, Lemoine knew little of what the Poles had achieved in breaking Enigma. Schmidt was not so lucky in 1943 when Lemoine was again arrested and this time, under torture by the Gestapo, gave up Schmidt who was duly arrested also. Schmidt died in September of that year in a German prison in Berlin, possibly by his own hand.[9]

Rejewski had worked out the precise interconnections of the Enigma rotors and reflector, after receiving documents and two pages of Enigma daily keys from Bertrand. He had also received an unexpected but extremely welcome surprise when one of the documents that Schmidt had provided contained a sample message in plain German and the same message in coded form using a particular machine setting. After he had worked out the military Enigma's logical structure, the Polish Cipher Bureau commissioned Palluth at the AVA to build replicas of the Enigma to Rejewski's specifications. His method of decrypting Enigma messages exploited two weaknesses of the German operating procedures. It used what Rejewski called 'characteristics' that were independent of the plugboard connections. This involved compiling a card catalogue of certain features of the set of indicator settings.

There was another obstacle to overcome, however. The military Enigma had been modified from the commercial Enigma, of which Rejewski had had an actual example to study. In the commercial machine, the keys were connected to the entry drum in German keyboard order, QWERTZU. However, in the military Enigma, the connections were different. Rejewski intuited that a German fondness for order would lead them to use normal alphabetic ordering, ABCDE. He later recalled that, after he had made this assumption, 'from my pencil, as by magic', began to issue numbers designating the connections in the right-hand rotor.

After Rejewski had discovered the wiring in the remaining rotors in early 1933, Różycki and Zygalski started devising methods and equipment to break Enigma codes. They now had the machine but no keys, whereas before they'd had the keys but no machine. The problem now was to find the daily keys. A number of methods and devices were required to counter the continual improvements in German operating procedure and to the growing sophistication of the Enigma machine itself. The earliest method for reconstructing daily keys was based on the fact that the plugboard's connections exchanged only six pairs of letters, leaving fourteen letters unchanged. Another method was Różycki's 'clock', which sometimes made it possible to determine which rotor was at the right-hand side of the Enigma machine on a given day. As an indication of the problems faced, after 1 October 1936, German procedure changed, and the number of plugboard connections became variable, ranging between five and eight. This almost totally negated all Rejewski's previous work, but a cyclometer method which created a catalogue of permutations could still be used.

The cyclometer comprised two sets of Enigma rotors and was used to determine the length and number of cycles of the permutations that could be generated by the Enigma machine. Even with the cyclometer, preparing the catalogue was a long and difficult task. Preparation of the catalogue had taken over a year, but when it was ready in about 1935, daily keys could be worked out in under twenty minutes. However, in November 1937, the Germans replaced the reflector in their Enigma machines, which meant that the entire catalogue had to be recalculated from scratch. It is worth noting that the cyclometer method was the forerunner of the code-breaking machine developed by Alan Turing at Bletchley Park in 1939/40.

The Germans increased the difficulty of decrypting Enigma messages by decreasing the interval between changes in the order of the rotors from quarterly, initially, to monthly in February 1936, then daily in October of that year, when they also increased the number of plugboard leads from six to a number that varied between five and eight. This made the Biuro's grill method much less easy, as it relied on unsteckered letter pairs. The German Kriegsmarine was more security-conscious than the Army and Air Force, and in May 1937 it introduced a new, much more secure, indicator procedure that remained unbroken for several years.

The next setback occurred in November 1937, when the scrambler's reflector was changed to one with different interconnections (known as Umkehrwalze-B). Rejewski worked out the wiring in the new reflector, but the catalogue of characteristics had to be compiled anew, again using Rejewski's cyclometer, which had been built to his specifications by the AVA Radio Company.

In 1937 Rejewski, along with the German section of the Cipher Bureau, transferred to a secret facility near Pyry in the Kabaty Woods south of

Warsaw. Disaster struck again in September 1938 when the Germans introduced new rules for enciphering message keys, which wiped out all the previous codebreaking advances. The system of pre-defining the indicator setting for the day for all Enigma operators on a given network, on which the deciphering method of characteristics depended, was changed. Operators now chose their own indicator setting. However, the insecure procedure of sending the enciphered message key twice, remained in use, and it was quickly exploited. The Poles responded immediately with new techniques. Henryk Zygalski devised a manual method that used twenty-six perforated sheets, which was later developed into a working decryption method at Bletchley Park, and Rejewski invented the 'bomba kryptologiczna', an electrically powered combination of six Enigma machines which solved the daily keys within about two hours. Six bomby were built by AVA and were ready for use within two months. The bomby worked on the fact that the plugboard connections applied to only some of the letters, but when the Germans increased the number of plugboard connections, the bomby struggled to keep up.

The Germans, once again, introduced another new level of complexity by adding two new rotors on 15 December 1938, giving a choice of three out of five to assemble in the machines on a given day. This increased the number of possible rotor orders from six to sixty. The Poles could now only read the small minority of messages that used neither of the two new rotors. Fortunately, however, the fact that the SD (Sicherheitdienst) network was still using the old method of the same indicator setting for all messages, allowed Rejewski to reuse his previous method of working out the wiring within these rotors. On 1 January 1939, the Germans made the military Enigma even more difficult to break by increasing the number of plugboard connections from between five and eight, to between seven and ten. The Poles were rapidly running out of resources to keep up with these changes. To carry on using Rejewski's bomby method would now require a combination of sixty replica Enigmas and not six. As war loomed, the Polish General Staff and government decided to appeal to the Anglo-Polish Agreement signed on 25 August 1939 and approached their Western Allies for assistance.

Polish Intelligence section BS-4 had moved into specially constructed new facilities in the Kabaty Woods, at Pyry, and it was there, well away from the prying eyes of German agents, on 25 and 26 July 1939, that a meeting took place. The Polish contingent consisted of Langer, Ciężki, Rejewski, Zygalski, Różycki and, to emphasise how seriously the Poles were taking things, Colonel Stefan Mayer, Chief of Polish Intelligence. They gave a detailed account of their work to date on Enigma. And offered both France and Britain a Polish-reconstructed Enigma, along with details of their equipment, including Zygalski Sheets and Rejewski's bomby. The British had sent Commander Alastair Denniston head of Britain's GCCS, Dilly Knox, chief British cryptanalyst and Commander Humphrey Sandwith, head of the Royal Navy's intercept and RD stations. The French party consisted of Bertrand, and Captain Henri Bracquenié of the French Air Force.

The first thing that Knox asked was about the connections in the entry drum. When Rejewski told him that he had guessed it would be ABCDE etc. Knox was embarrassed and annoyed that neither he nor anyone else at Bletchley Park had thought of such an obvious solution. His reaction clouded the meeting and threatened to derail negotiations not only because of his discomfort, but also at the realisation that the Poles had achieved so much more than the British and, up to that point, told them so little about it. The French were no better amused believing that the Poles had 'palmed them off with an unusable machine so that we and the British can find a way of making it work'.[10] For years they had been exchanging intercepts with the Poles but getting no deciphered texts in return. Neither the French nor the British felt that the meeting had been very productive for them, but at least Knox was gracious enough, a week later, to write thanking the Poles for their 'cooperation and patience'.

Rejewski was married with two children, Andrzej and 7-month-old Janina when the Germans invaded Poland on 1 September, and it was soon clear that Polish resistance was futile against the Wehrmacht military machine and that he would soon be separated from his family, evacuated along with other intelligence agents to continue his work elsewhere. Jerzy Różycki also had a wife, Maria Barbara Mayka, and a 6-month-old son Janusz. Some personnel of the Cipher Bureau's German section who had worked with Enigma, and most of the workers at the AVA Radio Company that had built replica Enigmas and cryptologic equipment for the German section, remained in Poland. Some were interrogated by the Gestapo, but no one gave away the secrets of Polish successes with Enigma. Rejewski, Zygalski and Różycki and their families left Warsaw with members of the Polish General Staff on the 6th on a special train, Echelon F, that came under frequent aerial attack while heading for Brest Litovsk. By the time they reached the Romanian border they had destroyed all sensitive documents and equipment and were down to a single very crowded truck. Upon arrival the truck was confiscated, and the civilians were separated from the military and shunted off to an internment camp. The dangers of being discovered there by German agents were apparent and so Rejewski and Różycki took the heart-breaking decision to leave their families and went south with Zygalski to Bucharest. In that city they sought asylum at the British Embassy but the staff there demurred and told them to call back in a few days after they had consulted London. Unwilling to waste a moment, the men then went to the French Embassy and used their connection to Bertrand to persuade staff there to give them immediate assistance. Crossing into Yugoslavia and passing through (still neutral) Italy, they eventually arrived in France but had to wait until Langer and Ciężki could make good their escape also and bring with them two replica Enigma machines.

The British now regretted their initial hesitation, and when Langer and Bracquenié visited Bletchley Park in December 1939, they asked that the Polish cryptanalysts be turned over to them. Langer, however, was not persuaded and argued that his team of cryptanalysts must remain in France where the Polish Armed Forces in exile were being formed. Instead 'Mohammed went to the mountain', in the form of Alan Turing, who visited the Poles at Bertrand's codebreaking headquarters in the Château de Vignolles in Gretz-Armainvilliers, codenamed PC Bruno, some forty kilometres southeast of Paris. The staff there now included fifteen Poles, fifty Frenchmen, and seven anti-fascist Spaniards who worked on Spanish and Italian ciphers. Turing had brought the Poles a full set of Zygalski Sheets that had been produced at Bletchley Park by John Jeffreys using Polish-supplied information. On 17 January, the Poles made the first break into wartime Enigma traffic by decrypting a message that had been sent three months earlier on 28 October.

There was close cooperation between Bletchley Park and PC Bruno which avoided duplication of effort and ensured sharing of knowledge. In April, PC Bruno staff succeeded in breaking the Luftwaffe 'red' codes by reference to work the Poles had done back in 1932 by employing the 'exclusivity principle', which had exposed, and relied upon, lax Luftwaffe operating procedures. There were reasons for optimism and anticipation of progress, but all was to change on 1 May when most Enigma operatives were instructed to stop encoding the message setting twice at the beginning of a signal. This completely nullified all Allied efforts which had been developed to that time and would have set them back to square one had it not been for two things (explained in detail elsewhere) Cillis and the Herivel tip.

On 10 May the Germans launched Fall Gelb, a Blitzkrieg attack against France and the Low Countries. On 10 June Bertrand abandoned PC Bruno and on the 24th, two days after the French surrender, the whole of the PC Bruno staff were evacuated by air to Algeria. Once it became clear that Vichy France was to be left unoccupied by the Germans, Bertrand made arrangements to bring the men back and, in September, set them up at the Château des Fouzes, codenamed Cadix, at Uzès, just west of Avignon. All were given cover names, Rejewski became Pierre Ranaud, a professor at the local lycée. Cadix retained contact with exiled cryptanalysts at Château Couba in Algeria under the command of Ciężki and there were frequent exchanges of personnel. Różycki had been to Algeria for a while and was returning to France on 9 January 1942 along with fellow Poles Piotr Smoleński and Jan Graliński and French agent Captain François Lane when their ship, the *Lamoricière*, was sunk in the Mediterranean with the loss of all on board.

On 8 November 1942, Bertrand learned from the BBC that the Allies had landed in French North Africa which, he knew, meant that the Germans would now occupy the Vichy Zone and the German Funkabwehr units would quickly detect radio transmissions from Cadix. Bertrand had a lucky escape on 6 November when a German truck equipped with a circular antenna had arrived at the gate of the Château des Fouzes but had not attempted to make entry, investigating nearby farms instead. He managed to evacuate Cadix just two days before the Germans marched in on the 12th.

The Poles were split into groups of two and three. On 11 November 1942, Rejewski and Zygalski were sent to Nice in the Italian-occupied zone, but there they attracted attention and were forced to move constantly to avoid capture. They passed through Cannes, Antibes, Marseilles, Toulouse, Narbonne, Perpignan and then on to the Spanish border. On 29 January 1943, accompanied by a local guide, Rejewski, and Zygalski, set out to cross the Pyrenees into Spain They managed to avoid patrols and thought themselves safely across the border when their guide challenged them at gunpoint and robbed them of all their money before abandoning them.

Arriving in Spain, penniless and without support, they were quickly arrested and imprisoned at Séo de Urgel and then at Lerida. The Polish Red Cross learned of their arrest and intervened on their behalf, after which the two men were released but remained in Madrid. They eventually managed to cross over into Portugal in July, where they were able to board the SS *Scottish*, which took them to Gibraltar. From there they were flown to RAF Hendon on 3 August. They were inducted into the Polish Armed Services as privates and set to work at Boxmoor, breaking German Doppelkassettenverfahren ciphers, which the two cryptanalysts had already worked on in France.

Having been in occupied France for so long, the British considered it too risky to invite them to work at Bletchley Park. British cryptanalyst Alan Stripp said that, 'Setting them to work on the Doppelkassetten system was like using racehorses to pull wagons.'[11]

Rejewski and Zygalski had fared better than some of their colleagues. Langer and Ciężki were betrayed by their French guide and were captured by the Germans as they tried to escape from France into Spain on the night of 10 March 1943, along with Palluth, Edward Fokczyński and Kazimierz Gaca. Palluth and Fokczyński died as slave labourers in Germany. Ciężki and Langer were sent to an SS concentration camp where, during interrogations, they managed to protect the secret of Enigma decryption. They convinced their interrogators that, while the Poles had had some success with solving the Enigma early on, changes introduced by the Germans just before the start of the war had prevented any further decryption.

On 5 January 1944, Bertrand was captured by the Germans at Sacré Couer in Montmartre as he waited for a contact from London. The Germans tried to turn him and he persuaded them that he would indeed work for them as a double agent, but when he made contact again with British Intelligence, he and his wife Mary and a Jesuit priest, were picked up at an improvised airstrip in the Massif Central and whisked away to England in a Lysander aircraft. Bertrand moved into a house at Boxmoor next to the Polish radio-intercept station and cipher office at the nearby village of Felden.

The story of how the three Polish heroes were treated after the defeat of Germany in 1945 does not reflect well upon either the British or the Polish political establishment. In 1944 the Germans had sent Rejewski's wife and children west where they found refuge with her parents in Bydgoszcz, and when Rejewski was discharged from the Polish Army in Britain on 15 November 1946, he returned to Poland to be reunited with his wife and family. His old Poznań University professor, Krygowski, offered him a university mathematics post at Poznań but he was still suffering from rheumatism which he had contracted in the Spanish prisons and was unable to take up the appointment. Tragedy struck in the summer of 1947 when his 11-year-old son Andrzej died of polio after only five days' illness. After his son's death, Rejewski did not want to part, even briefly, from his wife and daughter, so they lived in Bydgoszcz with his in-laws, where he took a position as sales director of a local cable-manufacturing company, Kabel Polski. Between 1949 and 1958 he was repeatedly investigated by the Polish Secret Services, now controlled from Moscow, who could not be sure that he was not working for British Intelligence, especially since he had maintained a lively correspondence with Bertrand after the war. He retired in 1967 and moved with his family back to Warsaw in 1969, to an apartment he had acquired thirty years earlier with financial help from his father-in-law. He died of a heart attack on 13 February 1980, aged 74, after returning home from a shopping trip. He was buried with military honours.

In mid-1945, having been liberated, Ciężki and Langer arrived in London, where they were badly received by Colonel Gano, chief of the Polish Section II in Britain. Bertrand had deflected attention from his own failings by telling Gano that it was Langer who had been responsible for the late evacuation of his group from France in 1942 resulting in their capture. After all he had been through in captivity, Langer was distraught to find himself unjustly blamed. He became ill and died at the Polish Army signals camp at Kinross on 30 March 1948 and was buried, in accordance with his fervent wishes, in Wellshill Cemetery in Perth alongside the 381 Polish pilots also buried in there. Sixty two years later, on 1 December 2010, his remains were exhumed and reburied with full military honours in Poland, where he now has a headstone of black granite describing his role in the breaking of the German Enigma ciphers. Ciężki died in similarly ignominious circumstances on 9 November 1951, after living the previous three years on subsidies from the Assistance Board.

After the war Zygalski fared a little better, being employed as a mathematical statistics lecturer at the Polish University College based in eight buildings between Knightsbridge and Putney. In 1951 it was agreed that Battersea Polytechnic would take over the Putney Buildings of the Polish University College, as well as all their remaining students. However, possibly as a result of Poland now being firmly within the Soviet grasp, in a move that caused much resentment, only eight of the staff of the Polish University College were to be given positions in Battersea Polytechnic after the move. Zygalski, however, was one of the eight. In June 1957, Battersea Polytechnic became a College of Advanced Technology. Then, in September 1966, Battersea Polytechnic achieved university status and it became the University of Surrey. Zygalski was at last on the staff of a university but, sadly, his time as a university teacher was short when he suffered a stroke and died in 1968.[12]

When the full story of Polish involvement in the Enigma story was revealed and Poland had emerged from Soviet dominance to take its place in the free world, Poland's President posthumously awarded Poland's second-highest civilian decoration, the Grand Cross of the Order of Polonia Restituta, to Rejewski on 21 July 2000. In July 2005 Rejewski's daughter,

Janina Sylwestrzak, received on his behalf the War Medal 1939–45 from the British Chief of the Defence Staff, and on 1 August 2012 Rejewski posthumously received the Knowlton Award of the US Military Intelligence Corps Association. He had been nominated for the Award by NATO Allied Command Counterintelligence.

A three-sided bronze monument was dedicated in 2007 in front of the Imperial Castle in Poznań. Each side bears the name of one of the three Polish mathematicians who broke the Enigma cipher.

Appendix A

The Oslo Report (extracts)

One of the reasons the Oslo Report received such a chilly reception is that it was debated in Whitehall just as the British secret community reeled in the wake of [the Venlo Incident][1]

The Oslo report of November 1939 included the following information

1. The Junkers Ju88 twin-engine long-range bomber is being modified to give it a dive-bombing facility. Production of this aircraft is currently around 5,000 per month with a fleet of up to 40,000 anticipated by April 1940. [This prediction proved to be optimistic.]
2. The first German aircraft carrier, the *Franken*, is in Kiel Harbour and expected to be in service by April 1940. [In fact, this was quite incorrect. There were no aircraft carriers under construction at the time and the only known reference to a vessel called *Franken* was a large naval tanker.]
3. The Kriegsmarine is developing remote-controlled gliders (FZ 21 Ferngesteuerte Zielflugzeug) at Peenemünde which can be launched from an aircraft. [This possibly referred to the Blohm & Voss Bv 143 or the Henschel Hs 293. The gliders had:
    a) an electric altimeter that enables it to fly at wave-top height under rocket propulsion.
    b) a remote-controlled apparatus using short-wave telegraphic signals for guidance.]
4. A pilotless aircraft is being developed at Diepensee, near Berlin, that can be controlled from a manned aircraft.
5. The Heer [German Army] was developing remote-controlled shells [Geschoss] with rocket propulsion and gryo stabilisers.
6. Rechlin was the home of Luftwaffe laboratories and test ranges [a fact well-known to RAF Intelligence].

7. Techniques of attack against reinforced bunkers developed during the Polish campaign used smoke shells to disorientate occupants prior to assault by flame-throwers.

8. Short-wave transmitters sited all along the German coastline were capable of detecting approaching aircraft at a range of 120km. [The level of detail included about wavelengths used was crucial in the development of 'Windows' counter-measures employed later in the war to 'jam' German radar and protect allied bombers.]

9. A method had been developed at Rechlin to guide Luftwaffe bombers onto their target. It used a single pulse of transmission which allowed an aircraft to determine its distance from the transmitter [the Y-Gerät apparatus].

10. The Kriegsmarine was developing two new types of torpedo:
    a) The first could be guided close to the target using radio and then proximity acoustic guidance would home it in.
    b) The second had magnetic proximity fuses designed to explode when it was directly underneath a vessel. The elaborate working of this devise is described in the report.

It goes on to describe how mechanical fuses were being replaced in all sorts of German ordnance by electrical fuses which had proved to be so successful and such a device was included with the report.

Appendix B

British Intelligence on Luftwaffe Aircraft

> None of the German Armed Services was of greater concern to the British government that the air force.[1]

The following is a resumé of intelligence files in the Public Records Office collected in 1939-40 pertaining to information about Luftwaffe aircraft development.

Heinkel He 113

An RAF pilot claimed to have shot a He113 down over the Dunkirk evacuation.

On 17 June a German PoW under interrogation said that only a few He113 have been produced, some of which were exported to the Soviet Union.

In July, the British Air Attaché in Bern reported that the He113 was in service with a number of gruppen.

Another PoW claimed that He113s were operating in Holland and Norway.

The RAF reported the shooting down of three He113s over England in August 1940.

It is now generally accepted that the He113 never actually existed at all, that it was an He100 repainted and photographed for propaganda purposes.

Messerschmitt Bf109

In September 1939, the French captured a Bf109 intact and discovered it to have many impressive revolutionary features. In July 1940 the RAF tested a captured Bf109 against a Spitfire and claimed that the Spitfire was superior in all respects. This must be viewed with some scepticism since the report also, incredibly, states that even the Bouton Paul Defiant was a match for the Bf109.

Messerschmitt Bf110

In May 1939 a Bf110, which had crashed at Pontarlier in France featured a bomb-release mechanism suggesting that it might be a fighter-bomber.

Days before the outbreak of war a British engineer was allowed to inspect a Bf110 at the Augsburg aircraft development site. He was told that shock absorbers had been fitted to soften the vibration caused by the nose mounted canon. He saw no bomb rack.

Dornier Do17

In May 1939, an intelligence source claims that the Do215 is a twin-engine fighter version of the Do17. Later that year the same source claims that the Do17 is a multi-task bomber/reconnaissance/ground attack aircraft, but a second source claimed that during the Spanish Civil war the Do17 was withdrawn from a bombing role due to its inability to carry a significant bomb load.

An alarming report claimed that the Do215 was being equipped to spray poison gas.

Dornier Do217

In May 1940 a report indicates the existence of the Dornier Do217 multi-purpose aircraft.

Heinkel He111

In 1938 a report claims that the He111, despite its old design and obsolete construction, has been re-equipped to be a formidable strike aircraft.

In 1940 a report states that the addition of two extra gun platforms have reduced the speed of the He111 by 15mph. The He111 suffers from severe icing at high altitude restricting its ceiling to 8,500 metres.

Heinkel He177

In January 1940 PoW interrogation reveals the existence of a new four-engine He177 heavy bomber.

In May a source reported that the He177 was in production.

In June a report claims the He177 has a speed of 310 mph and a range of 1800 miles and required extended runways to operate from.

Junkers Ju87

A report states that the Ju87 has an automatic apparatus for pulling out of steep dives to prevent crashing. It works on barometric pressure and must be calibrated every day.

In July 1940 PoWs report the sequence that aircraft in a formation adopt when attacking a target.

Junkers Ju88

A PoW reveals that the Junkers Ju88 is produced at the Desau Junkers factory. It is poorly armoured and cramped for the crew.

Appendix C

How the Enigma Machine Worked

> …the wheel order and ring settings provide more than a million variations, so the total number of possible keys is more than 200 quintillion (two hundred million million million million.)[1]

For those who wish to explore the hugely complicated procedures employed to break the Enigma codes the following are recommended: 'The Hut Six Story' by Gordon Welchman, 'Top Secret Ultra' by Peter Calvacoressi and 'Enigma' by Hugh Sebag-Montefiore.

Enigma was used for encoding communications between units that did not have a fixed telephone line link. The Enigma machine did not send or receive messages, it merely encrypted and decrypted the message which was then transmitted, usually by Morse code, through radio communications.

The Enigma (referred to by the Germans as Glühlampenmaschine (Glowlamp Machine)) looked superficially like a typewriter but internally was much more complicated. It had a 26-letter keyboard but no numerals, which had to be entered as the word not the numeral (i.e. eighteen not 18). The letters were also arranged slightly differently to a conventional typewriter keyboard. Above this were the same letters in the same order but on a glass plate (lightboard) where a different letter lit up when a key on the machine was depressed. The letter lit up was the encrypted form of the letter on the key depressed

The internal workings of the machine determined which letter lit up when a key was depressed. The whole message was then fed through the machine one letter at a time and the series of lit letters became the encrypted message which was transmitted by Morse code. To work out the original message, the receiver had to enter the received letters in his own Enigma machine (by depressing the appropriate key) and record the sequence of letters which showed up in his lightboard. The crucial element in decryption was to know the settings on the encrypting machine and set up the receiving machine in exactly the same way. Some of this information was in the code

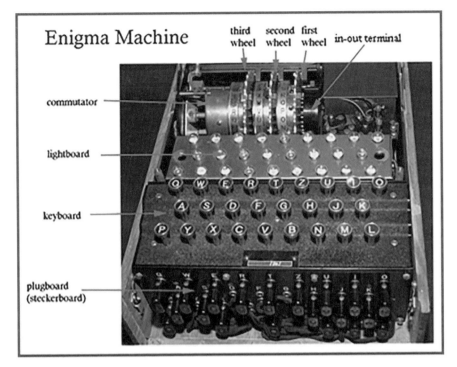

An enigma machine had a superficially similar appearance to a large typewriter.

books which were distributed to all units and the rest was included in the first part of the message (in plain text with no encoding).

The encrypting components of an Enigma machine were:

> A **keyboard** on which a key (e.g. F) could be depressed to make an electrical connection which sets up an electric current from the battery to the plugboard (steckerboard).

The plugboard (steckerboard) displays the twenty-six keyboard letters (in the same order), each letter having two sockets. One socket connects to the keyboard and one to the lightboard. Any two letters can be connected by inserting twin plugs in their two sockets. There are now two connections between the pairing allowing the current to flow both ways (reciprocity). The current flows to the letter which is identical to the letter depressed on the keyboard (F) via the keyboard plug. Now suppose that F is connected to B. The current now flows from F to B. Note that not all letters need to be connected to another one and if one is not it is said to be 'self-steckered', in which case the current flows directly to the same letter on the lightboard.

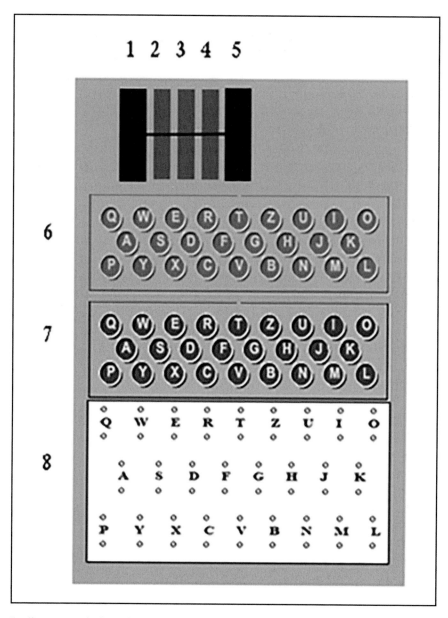

In diagrammatic form it looks like this

1 commutator	4 first wheel	7 keyboard
2 third wheel	5 in-out terminal	8 plugboard
3 second wheel	6 lightboard	

The top row of plugs for each letter in the plugboard connect it to the same letter on the keyboard and the bottom row to the same letter on the lightboard

There are thirteen possible couplings called steckerverbindungen (e.g. F/B, W/T, S/G, C/Y, B/A, X/E, Q/U, etc) but in practice only between seven and ten were ever used at any one time in 1940. The number of ways in which the letters can be cross-plugged if all thirteen pairings are made is a staggering eight trillion (8,000,000,000,000). Surprisingly, if only nine pairings are made, leaving eight letters 'self-steckered' the number of possible combinations increases to 200 trillion.

The current now flows to the in-out terminal or commutator (umkehrwalze) where it connects to the letter B. Each letter on the in-out terminal is connected to a pin. The in-out terminal is fixed in place so that it makes an electrical connection with the first wheel through one of its twenty-six pins arranged in a circular pattern on its side touching one of twenty-six studs on the first wheel.

This wheel is one of five (numbered I, II, III, IV, V) and any three can be chosen and placed in the machine in any order. The three chosen wheels when inserted in the machine are collectively called the 'scrambler'. There are sixty possible combinations (wheel order) (e.g. IV I V, II III V, I IV III, etc). The wheel studs and pins are connected by internal electrical wiring. The internal wiring of the wheels is fixed but each wheel is wired differently. The code book indicated which wheels were to be used and in which order over a given timescale, usually one month, after which the instructions were changed.

The **wheel**, in appearance, has the twenty-six keyboard letters arranged around the circumference so that when they are in place in the machine and the lid is closed, the topmost letter will be visible through a small window and the sequence of the three letters recorded and included in the message. The wheel has twenty-six pins arranged in a circular pattern on one side and twenty-six studs on the other. This means that a current entering the wheel through a stud could exit from any one of twenty-six pins on the other side according to which letter was against the marker

Each wheel came apart with the two halves connected by internal wiring. This wiring was sufficiently long to allow a full rotation of one half relative to the other. The half without letters had a red dot in one position and the two halves were reconnected with a particular letter opposite the dot. The identity of the letter selected was included in the un-encoded part of the message and was given by the code book instructions for that month. A clip would then hold the wheel in that position in the machine. This is now the 'ring setting' (ringstellung) for the wheel and identified by quoting the letters fixed against the marker. With twenty-six possible ring settings for each wheel there are $26 \times 26 \times 26$ (17,576) possible combinations for any three given wheels. Since there are sixty possible combinations of wheels, we get 1,054,560 possible ways of setting up the

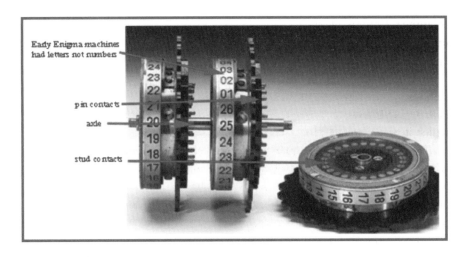

Early Enigma machines
had letters not numbers

pin contacts

axle

stud contacts

scrambler. Combined with the possible plugboard settings there are 1,054,560 multiplied by 200 trillion possible routes the electrical current can take in encrypting a letter on the keyboard into a letter on the lightboard.

The scrambler setting (ring setting and wheel order) and the plugboard settings are collectively known as the **key** (e.g. PYR I IV III F/B W/T S/G C/Y B/A X/E Q/U), which was issued to a unit for use over a specified period, after which it was changed. Note that different units would have different keys.

The electrical current now flows from the first wheel through the pin which is connected to the stud, taking the current from the in-out terminal and into the second wheel by contact with the opposing stud. The electrical current has twenty-six ways of passing through this wheel according to the setting before exiting via the pin connected to the live entry stud. This pin will be in a position which corresponds to a new letter.

The electrical current now flows from the second wheel to the third in a similar manner. The electrical current has twenty-six ways of passing through this wheel according to the setting before exiting via the pin connected to the live entry stud. This pin will be in a position which corresponds to another new letter,

The current now flows from the third wheel to the commutator fixed inside the machine, via an electrical contact between the live pin on the third wheel and one of twenty-six studs arranged in a circular pattern on the side of the commutator.

The twenty-six studs of the commutator are connected internally in pairs so that the current now passes through it and back to the third wheel by a completely different connected pair of commutator stud and wheel pin. This pin will be in a position which corresponds to another new letter,

The current now flows back through the wheels taking one of twenty-six possible routes through each wheel (note that these routes are via different connections to those used in the forward passage) and re-enters the entry disc at a pin which is associated with a particular letter (say C). The current now flows back to the plugboard where it connects to the same letter (C) via the lightboard plug.

The current now flows from C to Y in the plugboard and then to Y in the lightboard which is lit up. So now the letter F has been encrypted into the letter Y via nine transitions but note that a second depression of the letter F on the keyboard immediately after will NOT be encrypted into Y for the following reason.

Whenever a key is depressed on the keyboard, setting up a current as described above, the first wheel (and only the first wheel) is rotated by one position. Now if the same key is depressed again the current will take the same path through the plugboard and entry disc but will now make contact with a different pin on the first wheel. This will take it along a different internal path to a stud corresponding to a different letter. And so on through all the commutator and wheel transitions. This, naturally, will result in a different letter being illuminated on the lightboard.

Furthermore, when the first wheel has made twenty-six position changes and returns to its original setting, it causes the second wheel to advance by one position. Likewise, when the second wheel has advanced by twenty-six positions it causes the third wheel to advance by one position. In this way there will be 26 x 26 x 26 different wheel positions before returning to the start setting.

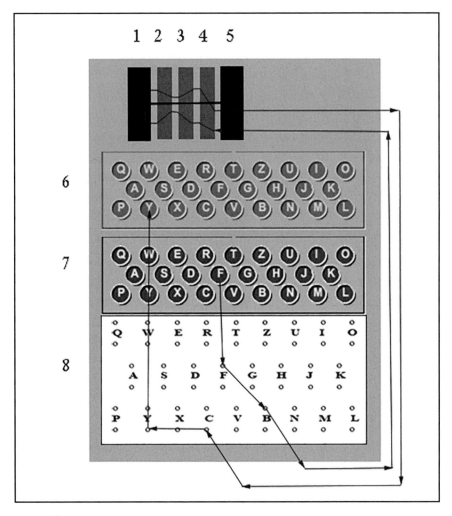

Encryption route.

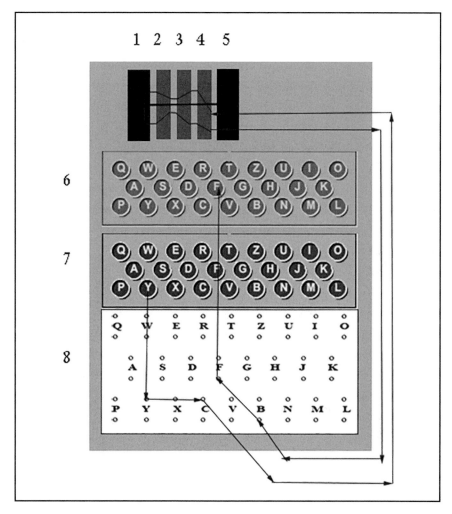

Decryption route.

Once encrypted, the message would be transmitted by radio link using Morse code in blocks of five letters. Every Enigma user within a network was given a 'key' to set up his machine. The key was changed periodically at intervals ranging from months to hours according to the level of security required. The key consisted of

- the ring setting (e.g. PYR) ringstellung
- the order and number of the wheels in the scrambler unit (e.g. I IV III)
- the cross-plugging connections (e.g. F/B W/T S/G C/Y B/A X/E Q/U etc).

When two Enigma machines were set with the same key the internal electrical connections within them were identical.

Already having his machine set up with the correct key, to decipher the message the recipient would also need to be told how the wheels in the encrypting machine had been set and the simplest way to do this was to say which letter of each wheel was in the topmost position at the start of encryption.

The exact starting configuration of the encrypting machine will need to be known by the recipient in order to decrypt the message. As well as the key, this will consist of information relating to the starting positions of each of the three wheels. Each wheel had a protruding indented flange allowing it to be separately rotated by hand round its axis and fixed in place by a spring clip. By turning the wheels, the operator could choose three letters at random to appear in the topmost positions and be visible through a glass window (wheel setting).

Firstly, he decides which wheel setting he will adopt when encrypting his message (e.g. ESN), but does not yet set the wheels in that position. Instead he chooses a second random wheel setting (e.g. XFO, indicator setting) to which he now sets the wheels. With XFO now showing in the window he depresses the letter E on the keyboard and notes which letter is illuminated on the lightboard (e.g. Z). Note that a different letter will now appear in place of X in the window (*FO). Now he depresses S and again notes the illuminated letter (e.g. W) and repeats for N (B). He now depresses E again and notes the illuminated letter (e.g. T) which is not the same one as illuminated for the first depressing of E since the first wheel has moved by three positions. He does the same for S and N and records a new sequence which may be something like ZWBTGL. This is the encoding of ESNESN with a starting wheel position of XFO. The operator now sets his wheels to the first setting ESN and begins encryption of his message. As each key is depressed, he notes the letter illuminated in the lightboard and writes it down.

He now passes the series of encrypted letters to the radio operator who prepares to transmit it, but first must prepare a preamble to the encryption. The preamble will be transmitted in plain text (i.e. not encrypted). This preamble will consist of:

- His call sign (identifier) and the call sign of the unit the message is intended for and possibly the call sign of any other unit to which the message may be forwarded.
- The time of sending.

- The total number of letters in the encrypted text.
- Whether the message was complete or part of a larger message.
- A 'discriminant' indicating the type of traffic (level of command, type of military unit etc.). This will tell the recipient if that message is intended to be read and decrypted by his unit.
- The letters XFO (indicator setting) to inform the receiver how to set his own wheels.

Now he transmits the encrypted part which consists of the six letters of the twice encoded wheel setting ESN which is ZWBTGL followed by the encrypted message. The recipient would know to set his wheels to XFO. He would then press the letters ZWBTGL on his keyboard and, having his Enigma machine set up with the correct key, note that they are decrypted as ESNESN. He now sets his wheels to ESN and begins entering the letters of the encrypted message into his machine. Noting the sequence of illuminated letters each time will reveal to him the full plain text of the message.

The transcript of the preamble of a typical Enigma message (plain text; no encryption) may look like:

YTZ DP C 1525 = 163 = BSL YWK =

Call Sign	(from) YTZ (to) DP (and) C
Time	15.25
Characters	163
Discriminant	BSL
Indicator Setting	YWK

And this would be followed by the body of the message (encrypted) which would be blocks of five letters

KRSTB YHBTT PRNST JHHFF LRSDM …. Etc
(The operator might also add the frequency of transmission and the time of interception.)

If the cryptanalyst had an Enigma machine similar to the one used and a current code book, they would be able to decrypt the message by setting the wheels and steckerboard accordingly and feeding the letters through one at a time. Of course, that did not happen, so they had to try and work out the wheel setting and steckerboard settings from a standing start. It seems an almost impossible task given the vast number of possibilities.

The methods used were ingenious and complex. The people involved were mathematicians, chess champions, crossword puzzlers; clear thinkers who relished the challenges of word games, logic problem and puzzles in general.

Inspired guesswork and supposition were the first important means. 'What if' or 'suppose that' were the first questions asked. Intuitive leaps such as that made by John Herivel played an important part. Sometimes it was pure observation as when, in January 1940, Dilly Knox discovered a serious breach of German operating protocol when sending messages of more than 250 characters (the maximum permitted for a single transmission). At the start of the second part, which would also have its own preamble, the operator might leave the machine configuration unchanged so that the wheel setting for the last character of the first message was the same as the wheel setting for the first character of the second part, and this setting was included in plain text in the preamble to the second part. The analysts then, knowing how many characters had been in the first part could set their replica machine to the discovered setting and click the wheels back through that number of turns to find the original setting. This did not open the box immediately, but it prised the lid enough to let the light in. These clues were called 'cills' after the first setting uncovered, CIL, and came to be known as 'cillies' (or sillies in recognition of the German operators contribution to their own downfall).

The main tools of decryption, however, were 'cribs'. Cribs gave cypher clerks clues about the type of information in the message. Weather reports, for instance, usually contained the same words and often in the same order, while the name of a unit, identified by the direction of the signal and maybe by some idiosyncrasy of the operator, would appear often. The latter made a little easier to spot since many units sent reports at exactly the same time every day. One operator even sent, day after day, the repeated message that he had 'nothing to report'.

In the main, Enigma traffic was routine, humdrum, and apparently of no great significance in terms of security which may have contributed to lazy practices becoming commonplace when operators were not under close scrutiny. The temptation to circumvent elaborate procedure when reporting wind speed and cloud cover every day must have been irresistible to more than just a few operators. The problem for them was that the decryption of such seemingly unimportant communications were a gateway through which analysts were able to enter a much bigger field of intelligence. The common short-cuts employed by Enigma operators were frequent use of common short words such as 'ist', or repeated use of short sequences of letters, which may have had meaning for the operator as in the initials of his girlfriend.

Appendix D

Giulio Douhet

Aviation is a strike force, a force of pure attack. By its almost unlimited destructive capacity, it can decide by itself the outcome of a war .[1]

Much government opinion throughout Europe about aerial warfare in the 1930s was founded on the work of Giulio Douhet, the 'arrogant and quarrelsome'[2] author of a 1921 book, *Command of the Air*, championing air forces as the pre-eminent player in any future war. On 15 October 1916, an Italian Court Martial had found Colonel Douhet guilty of expressing a 'point of view on the war effort that was contrary to information published by the High Command',[3] and sentenced him to a year's imprisonment. His 'crime' was to have written a criticism of the Italian action in taking the town of Gorizia which had left them 'without reserves and a scarcity of ammunition' in the face of renewed attacks by German forces. Douhet was a military strategist within the Italian General Staff, whose speciality was the 'mechanisation of warfare' and who, through the course of the First World War, had become increasingly critical of the Italian war effort.

At the time of Douhet's release from prison in October 1917, the Italians had suffered a catastrophic defeat in the Battle of Caporetto which, a committee of inquiry later found, could have been avoided if more attention had been paid to Douhet's critique of Italian military preparedness; the document for which he had been imprisoned. Upon appeal against his conviction, Douhet was pardoned, rehabilitated and promoted to major-general.

After the war, while continuing to pursue his interest in the techniques of modern warfare, he became a journalist and was actively involved in the burgeoning Fascist movement under Mussolini. In 1921 he published his seminal work in which he explained his theories of strategic bombing. This publication unequivocally endorsed air power as the supreme military force, superior to armies or navies and capable of playing a decisive role in any future war by the destruction of an enemy's infrastructure, especially industrial centres. Heavy bombers would cause massive damage in a very short time achieving results that could only otherwise be got by invasion and occupation by land forces over the course of a protracted and costly battle. Civilian lives would be lost by putting non-combatants in the firing line, but he argued that many soldiers' lives would be saved as a consequence. Douhet's opinions seem to have undergone a dramatic change, since this doctrine was directly at odds with previous conclusions published by him before 1914 in which he had rejected the bombing of defenceless civilian areas as a 'barbaric act'.[4] Initially unimpressed with the potential of air power for uses other than reconnaissance, he had seen no offensive role for flying machines but the rapid advances in aircraft design and capabilities caused to him to review his opinions.

It cannot have been coincidental that Douhet, at the same time, was involved with Fascism, which saw nations as being the prime entity and armed forces simply instruments of achieving a nation's destiny, as well as being an expression of pride. War was increasingly seen as a 'national' enterprise in which everyone played a part, not just armies in the field. The concept of 'terror bombing' was conceived, whereby the whole enemy nation would be viewed as culpable for the actions of its leaders, whom it voted into power or at the very least whose decision to go to war was not challenged by the people. By November 1915, Douhet 'openly called for the strategic bombing of urban centres.'[5] Even during the First World War there had been calls from French strategists to bomb German cities. This was clearly a move towards 'terror bombing', as any attempt to justify such actions by reference to bombing strategic locations within the cities could be completely ruled out by the sheer inadequacy of bomb-aiming techniques that rendered precision bombing impossible. However, an 'Inter-Allied Aviation Committee', convened in 1918, adopted the British proposal to launch a massive air offensive against German cities which was subsequently abandoned when Germany capitulated. Although never activated, this policy decision coloured military opinion during the post-war years. The French were less than enthusiastic given the proximity of their cities to the German border, but conceded that a massive bombing action against civilian centres could break the morale of the working population and thus jeopardise the supply of military materiel to the armed forces, as well as destabilising the social contract between the government and the governed. Douhet was to declare that 'the distinction no longer exists between belligerents and civilians since all are working for the war effort'. This was justified by making it equivalent to a naval blockade, widely practised, which caused death and hardship to all citizens of the beleaguered nation. It was also simply an extension of the terror bombing of non-combatants which had been commonly practised by Britain and many other European nations against 'tribal' populations in colonial Africa and the Middle East for some years. British air war strategists declared that it was the object of any warring nation to break the willpower of the enemy nation to resist.

Having accepted the concept of strategic bombing as a paradigm shift in military thinking and one with dramatic possibilities, the victorious allied nations in the Treaty of Versailles strictly prohibited Germany from building an air force. The Reichswehr, however, were able to acquire secret training facilities as early as 1925 for pilots at Lipetsk in the Soviet Union which was essentially a fighter school but began testing bombers in 1930.[6]

Alongside the growing enthusiasm for air power there was still a debate about its morality. Douhet had achieved prominence as a revolutionary strategic theorist in the field and his views, which gave coherent justification for air warfare, were consequently given serious consideration. The military were anxious for their new concepts to be given legitimacy, given their contentious consequences. Douhet, while championing the use of massive force against civilian centres, was clear that it could only be justified in terms of 'justice' against a 'criminal act' of aggression by a nation in the grip of militarism and should be carried out by an international (or supranational) power. The theory, of course, lacked credibility in the absence of any such organ of 'universal justice', but the underlying idea of justified force inherent in the doctrine survived this impediment.[7]

The essential concepts of Douhetist air warfare were: first, that command of air space is of paramount importance in any conflict; second, that control of air power should be wielded independently of land and sea forces although, of course, all three could be combined within a tactical or strategic initiative; under no circumstances should air power be subordinated to the other military arms. Third, that air power is an offensive not a defensive weapon. This was seen as axiomatic since it was clearly extremely difficult to defend a wide area of sky, some tens or hundreds of miles across, on a continuous basis, while a concentrated force falling unexpectedly upon a given target would be almost impossible to resist. The concept that 'the bomber would always get through' became the mantra of many, including the British Air Ministry, and underlay much of their investment and policy decisions during the 1920s and early 1930s.

While Britain was fixated on the notion of the invincibility of the bomber, which severely restricted production of fighter aircraft thought to be of little use as deterrents or a defence, Germany was equally under the influence of Douhetist doctrine as clearly shown in the approach taken by Göring during the Battle of Britain when all three strategies were employed. After initially resisting calls for the terror bombing of London, Hitler too, was following Douhetist theory when he eventually gave in to calls from Göring and Sperrle to initiate the 'Blitz', which was specifically designed to break the will of the British people, turn them against Parliament and force the government to seek peace terms. It seems clear that the near-catastrophe of British un-preparedness for war in 1939 and the failure of German air policy against Britain in 1940 are bold refutations of Douhetist theory, but they also owe much, in the British case, to the intransigence of embedded but redundant doctrine and, in the case of the Luftwaffe, to the power of uneducated and unimaginative leadership to wilfully court disaster.

Sources

Barley, M.P., *Contributing to its Own Defeat: The Luftwaffe and the Battle of Britain* (Defence Studies, 2006)

Calvacoressi, Peter, *Top Secret Ultra* (M & M Baldwin, 2011)

Clark, Gregory C., *Deflating British Radar Myths of World War II* (The Research Department of Air Command and Staff College, 1997)

Collier, Basil, *The Defence of the United Kingdom* (The Naval and Military Press, 2004)

Corum, James S. *The Luftwaffe, Creating the Operational Air War 1918-1940* (University of Kansas Press, 1997)

Deichmann, Paul D.*, The System of Target Selection Applied by the German Air Force in World War II* (USAF Historical Studies 186, 1956)

Deighton, Len and **Hastings**, Max, *Battle of Britain* (Jonathan Cape, 1981)

Fisher, David, *A Summer Bright and Terrible* (Shoemaker and Hoard, 2005)

Forczyk, Robert, *We March against England, Operation Sea Lion 1940-41* (Osprey, 2016)

Gottschling, Kurt *The Radio Intercept Service of the German Air Force* (USAF Historical Studies 191, 1955)

Hastings, Max, T*he Secret War* (William Collins, 2015)

Hinsley, F.H., Thomas, E.E., Ransom C.F.G., Knight, R.C. *British Intelligence in the Second World War Volume 1* (Her Majesty's Stationery Office, 1979)

Hippler, Thomas, *Governing from the Skies* (Verso, 2017)

Hooton, E.R., *Eagle in Flames, The Fall of the Luftwaffe* (Arms and Armour, 1997)

Jacobs, Peter, *Airfields of 11 Group* (Pen and Sword, 2005)

James T.C.G., *The Battle of Britain* (Frank Cass, 2000)

Jennings, Christian, *The Third Reich is Listening, Inside German Codebreaking 1939-45* (Osprey, 2018)

Jones R.V., *Most Secret War* (Penguin, 1978)

241

Kahn, David, *Seizing the Enigma* (Houghton Mifflin, 1991)

Kahn, David, *Hitler's Spies, German Military Intelligence in World War II*, (Macmillan, 1978)

Kesselring, Albert, *The Memoirs of Field-Marshal Kesselring* (The History Press, 2015)

Kieser, Robert, *Operation Sea Lion* (Cassell, 1998)

Kreipe, Werner, Diary entry for 11 August 1944.

LaSaine, John T. Jnr., *Air Officer Commanding; Hugh Dowding Architect of the Battle of Britain* (University of New England Press, 2018)

Mahlke, Hans Ulrich, *Stuka Pilot* (Black House, 2016)

Matthews, Peter, *Sigint, The Secret History of Signals Intelligence inn the World Wars (*The History Press, 2018*)*

Mckay, Sinclair, *The Secret Listeners (*Aurum Press, 2013)

McKinstrey, Leo, *Operation Sealion* (John Murray, 2014)

Mitcham, Samuel W., *Eagles of the Third Reich* (Stackpole Books, 2007)

Nielsen, Andreas L., *The Collection and Evaluation of Intelligence for the German Air Force High Command* (USAF Historical Studies 171, 1955)

Nielsen, Andreas L., *The German Air Force General Staff* (USAF Historical Studies No 173, 1959)

O'Connor, J.J. and **Robertso**n E.F., (School of Mathematics and Statistics, University St Andrews, Scotland 2017)

Overy, R.J., *Goering, The Iron Man* (Routledge and Kegan Paul, 1984)

Paine, Lauran, *German Military Intelligence in World War II* (Military Heritage Press, 1984)

Parkinson, Roger *Summer 1940, The Battle of Britain* (David McKay, 1977)

Parsinnen, Terry, *The Oster Conspiracy of 1938* (Pimlico, 2004)

Phelps, Stephen, *The Tizard Mission* (Westholme, 2012)

Price, Alfred Dr, *Instruments of Darkness, The History of Electronic Warfare 1939-1945* (Frontline Books, 1977)

Price, Alfred Dr, *The Luftwaffe Data Book* (Greenhill, 1977)

Pritchard, David *The Radar War* (Patrick Stephens, 1989)

Ray, John, *The Battle of Britain, New Perspectives* (Arms and Armour, 1994)

Robertson E.M., *Mussolini as Empire Builder* (London, 1977)

Robinson, Derek, *Invasion 1940* (Constable and Robinson, 2005)

Saunders, Andy, *The Battle of Britain RAF Operations Manual* (Haynes, 2015)

Sebag-Montefiore, Hugh, *Enigma, The Battle for the Code* (Weidenfeld & Nicolson, 2001)

Staerck, Christopher & **Sinnot,** Paul, *Luftwaffe; The Allied Intelligence Files* (Brassey's 2002)

Stripp, Alan, *Enigma, How the Poles Broke the Nazi Code* (New York, Hippocrene, 2004)

Suchenwirth, Dr Richard, *Command and Leadership in the German Air Force 1919-1939,* (New York, USAF Historical Studies No 174, 1968)

Suchenwirth, Dr Richard, *The development of the German Air Force 1919-1939* (New York, USAF Historical Studies No 160, 1968)

Tate, Tim, *Hitler's British Traitors, The Secret History of Spies, Saboteurs and Fifth Columnists (*Icon Books, 2018)

Taylor, Telford, *The Breaking Wave, World War in the Summer of 1940* (Simon and Schuster, 1967)

Taylor, Telford, *The Anatomy of the Nuremberg Trials* (Skyhorse, 2013)

Tremain, David, *The Beautiful Spy, The Life and Crimes of Vera Eriksen* (The History Press, 2019)

Wadman, David, *Aufklärer Luftwaffe Reconnaissance Aircraft and Units 1935-1941* (Midland, 2007)

Welchman, Gordon, *The Hut Six Story, Breaking the Enigma Codes* (M & M Baldwin, 2018)

Wilkins, Arnold, *The Birth of British radar*, (Radio Society of Great Britain, 2011)

Wood, Derek with **Dempster**, Derek, *The Narrow Margin* (Hutchison & Co, 1969)

Zimmerman, David, *Britain's Shield, Radar and the Defeat of the Luftwaffe* (Sutton Publishing, 2001)

Web sites

International Committee of the Red Cross; Geneva Convention, *https://www.icrc.org/en/war-and-law/treaties-customary-law/geneva-conventions*

Notes

Introduction

1. Kahn, p.41
2. Hinsley, p.6
3. Hastings p.61

Chapter 1: Luftwaffe Intelligence

1. Wood and Dempster p.119
2. Nielsen, USAF Historical Studies 171 p.16
3. Kahn p.63
4. Nielsen, USAF Historical Studies 171 p.9
5. Parsinnen
6. Hastings p.57
7. Jennings p.68
8. Kahn p.179
9. Jennings p.69
10. Kahn p.382
11. Nielsen, USAF Historical Studies 171 p.33
12. Holland p.536
13. Kahn p.382
14. Nielsen, USAF Historical Studies 171 p.53
15. ibid p.27
16. Mitcham
17. Kahn p.382
18. ibid p.383
19. Nielsen, USAF Historical Studies 171 p.37
20. Price p.14
21. Forczyk p.111

NOTES

22. Nielsen, USAF Historical Studies 171 p.55
23. Kahn p.384
24. ibid p.200
25. Jennings p.130
26. ibid p.133
27. Suchenwirth p.101
28. ibid p.102
29. ibid p.103
30. Nielsen, USAF Historical Studies 171 p.17
31. ibid p. 20
32. ibid p.17
33. Jennings p.68
34. ibid p.71
35. Nielsen, USAF Historical Studies 171 p.34
36. Kahn p.115
37. Wadman p.15
38. ibid
39. Nielsen, USAF Historical Studies 171 p.35
40. Wadman P.11
41. Nielsen, USAF Historical Studies 171 p.35
42. Forcyzk p.113
43. Nielsen, USAF Historical Studies 171 p.52
44. ibid p.111
45. ibid p.30
46. Phelps p.140
47. Taylor, *The Anatomy of the Nuremberg Trials*
48. Nielsen, USAF Historical Studies 171 p.91
49. Kahn p.138
50. Tate p.108
51. ibid p.48
52. Hastings p.62
53. Tate p.132
54. Kahn p.304
55. ibid p.306
56. ibid p.367
57. ibid p.351
58. ibid p.369
59. Taylor *The Breaking Wave,* p.106
60. ibid p.107
61. Nielsen, USAF Historical Studies 171 p.40

62. Deichmann p.3
63. ibid p.7
64. Taylor, *The Anatomy of the Nuremberg Trials*
65. Deichmann p.22
66. ibid p.32
67. Nielsen, USAF Historical Studies 171 p.60
68. ibid p.64
69. ibid p.124
70. Forcyzk
71. Jennings p.120
72. Wood and Dempster p.65
73. Nielsen, USAF Historical Studies 171 p.109
74. ibid p.66-7
75. Fisher p.164
76. Nielsen, USAF Historical Studies 171 p.124
77. Forcyzk p.116
78. Nielsen, USAF Historical Studies 171 p.128
79. ibid p.128
80. ibid p.99
81. Deichmann p.3
82. Barley p.407
83. Wood and Dempster p.70
84. Nielsen, USAF Historical Studies 171 p.130
85. ibid p.126
86. Suchenwirth, USAF Historical Studies 174 p.146
87. Nielsen, USAF Historical Studies 171 p.210
88. ibid p.221
89. ibid p.221
90. Nielsen, USAF Historical Studies 171 p.125
91. ibid p.122

Chapter 2: Reichsmarschall Hermann Wilhelm Göring

1. Suchenwirth p.143
2. Overy p.ix
3. Sucherwirth p.127
4. ibid p.133
5. Blood-Ryan p.25
6. Suchernwirth p.114

7. Blood-Ryan p.26
8. ibid p.40
9. Suchenwirth p.115
10. Blood-Ryan p.38
11. Overy p.13
12. Suchenwirth p.117
13. Blood-Ryan p.61
14. ibid p.71
15. Suchenwirth p.107
16. ibid p.121
17. ibid
18. Overy p16
19. Suchenwirth p.135
20. ibid p.54
21. Overy p.1
22. Suchenwirth p.132
23. Taylor, *Nuremberg* p.329
24. Suchenwirth p.142
25. ibid p.140
26. Suchenwirth p.174
27. Nielsen, USAF Historical Studies No 173 p.143
28. Ray p.36
29. Kreipe
30. Suchenwirth p.127
31. Robertson p.57
32. Nielsen, USAF Historical Studies No 173 p.138
33. Overy p.91
34. Taylor, *Nuremberg* p.331
35. Overy p.94
36. Suchenwirth p.131
37. ibid p.142
38. Nielsen, USAF Historical Studies No 173 p.148
39. Overy p.153
40. ibid
41. ibid
42. ibid
43. ibid p.154
44. ibid p.13
45. Overy p.157
46. Taylor, *Nuremberg*

47. Overy p.84
48. ibid p.159

Chapter 3: German Radar

1. Pritchard p.55
2. ibid p.35
3. ibid p.15
4. Clark p.3
5. Pritchard p.22
6. ibid p.36
7. ibid p.41
8. Phelps p.27
9. Pritchard p.44
10. Clark p.19
11. Baughen p.66
12. ibid p.14
13. Pritchard p.35
14. ibid p.65
15. Keiser p.172
16. Zimmerman p.204
17. Pritchard p.55
18. Malke p.125
19. Zimmerman p.205
20. Wood and Dempster p.209

Chapter 4: RAF Intelligence

1. Jones p.92
2. Hinsley p.3
3. ibid p.4
4. ibid p.10
5. Wood and Dempster p.74
6. Hinsley p.78
7. Hippler p.119
8. Hinsley p.79
9. ibid p.182

10. McKay p35
11. Hinsley p.178
12. ibid p.179
13. ibid p.269
14. ibid p.179
15. Calvacoressi p.55
16. McKay p.42
17. Calvacoressi p.58
18. Hinsley p.181
19. ibid p.320
20. ibid p.321
21. Sebag-Montefiore p.103
22. Welchman p.77
23. Hinsley p.29
24. Baughen p.60
25. McKinstry p.263
26. Hinsley p.102
27. Forczyk p.94
28. ibid p.95
29. Hinsley p.101
30. Ray p.36
31. Kreipe
32. Hinsley p.56
33. ibid p.95
34. Jones p.58
35. Hinsley p.100
36. Collier p.232
37. Hinsley p.170
38. ibid p.166
39. ibid p.167
40. McKinstry p.193
41. Taylor, *The Breaking Wave* p.22
42. Hinsley p.188
43. ibid p.90
44. Parkinson p.59
45. ibid p.40
46. James p.399
47. Hinsley p.316
48. Taylor, *The Breaking Wave* p.120

49. Jones p.85
50. ibid p.93
51. ibid p.96
52. ibid p.100
53. ibid p.101
54. ibid p.103
55. Price, *Instruments of Darkness* p.22
56. Jones p.120
57. ibid p.23
58. ibid p.25
59. ibid p.38
60. ibid p.40
61. ibid p.41
62. ibid p.44

Chapter 5: Air Chief Marshal Sir Hugh Caswall Tremenheere Dowding

1. Taylor, *The Breaking Wave* p.85
2. Holland p.158
3. LaSaine p.42
4. Deighton and Hastings p.42
5. LaSaine p.58
6. Holland p.158
7. LaSaine p.66
8. ibid p.76
9. ibid p.74
10. Orange p.99
11. ibid p.89
12. ibid p.90
13. ibid p.123
14. ibid p.124

Chapter 6: British Radar

1. Galland p.17
2. Zimmerman p.12

3. ibid p.31
4. ibid p.43
5. ibid p.44
6. Jones p.16
7. Wilkins p.35
8. Zimmerman p.78
9. Wilkins p.27
10. ibid p.84
11. ibid p.84
12. Wilkins p.36
13. Zimmerman p.87
14. Wilkins p.43
15. Zimmerman p.58
16. ibid p.90
17. Orange p.88
18. ibid p.81
19. Jones p.40
20. Zimmerman p.119
21. ibid p.170
22. ibid p.135
23. ibid p.137
24. ibid p.138
25. ibid p.137
26. ibid p.139
27. Saunders p.80
28. Wilkins p.61
29. Zimmerman p.186
30. Pritchard p.182
31. Zimmerman p.185
32. ibid p.171
33. ibid p.183

Chapter 7: The Dowding System

1. Wood and Dempster p.116
2. Collier p.34
3. Orange p.86
4. Wood and Dempster p.96

 5. Saunders p.19
 6. Wood and Dempster p.96
 7. ibid
 8. Zimmerman p.40
 9. ibid p.110
10. ibid p.113
11. ibid p.116
12. Orange p.86
13. Zimmerman p.41
14. Orange p.118
15. Wood and Dempster p.119
16. ibid p.118
17. Saunders p.66
18. Wood and Dempster p.121
19. Zimmerman p.113
20. ibid p.164
21. ibid p.111
22. ibid p.166
23. ibid p.167
24. ibid p.168
25. ibid p.174
26. Orange p.118
27. Ibid p.118-9
28. Jacob p.78

Chapter 8: Testing the Dowding System to Destruction

 1. Price p.83
 2. Orange p.153
 3. Zimmerman p.198
 4. ibid p.200
 5. ibid p.201
 6. ibid
 7. ibid p.202
 8. Zimmerman p.206
 9. Mahlke p.125
10. Saunders p.86
11. James p.311

12. Wood and Dempster p.290
13. Wilkins P.59
14. Zimmerman p.209
15. Orange p.179

Chapter 9: The Tizard Committee

1. Phelps p.xi
2. LaSaine p.40
3. Phelps p.20
4. ibid p.23
5. Zimmerman p.44
6. Phelps p.18
7. ibid p.32
8. Jones p.83
9. Hastings p.42
10. Jones p.40
11. ibid p.42
12. ibid p.43
13. ibid p.74
14. ibid
15. ibid p.75
16. ibid p.77
17. Phelps p.57
18. ibid p.59
19. Kahn p.331
20. Phelps p.61
21. ibid p.63
22. ibid p.66
23. ibid p.70
24. Jones p.95-6
25. Phelps p.84
26. ibid p.122
27. ibid p.92
28. ibid p.129
29. ibid p.101
30. ibid p.129
31. Phelps p.133

32. ibid
33. ibid p.141
34. ibid p.152
35. ibid p.159

Chapter 10: Enigma

1. Hastings p.xvii
2. ibid p.73
3. Jennings p.40
4. ibid p.65
5. ibid p.311
6. Sebag-Montefiore p.22
7. ibid p.61
8. ibid p.99
9. Welchman p.56
10. ibid p.153
11. Sebag-Montefiore p.102
12. Welchman p.35-6
13. Welchman p.53
14. ibid p.88
15. ibid p.91
16. ibid p.58
17. Sebag-Montefiore p.91
18. Hinsley p.144
19. Jones p.125
20. ibid
21. Welchman p.96
22. Hastings p.75

Chapter 11: Polish Codebreakers

1. Kahn, *Seizing the Enigma*
2. Calvacoressi p.70
3. ibid p.65
4. O'Connor and Robertson
5. Sebag-Motefiore p.36

6. ibid p.18
7. Welchman p.15
8. Sebag-Montefiore p.31
9. ibid p.290
10. ibid p.50
11. Stripp
12. O'Connor and Robertson

Appendix A: The Oslo Report (extracts)

1. Hastings p.44

Appendix B: British Intelligence on Luftwaffe Aircraft

1. Staerck and Sinnott

Appendix C: How the Enigma Machine Worked

1. Welchman p.52
2. Calvacoressi p.7

Appendix D: Giulio Douhet

1. Hippler p.138
2. ibid p.119
3. ibid p.120
4. Douhet, p.133-4
5. Hippler p.123
6. Corum p.115-6
7. Hippler p.134

Index

11 Group, 35, 38, 41, 45, 97, 101, 107, 120–2, 147, 150, 157, 159, 168–9, 172–3

3rd Abteilung, Funkhorchdienst; 3rd Branch Foreign Powers Section, 7–9, 37, 42, 170

5th Abteilung, 5th Branch Foreign Powers Section D5, 2, 4–6, 9, 15, 25, 38–9, 47, 72

8th Abteilung, 8th Branch Foreign Powers Section, 15

Abwehr, OKW Counterintelligence Office, 1, 12–13, 19–21, 183, 212

ADEE (Air Defence Experimental Establishment), 125

Adlerangriff, 14, 29, 40–2, 44, 80–1, 104, 145, 169–70, 172

Adlertag, 40

ADRC (Air Defence Research Committee), 133, 160, 176, 179–80

Air Intelligence, x 87, 181, 204–205

Alexander, Hugh, 89–90

AMES (Air Ministry Experimental Station), 135

Anderson, Admiral, 189

Anschluss, 25, 85, 117, 132

ASDIC, 184–5

aspirins, navigation beams, 111

ATB (Advisory Committee on Trade Questions in Time of War), 83

Atlee, Clement, 132

Aufklärer, Luftwaffe Reconnaissance Units, 12

AVA Radio Company, 207, 213, 215

Bade, Lily, 20

Bader, Douglas, 122, 174

Baldwin, Stanley, 123, 176

Baroness Carin von Ganzow, 56

BATDU (Blind Approach Training and Development Unit), 111

Battle of Barking Creek, 165, 167

Bawdsey Manor, 80, 128, 130–2, 136, 138–9, 155, 159

B-Dienst, 29

Beaumanor, 87, 90

Beaverbrook, Lord, 45, 47, 52, 185, 187

Becket, Thomas Hubert, 19

BEF, 203

Bell Telephone Laboratories, 190

Bentley Priory, 42, 88, 113, 116, 129, 131, 137–8, 141, 147–52, 156–7, 162, 171

Bertrand, Gustave, 195, 209–12, 215–18

Messerschmitt Bf109, 33, 35, 41, 72, 78, 84–5, 91, 145, 223–4

Messerschmitt Bf110, 33, 35, 49, 78, 105–106, 145, 169–71

Biggin Hill, 44, 125, 146, 153, 163, 173

Biuro Szyfrów, 207–208, 213

Bletchley Park, viii, 85, 87, 90, 104, 111, 181, 192, 195–7, 200–202, 205, 207

Boetzel, Oberstleutnant Fritz, 7, 15

bomby, 195, 200, 214–15

Boniface, Enigma intelligence, 87, 192, 203, 205

Boot, Henry A.H., 186

Boulton Paul Defiant, 114, 117, 224

Bowen, Edward, 188–90

Boyes, Hector, 94

Bracquenié, Henri, 215–16

Bredstedt, 109

Brinker, Dr., 135

British Intelligence, ix, 11, 15, 17, 20–1, 83–6, 89, 93, 95–6, 99, 101, 116, 153, 182, 195–6, 198, 201, 203, 205, 218

Bufton, Flight Lieutenant Harold, 109

Buggisch, Otto, 15

Byrne, Vincent, 166–7

Cadogan, Sir Alexander, 94

call sign, 88–9, 110, 197–8, 235

Calvacoressi, Peter, 207, 226

Canaris, Konteradmiral Wilhelm Franz, 1, 212

Canewdon, 80

Caroli, Gösta (codename 'Leonhardt), (codename 'Summer'), 21–2

CD (Coastal Defence Radar), 136–7, 139, 159

CH (Chain Home), 77, 79, 124, 135–9, 141, 158–9, 161, 171–3

Chamberlain, Neville, 64, 115, 165, 183

Château de Vignolles, 196, 216

Château des Fouzes, 196, 217

Château-Thierry, Anna Sonia de, 22

Chatham, 87, 89–90, 196, 198–200

Cheadle, x 86–7, 89, 102, 107

Cherbourg, 109–11

Chicksands Priory, 90

Chiffriermachinen Akteingesellschaft, 194

CHL (Chain Home Low), 77, 124, 127, 137–9, 159–60, 170

Churchill, Winston, 17–18, 39, 47, 86, 95, 97, 100, 109, 121, 129–30, 132–3, 143, 160, 165, 167, 174–7, 180, 184–8, 202

Ciężki, Maksymilian, 208, 214, 216–19

Cillies, 211, 216, 236

Cockcroft, John T., 188

Cockfosters, 104, 108

Comparative Study of RAF and Luftwaffe Striking Power, 32

Connolly, Cyril, 19

Cotton, Wing Commander Sydney, 91–2

Courtney, Air Chief Marshal Sir Christopher Lloyd, 120, 174

crib, 7–8, 236

Cromwell, Code for invasion, 103

CRT (Cathode Ray Tube), 126, 137

CSDIC, AII(k) branch at the Combined Services Detailed Interrogation Centre, 104

CSSAD (Committee for the Scientific Survey of Air Defence), 125, 176–7, 180, 185
cyclometer, 213
Czech intelligence, 90

Dahlerus, Berger, 64
Danilewicz, Ludomir, 209
Darley, Squadron Leader H.S., 106
Denniston, Alastair, 215
Dezimeter Telegraphie (De Te), 77
Dickens, Dr. B.G., 146
Die Luftwacht, 25
Dieppe, 111
discriminants, 197–8, 235
Donaldson, Squadron Leader E.M., 165–6
Donovan, William J., 187
Doppelkassettenverfahren, 217
Dornier Do 17, 224
Dornier Do 217, 224
Douhet, Guilio, 85, 123, 237–9
Dover, 45, 81, 98, 170–1
Dowding, Air Chief Marshal Sir Hugh Caswall Tremenheere, xi, 37, 52, 72, 97–9, 101, 104, 107–108, 112–22, 126, 129–30, 134, 141, 143–4, 146, 149, 152, 156, 158–63, 165, 167, 171, 174, 176–7, 179, 185, 204–205
Dowding System, viii, 10, 33, 97, 99, 101, 112–13, 141, 143–64, 167, 173
Driffield, 43
Drueke, Theodore, 22
Duchess of Richmond, 188–9
Dunderdale, Wilfred, 210
Dunkirk, 15, 17–18, 32–3, 37, 39, 47, 58, 70–1, 80, 92, 96–7, 99, 155, 167–8, 171, 203

Eastchurch, 43
Eckhardt, Heinrich von, 193
Economic Warfare Intelligence (EWI), 91–2, 95
Ellington, Sir Edward, 114–17
Emden, 8
Enigma red, 103, 192, 199–205, 216–17
Erfurt, 7
Erprobungsgruppe 210, 43, 80, 136, 170–1

Faulkner, Captain H.W., 188
FCI (Committee of Imperial Defence), 83
Fellgiebel, General Erich, 15
Felmy, General Helmuth, 23–4
Fenner, William, 11
Fernaufklärungsgruppe ObdL, Long-range reconnaissance for the C-in-C of the Luftwaffe, 13
Ferngesteuerte Zielflugzeug, 221
Fighter Command, vii, xi–xii, 9, 17, 19, 33, 35–47, 52–3, 72–3, 80–3, 86, 89, 96–9, 102–107, 112, 116–21, 142–9, 157–62, 167–8, 172–4, 178–82
FLAK GAST, 202
Flinders, Sergeant, 166
Focke Wulf Fw200 Condor, 14
Fokczyński, Edward, 218
Forbes-Sempill, William Francis, 19th Lord Sempill, 17
Foreign Office, ix, 83, 94
Forschungamt, x, 2, 11, 17, 64
Four Year Plan, 67–8, 93
Franken, 221
Frankfurter, Felix, 184
Freeborn, P.O., 166–7
Freudenfeld, Major Ulrich, 9

Freya radar system, 77–9, 104, 110, 127, 135
FuG 25a Erstling, 135

Gaca, Kazimierz, 218
Galland, Adolf, 3, 123
Gano, Colonel, 219
GC & CS (Government Code and Cypher School), 83, 88
Gema Company, 77, 135
German Air Field Manual, 25, 40, 74
Golovine, Michael, 84–5
goniometer, 128, 138
Göring, Reichsmarschall Hermann Wilhelm, vii, x–xi, 2–6, 9, 11–18, 23–7, 31, 33, 37–49, 53–74, 80–1, 93, 112, 129, 164, 170–2, 240
Gort, Lord, 203
Gosport, 43, 171
Gottschling, Kurt, 8, 44
Graf Zeppelin, 9, 80
Graliński, Jan, 217
Cavity magnetron, 186, 188–90
Grenfell, 152–4
Gretz-Armainvillieres, 196, 216
Grosvenor, Hugh Richard Arthur, 2nd Duke of Westminster, 18
Guderian, General Heinz, 48
Gutheridge, William, 23

Hague Conference, 40
Hague Convention, 25
Halder, General Fritz, 37
Halifax, 18, 64, 188, 190
Hansa Luftbild GmbH, 12
Hawkinge, 43
headaches, navigation beam jamming, 111

Heinkel,
  He111, 13, 21, 25, 86, 108, 111, 224
  He113, 223
  He176, 93
  He177, 68, 224
  Hs 59, 107
Herivel, John, 201, 216, 236
Hermann, mystic, 16
Hertz, Heinrich, 145
Heston Special Flight, 91
Hill, Professor Archibald Vivian, 184
Hintlesham, 166
Hinxton, 22
Hitler, Adolf, 2–3, 12, 15, 18, 21, 24, 30–2, 37, 39–40, 45–8, 56–61, 64–74, 93–4, 103, 116, 240
Hitler's Directive No. 6, 30
Hitler's Directive No. 9, 31
Hitler's Directive No. 13, 32
Hülsmeyer, Johan Cristel (Christian), 76–7
Husum, 8
Hut 3, 201–207
Hut 6, 200–204
Hutton-Harrop, Montagu, 166

IFF (Identify Friend or Foe), 119, 126, 134–5, 189
IIC (Industrial Intelligence Centre), 83
III./Luftnachrichten-Regiment 2, 37
indicator, 197, 210, 212–14, 234–5
Ing, Oberst, 38
Ironside, Edmund, 64, 100

Jeffreys, John, 200, 216
Jeschonnek, Chief of the Luftwaffe General Staff Hans, 2, 5–6, 13, 24, 27, 45, 66, 80, 170

Jever, 78
JIC (Joint Intelligence Sub-
Committee), 83–5, 94, 97,
100, 103
Jones, Professor Reginald Victor,
78, 95, 108–11, 130, 177–86
Joubert de la Ferté, Air Marshal
Philip, 174
Junkers,
Ju87, 72, 81, 171, 225
Ju88, 49, 221, 225

Keppler, Wilhelm, 67
Kerr, Philip, Marquis of Lothian, 184
Kesselring, Generalfeldmarschall
Albert, 27, 38, 41, 44, 49, 60–3,
80–1, 170
key, 197–204, 214, 226–7, 231–5
KG 100, 89, 110–12
KG 54, 110
Knickebein, 107–11, 160, 182, 185–6
Knox, Alfred Dillwyn (Dilly),
215, 236
Kriegsmarine, 8
Krygowski, Zdzisław, 208, 218
Kühnhold, Rudolf, 76–7

Lamoricière, 217
Lane, François, 217
Lang, Wing Commander
Thomas, 168
Lang, Hermann W., 183
Langer, Gwido, 207, 210, 214, 216,
218–19
Lee-on-Solent, 43, 171
Leigh-Mallory, Air Vice-Marshal
Trafford, 121–2
Lemoine (Stallmann), Rodolphe,
209–12

Lichterfelde Cadet School, 54
Lindemann, Frederick, 109, 111,
125, 129–33, 175–80, 185
Londonderry, Lord, 175
Lorenz Company, 77
Lorenz system, 110
Lörrach, 110
Lörzer, Bruno, 54–5
Lucking, Captain D.F., 166–7
Lucy spy ring, 15
Luftsreitkräfte, 13
Luftwaffe Air Field Manual, 40, 74
Lympne, 43
LZ127 Graf Zeppelin, 80

Mackey, Corporal Dennis, 109
Manston, 19, 43, 82, 109, 154
Marconi, 76
Martini, Generalleutnant Wolfgang,
7–11, 37–8, 77–80, 135, 164, 170
Martlesham Heath, 43
Mautendorf, 54
Mayer, Hans Ferdinand, 95
Mayer, Stefan, 215
Mayka, Maria Barbara, 215
Mechelen Incident, 24
Mers-el-Kebir, 186
Milch, General Erhard, 4–6, 27,
61–3, 75, 129
Ministry of Economic Warfare
(MEW), 91–2
Molotov-Ribbentrop Pact, 180
Mosley, Sir Edward, 18
Muehlhausen, 54
Munich Crisis, 6, 85, 90, 134

Neurath, German Foreign Minister,
Konstantin von, 2
Newall, Sir Cyril, 120–1, 174

Noisy, 9
Norden Mk XV bombsight, 16, 183–4, 187–90
Nuffield Spitfire Factory, 111
Nuremberg War Trials, 16, 25, 54, 58, 68

ObdL, Oberfehlshaber der Luftwaffe, 13, 25, 59
Oberursel, Dulag Luft, 16–17
Observer Corps, 79, 98, 119, 139, 142–5, 149, 155–9 162, 166, 173
OKH (Oberkommando der Heer), Army, 59, 61, 101
OKH/In 7/VI, German Amy Cryptanalytic Agency, 15
OKL (Oberkommando der Luftwaffe), 1
OKL Chi-Stelle, Luftwaffe equivalent of OKW-Chi, 7, 29
OKW, Armed Forces High Command, 1, 3, 7, 11–12, 15, 25, 37, 39, 44, 46–7, 59, 61–5, 135
OKW Chi, Oberkommando der Wermacht Chiffrierabteilung, 7, 11
Ondarza, Dr. Ramon von, 58
Operation Smith, 202
Orfordness, 126–8
Orientation Book Great Britain, 25
Oslo Report, 78, 95, 125, 221
Oster, Colonel Hans, 1, 15
Osterkamp, Generalmajor Theodor, 41
Owens, Arthur Graham (White), 20–3

Palluth, Antoni, 207–209, 212, 218
Paris, Dr. E. T., 139

Park, Sir Keith, viii, 35, 38, 97, 101, 107, 117, 120–2, 151, 157–8, 161–2, 165, 169, 172–4
PC Bruno, 216–17
Pearce, Group Captain F.L., 188
Peenemünde, 221
Pevensey, 81, 171
Photographic reconnaissance, 24, 85, 91
Plocher, Hermann, 3
Pokorny, Franciszek, 207–208
Portsmouth, 43, 128, 171
Potsdam, 5, 8–9, 29, 66
Preikschat, Herr, 135
Proposal for the Conduct of Air Warfare Against Britain, 30
PRU (Photographic Reconnaissance Unit), 91–2, 97, 100, 103
Pryn, 195

quartz crystal, 156

Raeder, Grossadmiral Erich, 101
Ramsay, Archibald Henry Maule, 18
Ramsgate, 19, 43
Randall, John T., 186
RCA, 190
RDF (Radio Direction Finding), 126–9, 134–6, 145–6, 155–6, 159, 162, 169, 173
Rechlin, 16, 60, 64, 93, 221-222
Referat Radiowywiadu, 208
Referat Szyfrów Własnych, 208
Rejewski, Marian, 195–6, 207–208, 210–20
Ribbentrop, Joachim von, 18, 64, 69, 180
Rights Club, 18

Ritter, Nikolaus (Dr. Ranzau),
19–22, 183
Roberts, G.A., 138
Robinson, Sonderzug, 5
Rochester, 43
Roosevelt, Theodor, 184–90
Rose, Frank C., 166
Round, Mitzi (Smythe), 19
Rowe, A.P. 158, 175
Rowehl, Oberst Theodor, 6, 12
Royal Navy Cypher No. 2, 29
Różycki, Jerzy, 195–6, 208, 210–17
Ruffian, signal, 111
Rumpel, Major, 16–17
Runge, Professor Wilhelm, 79
Russell, Hastings William
Sackville, Lord Tavistock, 18
Rye, 81, 171

Sandwith, Hunphrey, 215
Schacht, Hjalmar, 67
Schallberg, Vera de (Eriksen), 22
Scherbius, Arthur, 194
Schmid, Oberst Josef 'Beppo',
vii, x, 2–6, 10, 12, 16, 24–5, 27,
29–32, 35–41, 43–4, 46–9, 72–3,
164, 170, 194, 212
Schmidt, Hans Thilo, 194, 209
Schmidt, Dietrich Christian
(aka Hans Hansen, aka Bjorn
Björnson), 21
Scott, Walter John Montagu
Douglas, 8th Duke of
Buccleuch, 18
SCR-268, radar system, 189
SEE (Signals Experimental
Establishment), 124
Seelöwe, 202, 204
Seenotdienst, 107

Service de Renseignement, French
Intelligence Service, 209
settings, Enigma, 194, 197, 199-
201, 210–12, 226, 229, 231, 235
Sholto-Douglas, Air Marshal
William, 82, 117, 122, 129
Sicherheitdienst, SD, 214
Siebel, Fritz, 45
Siemens Research Labor, 95, 138
Simon, Walter, 19
Sinclair, Sir Archibald, 186
SIS (Secret Intelligence
Service), 83
Slessor, Sir John, 117
Smith, Reginald, 19
Smoleński, Piotr, 217
Southend, 43, 166
Spender, Michael, 92
Sperrle, Generalfeldmarschall
Hugo, 38, 41, 44, 66, 73, 80–1,
171, 240
Spitfire Mk 1, 91
Station Bruno, 196, 216–17
Station X, 181
steckerboard, 200, 202, 227,
235, 199
Stickleback, 134
Stollberg, 109–10
Strategic Reconnaissance
Group of the Luftwaffe High
Command, 12
Studie Blau, x, 27–9, 31, 36, 46–8
Stumpff, General Hans Jürgen, 23
Sub-Committee on the
Reorientation of Air defence
Systems of Great Britain, xi
Svenska Lufttrafik, 56
Swinton, Lord, 129, 176–7
Syko, Encryption system, 7–8

Tangmere, 43, 150
Telefunken, 77–9, 110
Telemobiloskop, 76
Telgte, 8
The Link, pro-Nazi propaganda organisation, 17
Thiele, Generalleutnant Fritz, 15
Tizard Committee, 82, 124–9, 131, 175–91
Tizard Mission, 16
TR-9B, 147
Trenchard, Lord, 114–15
Turing, Alan, 213, 216
Tuttle, Wing Commander Geoffrey W., 91–2
Twinn, Peter, 196
Type-X, 15

Udet, Ernst, Luftwaffe Director General of Equipment, 27, 45–6, 59, 66
Ultra, 205

Vannes, 111
Veldenstein, 54, 66
Venlo Incident, 96, 221
Ventnor, 42, 81, 138, 171
Versuchsstelle für Höhenflüg, Experimental High-Altitude Unit, 13
VHF, 80, 88, 156, 160, 173
Voegele, Ferdinand, 7

WAAF (Women's Auxiliary Air Force), 87, 151
Wallace, Brigadier F.C., 188

Walti, Werner Heinrich, 22
Wangerooge, 78
War Office, ix, 94, 135, 139, 143
Watt, Robert Alexander Watson, 124–9, 131–5 139, 157–61, 174, 176, 179, 187
Weelchman Specials, 200
Welchman, Gordon, 89, 200, 226
Wever, Walter, 61–2
Whaddon Hall, 87
Wildpark-Werder, 5
Wilhelmshaven, 78
Wilkins, Arnold, 124–6, 133, 173
Williamson, Harry, 21
Wimperis, Harry Egerton, 124, 175
Wissant, 37–8, 81
Wood, Dr. A.B., 139
Wood, Kingsley, 131
Woodward-Nutt, Arthur, 188
Woolwich, 76, 124
Wormwood Scrubs, 87
Wotan, 109–10
WRNS, 87
Würtzburg, 78, 134

X-Gerät, 108–12, 182

Y-Service, 86–7, 142, 156, 205

Zeiss Rb /30, Reihenbildapparat, 14
Zimmerman, Arthur, 193
Zygalski, Henryk, 195–6, 208, 210–12, 214–19